10年

2004~2014 – THE DECADE AFTER HUMAN RIGHTS WAS ARTICULATED IN THE *CONSTITUTION OF THE PEOPLE'S REPUBLIC OF CHINA*

中国“人权入宪”十年 2004～2014

中国外交部国际司 主编

世界知识出版社

图书在版编目（CIP）数据

中国“人权入宪”十年：2004 ～ 2014 = 2004~2014 –The Decade after Human Rights Was Articulated in the *Constitution of the People's Republic of China* / 中国外交部国际司主编 .—北京：世界知识出版社，2014.12

ISBN 978–7–5012–4774–5

Ⅰ. ①中… Ⅱ. ①中… Ⅲ. ①人权—问题—进展—中国—2004～2014 Ⅳ. ①D621.5

中国版本图书馆 CIP 数据核字（2014）第 271389 号

书　　名	中国“人权入宪”十年：2004 ～ 2014 Zhongguo “Renquan Ru Xian” Shi Nian: 2004~2014
主　　编	中国外交部国际司
责任编辑	柏　英
责任出版	刘　喆
责任校对	张　琨
出版发行	世界知识出版社
地址邮编	北京市东城区干面胡同 51 号（100010）
电　　话	010–65265923（发行）　010–85119023（邮购）
网　　址	www.wap1934.com
经　　销	新华书店
印　　刷	北京盛通印刷股份有限公司
开本印张	787 × 1092 毫米　1 / 16　26 印张
字　　数	402 千字
版次印次	2015 年 5 月第一版　2015 年 5 月第一次印刷
标准书号	ISBN 978–7–5012–4774–5
定　　价	198.00 元

Contents
目录

序　言

外交部部长　王　毅

2004年，第十届全国人大第二次会议通过了《宪法》修正案，明确规定“国家尊重和保障人权”，将“人权”由一个政治概念提升为法律概念。“人权入宪”开启了用《宪法》保障人权的新时代。

2014年，中国共产党十八届四中全会就全面推进依法治国作出了战略部署，这是我党首次以依法治国为主题的中央全会。法治中国的建设将由此展开新的蓝图，迈向更高的阶段。

这是两件在中国人权与法治建设史上具有重要意义的事件。值此“人权入宪”十年之际，编辑出版《中国“人权入宪”十年：2004～2014》一书，承前启后，旨在推动中国人权事业不断发展。

“法者，天下之准绳也。”过去十年，中国人权事业伴随民主法治进程，取得了举世瞩目的新进步。

十年来，中国人民生活水平全面提高。“民为邦本，本固邦宁。”中国经济一跃成为世界第二，解决了13亿中国人民的温饱问题；中国率先实现贫困人口减半的千年发展目标，为人类减贫事业作出了巨大贡献；中国为7.7亿人口提供了就业，实现了9年义务教育全覆盖，初步形成了世界上规模最大的全民医疗保险体系和社会保障制度。中国人民千百年来“学有所教、劳有所得、病有所医、老有所养”的愿望正在成为现实。

十年来，中国民主法治建设持续推进。“法令行则国治。”人民依法享有的民主权利和自由更加广泛，选举民主和协商民主相互补充，民主监督质量和实效进一步提高，权力在阳光下运行。人权法治保障水平进一步提高，依法治国建设加快推进，司法领域人权保障取得重大进展，已建成中国特色社会主义法律体系。

十年来，中国积极促进国际人权事业发展。中国全面深入参与全球人权合作与治理，推动国际人权机构健康发展。中国认真履行国际人权义务，多次接受国别人权审查和人权公约履约审议。中国与全球近 40 个国家举行人权对话和交流，与联合国人权机构开展务实合作。中国已成为国际人权事业的积极建设者和推动者。

我们坚定不移地走中国特色人权发展道路；坚定不移地将人权的普遍性原则与中国自身国情相结合；坚定不移地坚持一切为了人民、依靠人民和服务人民；坚定不移地平衡推进各类人权，学习借鉴他国有益经验。这条道路深深扎根于中华民族悠久历史文化，承载着中国人民自强不息的精神追求，具有强大的道路优势、理论优势和制度优势。

世界上没有放之四海而皆准的发展模式，也没有一成不变的发展道路。治理一个国家，各国完全可以走出自己的道路，发展人权也不例外。人权与各国的价值观标准、特定文化传统、政治经济制度相关联，由此产生的人权保护手段也各有差异。“物之不齐，物之情也。”中国的人权事业，是中国经济社会发展重要而不可缺少的组成部分，必须也只能按照中国国情和人民要求予以推进。

在人权问题上，没有最好，只有更好。当前，中国人民正在为实现中华民族伟大复兴的中国梦而奋斗。中国梦归根结底也是中国人的人权梦。我们站在 960 万平方公里的广袤土地上，吸吮着中华民族漫长奋斗积累的文化养分，拥有 13 亿中国人民聚合的磅礴之力，走自己的人权发展道路，具有广阔的舞台，深厚的历史底蕴，不竭的前进动力。我们对此具有坚定的自信。

王毅

2014 年 12 月

Preface

Wang Yi, Minister of Foreign Affairs

In 2004, the Tenth National People's Congress passed at its second session the Constitutional Amendment, which clearly stated that "[t]he State respects and protects human rights". The human rights concept was thus upgraded to a legal matter from a political concept. The articulation of human rights in the *Constitution of the People's Republic of China* started a new era of promoting and protecting human rights in China.

In 2014, the 18th Central Committee of the Communist Party of China (CPC) set out at its fourth plenary session the strategy for governing the country in accordance with law. It was CPC's first plenary session about governing the country in accordance with law and marked a new chapter and a greater height for law-based governance in China.

These two events have important significance in terms of the human rights and legal development in China. Now, it has been ten years since human rights were written in the *Constitution of the People's Republic of China.* The publication of *2004-2014 – The Decade after Human Rights Was Articulated in the Constitution of the People's Republic of China* takes place at a new starting point for the cause of human rights in China.

"Law is the yardstick for measuring all things under heaven." In the past ten years, remarkable progress has been made in protecting human rights and promoting democracy in China.

In the past ten years, the living standards of the Chinese people have been substantially improved. "People are the basis of a country. The country will be in a peaceful state when its basis is solid." China has become the second largest economy in the world, and the subsistence concerns of the 1.3 billion Chinese people have been solved. China is the first country to successfully achieve the UN Millennium Development Goal to reduce impoverished population by half and has made great contribution to the world's poverty reduction efforts. China provides jobs for 770 million people as well as nine-year compulsory education for all. The world's largest medical insurance system and social security system have been basically established. The Chinese people cherish a centuries-old dream of "education, employment, medical service and old-age care for all." Now this dream is becoming a reality.

In the past ten years, democracy and rule of law continues progressing. "If the laws are enforced, the country is in order." Now people enjoy more freedom and democratic rights according to law. Democratic election and democratic consultation complement each other. The quality and efficiency of democratic supervision are further enhanced. Power is exercised in the sunshine. The legal guarantee of human rights is further improved. Law-based governance is further advanced. The protection of human rights in the judicial domain has made significant headway and a socialist legal system with Chinese characteristics has been set up.

In the past ten years, China has actively promoted development of human rights on international stage. China is deeply engaged in global human rights cooperation and governance and promotes the sound development of international human rights institutions. China takes seriously its international human rights obligations and receives Universal Periodic Reviews and reviews of its implementation of international human rights conventions. China engages in human rights dialogues and exchanges with nearly 40 countries and carries out practical collaborations with UN human rights institutions. China has become an active force that pushes forward international human rights cause.

China pursues a path of human rights development with Chinese characteristics and combines its own situation with principle of universality of human rights. China believes that all efforts should be made for the people, rely on the strength of the people and serve the interests of the people. China promotes all categories of human rights in a balanced manner and draws on useful experience of other countries. Such an approach is deeply rooted in China's long history and cultural tradition and embodies the pursuit of the Chinese people for constant self-improvement. Therefore, it has great strength in path, theory and system.

There is no one-size-fits-all development model in the world. Neither is there a path of development that never changes. Every country may find its own way of governance. The same is true for the development of human rights. Human rights are closely related to the values, cultural traditions as well as political and economic systems of a country. Thus the ways to protect human rights vary. "It is only natural for things to be different." The human rights cause is an important and integral part of China's economic and social development. It should and can only be pushed forward in accordance with China's own situation and needs of the Chinese people.

In protecting human rights, there is always room for improvement. Now, the Chinese people are striving to realize the Chinese Dream of great national renewal. The Chinese Dream is also about human rights. Standing on a land of 9.6 million square kilometers and nurtured by the long history of a hard-working nation, we, the 1.3 billion Chinese people, have a vast stage to pursue our own path for human rights development, a pursuit endowed with profound historical heritage and inexhaustible energy. We have every confidence in its success.

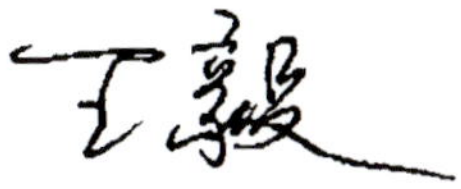

December 2014

(original translation by Yang Ji)

谱写人权司法保障新篇章

最高人民法院院长　周　强

2004年3月14日，十届全国人大二次会议通过《宪法》修正案，首次在《宪法》中明确宣示“国家尊重和保障人权”。十年间，人民法院忠实履行《宪法》和法律赋予的职责，坚持司法为民、公正司法，不断完善人权司法保障制度，为全面落实人权保障的宪法原则、促进中国人权事业的全面发展作出了积极贡献。

一、严格贯彻宽严相济刑事政策，依法保护被害人和被告人的合法权益

宽严相济是中国的基本刑事政策，是司法机关惩治犯罪、保障人权的重要指南。最高人民法院印发《关于贯彻宽严相济刑事政策的若干意见》，对贯彻落实宽严相济刑事政策提出明确、具体要求。各级法院严格贯彻宽严相济刑事政策，坚持尊重和保障人权，依法保护被害人和被告人的合法权益，最大限度地实现刑事审判惩治犯罪和保障人权的有机统一。

一是依法惩治各类刑事犯罪。严格依据法律规定，准确把握社会治安形势变化，坚持宽严相济刑事政策，充分考虑维护人民群众安全和惩治犯罪的实际需要，注重从严惩治严重危害国家安全、公共安全、社会治安和人民群众利益的犯罪，切实维护广大人民群众的人身权利、财产权利、民主权利

和其他权利，保障社会主义建设事业顺利进行，为充分实现广大人民群众的人权提供有力司法保障。10 年间，各级法院审结一审刑事案件 784.51 万件，判处罪犯 982.06 万人。

二是充分保障被告人的各项诉讼权利和合法权益。尊重和保障被告人的各项诉讼权利和合法权益，是刑事审判尊重和保障人权的重要体现。人民法院坚持实体公正与程序公正的统一，采取多种行之有效的措施，保障被告人依法享有辩护权、申请回避权、控告权、上诉权、申诉权等广泛的诉讼权利，保证被告人受到合法、公正、文明的审判。2013 年修改后的《刑事诉讼法》施行以来，各级法院进一步牢固树立惩罚犯罪与保障人权并重的观念，强化对被告人诉讼权利的保障，充分保障辩护律师依法履行辩护职责，进一步扩大了法律援助的适用范围，更加有力地保障被告人的各项诉讼权利和合法权益。

三是加强对未成年被告人的权益保障。对犯罪的未成年人实行教育、感化、挽救的方针，坚持教育为主、惩罚为辅的原则，尽最大努力促进失足未成年人回归社会。审理未成年人刑事案件时，由熟悉未成年人身心特点、善于做未成年人思想教育工作的审判人员进行，并保持有关审判人员工作的相对稳定性。截至 2014 年，全国已经建立少年法庭 2331 个。对未成年人刑事案件，在审判时依法通知法定代理人、合适成年人到场。对未成年被告人的成长经历、犯罪原因、监护教育等情况进行调查并作为办案的参考。审判时被告人不满 18 周岁的案件，不公开审理。对犯罪时不满 18 周岁、被判处五年有期徒刑以下刑罚的，实行犯罪记录封存。经过不懈努力，近年来，未成年人重新犯罪率基本控制在 2% 左右，未成年人犯罪案件呈现下降趋势，未成年罪犯占全部罪犯的比例逐渐下降。

四是确保量刑公开公平公正。规范量刑裁判权，落实量刑公开公平公正的目标，对于提高司法透明度和公信力，强化司法人权保障具有重要意义。2010 年 9 月，最高人民法院在总结试点经验的基础上，制定《人民法院量刑指导意见（试行）》，并会同有关部门联合下发《关于规范量刑程序若干问题的意见（试行）》。从 2010 年 10 月起，在全国法院试行量刑规范化改革，规范统一了 15 种常见犯罪的量刑标准。2013 年 12 月，最高人民法院发布《关于常见犯罪的量刑指导意见》，从 2014 年 1 月 1 日起在全国法院正式实施量刑规范化工作，进一步促进量刑公开公平公正。

五是切实维护被害人合法权益。被害人是犯罪行为的直接受害者，通过刑事审判惩罚犯罪分子，切实维护被害人的合法权益，是尊重和保障人权的应有之义。做好附带民事诉讼案件的审理工作，使被害人因犯罪行为遭受的物质损失依法得到赔偿，有利于切实维护被害人合法权益、有效化解社会矛盾。2013 年修改后的《刑事诉讼法》施行以来，各级法院严格按照法律规定和司法解释的要求，更加重视附带民事诉讼工作，进一步加大刑事附带民事调解工作力度，统一裁判标准，最大限度地挽回被害人的损失。推动建立健全被害人国家救助制度，对因遭受犯罪侵害无法获得有效赔偿而导致生活困难的当事人予以救助。2009 年 3 月，最高人民法院联合有关国家机关制定下发《关于开展刑事被害人救助工作的若干意见》。2014 年 1 月，最高人民法院又会同有关国家机关出台了《关于建立完善国家司法救助制度的意见(试行)》，明确了救助的条件和范围，细化了救助的标准和程序，地方各级财政部门将国家司法救助资金列入了预算。各级法院积极、稳妥、有序地开展国家司法救助工作，切实维护了被害人的合法权益。

二、审慎适用死刑，确保死刑案件审判质量

人民法院始终坚持严格控制和慎重适用死刑，严把死刑案件事实关、证据关和法律关，确保死刑案件审判质量，依法保障生存权这一最基本、最重要的人权。

一是严格贯彻国家的死刑政策。在死刑案件的审理、复核中，切实贯彻慎用死刑、严格控制死刑的政策，确保死刑只适用于极少数罪行极其严重的犯罪分子；同时，对于罪行极其严重、依法应当判处死刑的，坚决判处死刑，确保治安良好、社会稳定。自 2007 年死刑案件核准权统一由最高人民法院行使以来，死刑适用标准更加严格、统一，判处死刑的案件逐步减少。

二是确保死刑案件的审判质量。死刑案件，人命关天，必须慎之又慎。在死刑案件的审理及复核中，人民法院始终坚持证据裁判的最高标准和最严

要求，在办案质量上要求更加严格，在审判程序上更加规范，确保每一起死刑案件质量都经得起历史检验，经得起法律检验。

三是充分保障被告人的辩护权及其他合法权益。实行死刑第二审案件全部开庭审理，完善死刑复核程序，加强死刑复核监督。最高人民法院复核死刑案件时，注重依法讯问被告人，注重听取辩护律师的意见，确保把死刑案件办成铁案。

三、有效防范冤假错案，确保无罪的人不受刑事追究

人民法院在依法惩处各类刑事犯罪的同时，坚持“有罪依法追究，无罪坚决放人”的原则，建立健全防范刑事冤假错案工作机制，全面加强审判工作监督，坚守防止冤假错案底线。

一是完善刑事诉讼机制。2013 年 12 月，最高人民法院发布了《关于适用〈中华人民共和国刑事诉讼法〉的解释》。根据修改后的《刑事诉讼法》的规定，司法解释细化非法证据排除、证人鉴定人出庭、二审开庭、限制发回重审、上诉不加刑等保护当事人诉讼权利的原则，进一步完善刑事诉讼机制，从源头上防止冤假错案的发生。各级法院恪守罪刑法定、证据裁判、疑罪从无等原则，强化证据审查，严格排除非法证据，确保无辜者不受刑事追究。10 年间，各级法院依法宣告 14305 名被告人无罪。

二是坚决依法纠正冤假错案。以坚决果断的态度依法纠正“张氏叔侄强奸杀人案”等一批重大冤假错案，从错案中深刻吸取教训。通过依法纠正错案，匡扶社会正义，使依法纠错成为推进公正司法、保障人权的正能量。

三是建立健全防范冤假错案工作机制。2013 年 10 月，最高人民法院发布《关于建立健全防范刑事冤假错案工作机制的意见》，要求对定罪证据不足的案件，应当依法宣告被告人无罪，不得降格作出“留有余地”的判决；明确规定对采用刑讯逼供或者冻、饿、晒、烤、疲劳审讯等非法方法收集的被告人供述，应当排除；除情况紧急必须现场讯问以外、在规定的办案场所外讯问取得的供述、未依法对讯问进行全程录音录像取得的供述以及不能排除以非法方法取得的供述，也应当排除。

四、坚持司法为民，依法维护人民群众合法权益

人民法院始终强化司法为民、公正司法，充分发挥民事、行政等各项审判职能，妥善审理涉民生案件，加强司法便民利民工作，切实维护公民的生存权、发展权等基本人权和切身利益。

一是依法保障和改善民生。加强民商事审判工作，妥善审理与群众生产生活密切相关的案件。10年间，各级法院审结一审民商事案件5629.56万件，同比上升25.77%。注重保护妇女、老人和未成年人的合法权益，保障老有所养、幼有所教，促进家庭和睦，维护社会稳定。10年间，各级法院审结一审婚姻、家庭、继承案件1366.69万件。

二是加大知识产权司法保护力度。深入贯彻实施国家知识产权战略，加强知识产权案件审判工作，提高知识产权审判透明度，定期发布知识产权司法保护状况白皮书、年度报告和典型案例。10年间，各级法院审结一审知识产权案件450.91万件。

三是依法保护行政相对人的合法权益。坚持依法受理行政诉讼案件，保障公民、法人和其他组织的诉权。严格依照《行政诉讼法》和相关实体法审理行政诉讼案件，切实保护行政相对人的合法权益，监督行政机关依法行政。10年间，各级法院审结一审行政诉讼案件112.87万件。及时向行政机关反馈审判工作中发现的行政执法突出问题，支持行政机关提高执法水平。

四是保障公民享有依法取得国家赔偿的权利。高度重视国家赔偿审判工作，理顺国家赔偿工作机制，充实审判力量，注重工作联动，尽最大努力满足人民群众的赔偿诉求。10年间，各级法院审结国家赔偿案件20886件，决定赔偿金额45504.16万元。加大赔偿决定执行力度，确保赔偿请求人的权利尽快实现。

五是切实维护申请执行人的合法权益。健全高级人民法院统一管理本辖区执行工作体制，完善立案审判执行协调配合、执行流程管理、公开听证、异议复议等制度，规范委托评估、司法拍卖工作，加强执行联动机制建设，构建综合治理执行难的工作格局。开展集中清理执行积案、反规避执行、委

托执行案件集中清理等活动，努力提高执行质量和效率。10 年间，各级法院执结各类案件 2320.9 万件。

六是依法解决涉诉信访群众诉求。强化群众观念，认真落实信访工作责任制，坚持定期接访、法官带案下访、巡回接访等做法，畅通信访渠道。10 年间，各级法院共接待群众来访 1649.94 万人次。加强源头治理，推进涉诉信访工作机制改革，引导群众依法理性表达诉求，涉诉信访状况趋于好转。

五、深化司法公开，促进司法公正

公开是社会主义司法制度的基本运行方式，也是人民法院人民性的必然要求。为切实保障人民群众的知情权、参与权、表达权和监督权，各级法院不断创新司法公开形式，深化司法公开各项制度机制建设，努力以公开保公正。

一是加大庭审公开力度。积极推进阳光司法，全面客观公开案件事实、定案证据以及诉辩观点、判决理由，增进人民群众对司法裁判的了解和理解。建成中国法院庭审直播网，2013 年，各级法院直播庭审 4.5 万次。广受社会关注的薄熙来受贿、贪污、滥用职权案在济南市中级人民法院一审庭审时，实现了微博全程直播，引发海内外广泛关注，产生了很好的示范性效果。

二是加快推进裁判文书上网。公正不仅要实现，还要以看得见的方式实现。最高人民法院出台《关于人民法院在互联网公布裁判文书的规定》，建成中国裁判文书网，去年公布最高人民法院生效裁判文书 3858 份，地方各级法院上网公布生效裁判文书 164.6 万份。自 2014 年 1 月 1 日起，人民法院的生效裁判文书，除涉及国家秘密、个人隐私、未成年人违法犯罪、调解结案以及其他不宜在互联网公布的以外，均在互联网公开发布。

三是推进执行信息公开。2013 年，最高人民法院制定《关于公布失信被执行人名单信息的若干规定》，2013 年 10 月 24 日开通失信被执行人名单库，11 月 5 日通报了全国法院第一批失信被执行人名单信息，2014 年与人民网联合推出了"失信被执行人排行榜"。截至 2014 年 8 月 4 日，已发布失信名单信息 212867 条。一批失信被执行人主动履行了义务，有效缓解了执行难问题。

四是创新司法公开形式。依托现代信息技术，加强审判流程公开、裁判文书公开、执行信息公开三大平台建设，全面推进立案、庭审、执行、听证、文书、审务公开，防止暗箱操作。加强最高人民法院政务网站建设，开通最高人民法院微博、微信和新闻客户端，建成“全国法院微博发布厅”，方便人民群众通过新媒体了解法院工作。完善邀请人大代表、政协委员及各界人士旁听庭审制度，推行法院开放日制度，健全新闻发布制度，不断拓展司法公开的广度和深度。

党的十八大报告将“人权得到切实尊重和保障”确立为全面建成小康社会和深化改革开放的重要目标之一。党的十八届三中全会通过的《中共中央关于全面深化改革若干重大问题的决定》强调“国家尊重和保障人权”，要求“完善人权司法保障制度”。在全面推进依法治国进程的形势下，完善人权司法保障制度、促进人权保障事业不断进步，是党中央的要求和《宪法》的规定，也是人民群众的迫切期待。人民法院将坚持把人权司法保障作为贯穿审判工作始终的一条主线，不断完善人权司法保障制度，紧紧围绕“让人民群众在每一个司法案件中都感受到公平正义”的目标，忠实履行《宪法》和法律赋予的职责，为促进中国人权事业的全面发展作出新的更大贡献。

Writing down a New Chapter on Judicial Protection of Human Rights

Zhou Qiang, President, Supreme People's Court

On March 14, 2004, the Constitutional Amendment was adopted at the Second Session of the Tenth National People's Congress. It was the first time that the *Constitution of the People's Republic of China* made it clear that "[t]he State respects and protects human rights". In the ten years since then, the People's Courts have, in faithful performance of duties conferred by the Constitution, administered justice for the people, maintained judicial fairness and continuously improved the system of judicial protection of human rights, making much contribution to the comprehensive implementation of the constitutional principle that protects human rights and the all-round advancement of human rights protection in China.

I. The criminal policy of combining punishment with leniency is strictly followed and the lawful rights of both victims and defendants are protected according to law.

Combining punishment with leniency is a basic criminal policy in China and an important guide for the judicial organs in punishing crimes and protecting human rights. In the *Several Opinions on Implementing the Criminal Policy of Combining Punishment with Leniency*, the Supreme People's Court put forward specific and clear requirements in this regard. Courts at all levels have acted in strict accordance with the policy, persisted in respecting and safeguarding human rights, and protected the lawful rights of victims and defendants, achieving to the maximum an organic unity between punishment of crimes and protection of human rights through criminal trials.

First, criminal offenses are punished according to law. Acting in strict accordance with laws and the criminal policy of combining punishment with leniency, courts at all levels make effort to understand changes in social and public situation, take into full account the actual needs of safeguarding public security and punishing crimes and give emphasis to punishing crimes that severely endanger national security, public security, social order and people's interests. By so doing, the courts conscientiously protect people's right of person, property rights, democratic rights and other rights, ensure smooth progress of socialist undertakings and provide a strong judicial guarantee for the realization of human rights. In the past ten years, courts at all levels heard 7,845,100 first trials cases and gave sentences to 9,820,600 criminals.

Second, the various rights in litigation and other lawful rights and interests of the defendants are fully guaranteed. Respecting and protecting defendants' litigation and other lawful rights and interests is an important expression of the respect for and protection of human rights in criminal proceedings. The People's Courts upholds the unity of substantive justice and procedural justice and take various effective measures to secure the various litigation rights such as rights to defense, challenge, complaint, appeal and petition for the defendants so that the defendants are put to lawful, just and civilized trials. With the implementation of the revised *Criminal Procedure Law* since 2013, courts at all levels have further fostered the dual focus of punishing crimes and protecting human rights. With enhanced protection of defendants' litigation rights, full respect for defense lawyers' exercises of their defense duties and expanded scope of legal aid, the various rights in litigation and other lawful rights and interests of defendants are better protected.

Third, rights and interests of juvenile defendants are better protected. Bearing in mind that the policy is to educate, influence and save minors who have committed crimes and the principle is to rely primarily on education with punishment playing a secondary role, utmost efforts are made to help juvenile offenders back to society.

Criminal cases with juvenile delinquents are tried consistently by judges familiar with adolescent behavior adept at working with young people. By 2014, 2,331 juvenile courts had been set up around the country. Court proceedings are conducted in the presence of the offender's legal representative and appropriate adult. The minor's life experience, reasons behind the offense, and custody and education records are investigated into and taken as background information for the court. Juvenile offenders under eighteen years of age at the time of trial will have their cases heard in private sessions. Offenders under eighteen years of age and sentenced to less than five years in prison will have their court records sealed. With unswerving efforts in this area, in recent years, the incidence of juveniles committing crimes again has been kept at about 2%, juvenile delinquency has been decreasing and minors now account for a decreasing proportion among all criminals.

Fourth, measures have been taken to ensure open, fair and just sentencing. To standardize judge's power of sentencing and ensure open, fair and just sentencing is of great significance to enhancing judicial transparency and credibility and strengthening judicial protection of human rights. In September 2010, the Supreme People's Court formulated on the basis of pilot the *Guiding Opinion on Sentencing by People's Courts (for trial implementation)* and issued jointly with other relevant departments *Opinions on Several Issues concerning the Regulation of Sentencing Procedures (for trial implementation)*. Starting in October 2010, sentencing reform was tried out in all courts with sentencing for 15 common crimes standardized. Then the Supreme People's Court issued *Guiding Opinions on Sentencing of Common Crimes* in December 2013, with which sentencing standardization has been rolled out in all courts as of 1 January 2014 to ensure open, fair and just sentencing.

Fifth, the lawful rights of victims are earnestly protected. Victims suffer directly from crime. Punishing criminals through fair trials and protecting the lawful rights of their victims are natural contents of the respect for and protection of human rights. Trial according to law of civil suits collateral to criminal proceedings helps compensate the victims for their material losses, thus protecting their lawful rights and interests and greatly mitigating the potential for social conflict. Since the revised *Criminal Procedure Law* entered into effect in 2013, courts at all levels, in strict observance of legal provisions and the judicial interpretation, now pay more attention to civil suits collateral to criminal proceedings with increased mediation effort and unified judgement criteria with a view to helping victims to recover their losses to the maximum possible. A system of state aid system for crime victims has been created and substantiated to help those who are not effectively compensated for being crime victims and thus experience financial hardships. In March 2009, the Supreme People's Court and other relevant state organs issued *Several Opinions on Aiding Crime Victims.* In January 2014, the Supreme People's Court together with other state organs issued *Opinions on Establishing and Improving the System of State Judicial Aid System (for trial implementation),* which clarifies the conditions and scope of assistance and details the relevant standards and procedures. State judicial aid is now budgeted in local public finance and provided by courts at all levels in a positive, reliable and orderly manner, with the lawful rights and interests of victims thus well protected.

II. The death penalty is applied with great caution and the trial quality of death penalty cases is assured.

The People's Courts have always insisted on strictly controlling and cautiously applying death penalty and scrutinized facts, evidence and laws to ensure trail quality of each death penalty case, thus safeguarding the right to life, the most basic and important human right.

The first is to strictly adhere to the policy to apply death penalty with great caution and to strictly control death penalty during the trial and review of death penalty cases so as to ensure the imposition of death penalty only to extremely serious crimes. Meanwhile, death penalty is resolutely imposed to extremely serious crimes that are punishable by death according to law so as to ensure public security and social stability. Since the power to examine and approve death penalties was taken back by the Supreme People's Court in 2007, the criteria for the application of death penalty have become unified and more stringent and the number of cases in which the capital punishment is imposed has steadily declined.

The second is to ensure trial quality of death penalty cases. As human lives are involved, death penalty cases must be handled extremely cautiously. In the trial and review of death penalty cases, the Supreme People's Court has all along applied the highest standards and the most stringent requirements of evidence-based adjudication, exercised stricter case quality assurance and more standardized trial procedures, and made sure that the quality of each and every death penalty case will withstand the tests of history and law.

The third is to fully protect the right to defense and other lawful rights and interests of the defendants. All second trial death penalty cases must be tried in court sessions. Death penalty review procedures have been improved and supervision over the review strengthened. When the Supreme People's Court reviews death penalty cases, emphasis is given to questioning the defendants according to law and hearing defense lawyer's opinions to make sure that all death penalty cases are borne out with ironclad evidence.

III. Effective measures are taken to prevent unjust, false, and erroneous charges and protect innocent people from criminal punishment.

When dealing with the wide variety of criminal offenses, the People's Courts follow the principle of "punishing those guilty according to law and releasing those innocent without hesitation". Robust working mechanism has been established to prevent unjust, false and erroneous charges, a bottom line in the judicial area, by comprehensively enhancing supervision over court proceedings.

First, criminal litigation system has been improved. In December 2013, the Supreme People's Court published *Interpretation on the Application of the Criminal Procedure Law*. Based on the amended *Criminal Procedure Law*, the Interpretation further improved the litigation system by detailing principles to protect litigation rights such as illegal evidence exclusion, attendance of witness, including expert witness, court session for second trial, restrictions on remand for retrial and no aggravating punishment on defendants from appeals, thus preventing unjust, false and erroneous charges at the source. Courts at all levels act in strict observance of the principles of legally prescribed punishment, evidence-based adjudication, and assuming innocence until proven guilty, take measures to strengthen review of evidence, and strictly exclude illegal evidence so that the innocent are not criminally punished. In the past 10 years, courts at all levels acquitted 14,305 defendants.

Second, resolute action is taken to rectify unjust, false and erroneous charges according to law. The courts have acted resolutely to rectify a series of unjust, false, and erroneous charges including raping and murder cases and drawn lessons from them. These moves serve social justice, promote judicial fairness and protect human rights.

Third, a working mechanism to avoid unjust, false and erroneous cases has been created and improved. In October 2013, the Supreme People's Court issued *Opinions on Establishing and Improving the Working Mechanism for Preventing Unjust, False and Erroneous Criminal Charges*. The Opinions stipulate that the defendants should be acquitted in accordance with law in case of insufficient incriminating evidence rather than being given "compromised" sentencing and that confession extorted by torture or other illegal means, such as food and water deprivation, excessive heat or cold and imposed duress, should be excluded, as should confession obtained from interrogation sessions conducted at undesignated sites, from interrogation sessions the whole procedure of which is not videotaped, and from interrogation sessions in which the possibility of the use of illegal means cannot be ruled out.

IV. Justice is administered for the people and legitimate rights and interests of the people are safeguarded according to law.

Bearing in mind the principle of administering justice for the people and maintaining judicial fairness, the People's Courts conscientiously protect people's rights to subsistence and development as well as other basic human rights and their vital interests by fully exercising their civil and administrative trial functions, properly handle cases with a bearing on people's livelihood and make effort to bring convenience and benefit to the people.

The first is to safeguard and improve people's life according to law. Capacity pertaining to civil and commercial cases has been built up with a view to properly handling cases closely linked to people's daily life. During the past ten years, courts at all levels heard and concluded 56,295,600 first trial cases, an increase of 25.77% over the previous decade. The courts lay great importance on protecting the legitimate rights and interests of women, senior citizens and minors so as to ensure that the aged be provided for and the young be educated to contribute to family harmony and social stability. Among the cases heard and concluded in the past decade, 13,666,900 were about marriage, family and inheritance.

The second is to reinforce judicial protection of intellectual property rights. In the implementation of the National Intellectual Property Strategy, the courts have increased work on IPR-related cases, enhanced transparency with regard to these cases and regularly issued white papers and annual reports on IPR protection, as well as typical cases. In the last ten years, courts at all levels heard and concluded 4,509,100 IPR cases.

The third is to protect the lawful rights and interests of administrative counterparts according to law. The courts insisted on hearing administrative lawsuits according to law to ensure the procedural rights of citizens, legal persons and other organizations. Administrative cases are tried according to the *Administrative Procedure Law* and relevant substantive laws, thus earnestly protecting the lawful rights and interests of administrative counterparts and overseeing the process of administration according to law. In the past ten years, courts at all levels processed 1,128,700 administrative lawsuits. The courts have also provided feedbacks on problems found during trial for administrative organs so that the latter may improve the level of administrative law enforcement.

The fourth is to ensure citizens' rights to state compensation according to law. The courts have attached great importance to cases concerning state compensation, made effort to streamline the state compensation system, increased human resources and solicited cooperation from parties involved so as to best meet people's compensation needs. Over the past ten years, courts at all levels gave rulings over

20,886 state compensation cases, with a total amount of 455,041,600 yuan in state compensation. Enforcement of court rulings has also been improved to make sure that claimants get the compensation as soon as possible.

The fifth is to safeguard the lawful rights and interests of enforcement applicants. The system of higher People's Courts has overall control over enforcement of court rulings within their respective jurisdictions. Mechanisms for coordination between case registration, trial and ruling enforcement, enforcement process management, open hearings, objection and reconsideration have been set up and constantly improved. Process of entrusted assessments and judicial sale has been standardized and inter-agency enforcement mechanism has been strengthened with a view to addressing enforcement difficulties in a comprehensive manner. Campaigns have been conducted to close long-pending enforcement, counter enforcement evasion and strengthen entrusted enforcement with higher enforcement quality and efficiency. In the past ten years, courts at all levels enforced 23,209,000 cases.

The sixth is to address lawsuit-related petitions. Bearing in mind needs of the people, the courts take people's petitions seriously and keep communications with the people through regular acceptance and hearing of petitions as well as field visits by judges. In the past ten years, courts at all levels received 16,499,400 petitioners. The courts strengthened the system of managing origins of petitions, advanced reform of the petition system and guided the people to appeal according to law, thus greatly improving the overall situation of lawsuit-related petitions.

V. Judicial transparency is enhanced to promote judicial fairness.

The socialist judicial system operates transparently and the People's Courts naturally maintain an affinity with the people. In order to protect people's rights to know, to participate, to express themselves and to supervise over judicial operations, courts at all levels have worked together to increase transparency innovatively and to create institutions for increased transparency so that judicial fairness is fostered through transparency.

First, efforts have been expanded to make trials more open. The courts actively carry forward justice in sunshine with comprehensive and objective disclosure of case facts, incriminating evidence, prosecuting and defense arguments and grounds of decision, which has increased people's knowledge and understanding of judicial judgement. A special website has been created to broadcast live trials in Chinese courts. In 2013, over 45,000 trials sessions were on air. When Bo Xilai stood for the first trial at Ji'nan Intermediary People's Court on charges of taking bribes, embezzlement and abuse of power, the court sessions were live broadcasted on Weibo, which caused extensive attention from home and abroad and played a fairly good demonstrative role.

Second, action has been sped up to put judgements online. Justice should be not only realized but also realized in a highly visible way. The Supreme People's Court issued *Provisions on the Issuance of Judgments on the Internet by the People's Courts* and launched the website "Judicial Opinions of China". Last year, 3,858 effective judgments of the Supreme People's Court and 1,646,000 effective judgments of lower courts were make available online. As of January 1, 2014, all effective judgements, except those related to state secrets, personal privacy, juvenile delinquency, lawsuits settled through conciliation and other cases inappropriate for publication, have all been made public on the Internet.

Third, progress has been made to disclose enforcement information. In 2013, the Supreme People's Court enacted *Several Provisions on Announcement of the List of Dishonest Persons Subject to Enforcement.* On October 24, 2013, a database of such lists was launched. On November 5, the first list of dishonest persons was made public and a second list was published together with People's Daily Online in 2014. By August 4, 2014, 212,867 pieces of information concerning dishonest persons subject to enforcement had been published. As a result, many people on the list have taken the initiative to fulfill their obligations provided in the relevant court rulings, thus mitigating to a certain extent the enforcement problems in China.

Fourth, innovative methods have been used to make the judicial process more transparent. Latest information technology was used to build three platforms for making public respectively trial proceedings, judgments and enforcement information.

Black case work is prevented by providing the public with all information pertaining to case initiation trials, enforcement, hearings, documents and trial affairs. The Supreme People's Court continues developing its official website, operates interactive accounts with Weibo, WeChat and news applications and facilitates a "press room" for People's Courts on Weibo. With these, it becomes easier for people to understand better the judicial process via new media. The courts have also improved the system for inviting deputies to the National People's Congress, members of the Chinese People's Political Consultative Conference and other representatives from all walks of life to attend court trials, introduced court open days and improved the press release system with a view to expanding judicial transparency.

The report of the 18th CPC National Congress identified "the true respect for and protection of human rights" as an important goal in creating a well-off society in an all-around way and deepening reform and opening-up. The 18th CPC Central Committee adopted at its 3rd Plenary Session *Decision on Some Major Issues Concerning Comprehensively Deepening the Reform,* which stressed that "[t]he State respects and protects human rights" and vowed to improve the judicial system to protect human rights. Against the backdrop of comprehensively advancing law-based governance, improving the judicial system to protect human rights and promoting continued progress in human rights protection are both required by the CPC Central Committee and the Constitution and ardently expected by the people. The People's Courts will, as always, bear in mind judicial protection of human rights in their work and consistently improve the judicial system for human rights protection. Determined to bring justice through each and every case, they will faithfully fulfill the duties conferred by the Constitution and laws and by so doing make even greater contribution to human rights protection in China.

(original translation by Niu Ya'nan)

依法履行法律监督职责
切实强化人权司法保障

最高人民检察院常务副检察长 胡泽君

2004年，“国家尊重和保障人权”写入《宪法》，开启了中国人权保障法治化的新时代。2012年，“尊重和保障人权”作为重要任务写入《刑事诉讼法》，为人权司法保障提供了操作指南。检察机关作为国家法律监督机关，肩负着保障法律统一正确实施的神圣使命，为人权发展提供司法保障是检察职能的应有之义。“人权入宪”十年来，全国检察机关充分履行职责，既依法打击侵犯人权的犯罪，加强对侵犯人权问题的法律监督，努力提高保障人权的工作水平；又主动接受外部监督，加强内部监督制约，防止在自身执法活动中发生侵犯人权的问题，切实保障公民享有充分人权，促进人权事业的发展。

一、依法惩治犯罪，保障公民生命财产安全和人身权利、民主权利

各级检察机关认真履行批准逮捕、提起公诉、查办和预防职务犯罪等职责，依法打击刑事犯罪，严肃查办渎职侵权等职务犯罪，保障人民群众平等享有政治、经济、社会、文化权利。

一是依法严惩刑事犯罪，保障公民生命财产安全。深入开展反恐斗争，

坚决打击严重暴力犯罪、黑恶势力犯罪、多发性侵财犯罪、涉众型经济犯罪、毒品犯罪，严惩危害人民群众生命健康和切身利益的犯罪。积极参与食品药品安全专项整治，批准逮捕一批制售假药劣药、有毒有害食品犯罪嫌疑人。加强公民个人信息司法保护，及时批捕起诉非法出售、提供、获取公民个人信息的犯罪嫌疑人。严肃查处污染环境的违法犯罪行为，与有关部门共同制定办理环境污染刑事案件司法解释，明确定罪标准，加大处罚力度，保障人民享有良好环境的权利。

二是加大查办职务犯罪力度，保障公民权利不受侵犯。严肃查办发生在社会保障、劳动就业、征地拆迁、移民补偿、抢险救灾、医疗卫生、招生考试等民生领域的职务犯罪，认真查处涉嫌非法拘禁、非法搜查、刑讯逼供、暴力取证、破坏选举、报复陷害等侵犯公民人身权利、民主权利的犯罪行为。着力查办问题奶粉、瘦肉精、地沟油、毒胶囊等事件背后的渎职犯罪，依法同步介入矿难、火灾、爆炸等重特大事故调查，及时立案侦查造成人民群众生命财产重大损失的严重渎职犯罪。

三是更加注重特殊群体和困难群众权益的司法保护。加强对特殊群体和困难群众的司法保护，是保障人权的重要工作之一。近年来，检察机关不断加大对妇女、儿童、残疾人、农民工、下岗职工等特殊群体和困难群众的司法保护力度。修订人民检察院办理未成年人刑事案件规定，实行社会调查、合适成年人到场、分案起诉、犯罪记录封存等制度，帮助失足未成年人改过自新。积极参与打击拐卖妇女儿童专项行动，配合有关部门做好被拐卖妇女儿童的救助工作。会同有关部门出台加强残疾人法律援助工作的意见，协助建设残疾人法律救助工作站。认真办理涉及农民工劳资纠纷、下岗职工补贴救助等民事行政申诉案件，开展支持起诉工作。探索建立涉罪外来流动人员教育帮扶制度，协调有关单位为涉嫌轻微犯罪、取保候审的流动人员提供担保、食宿等，平等保护其诉讼权利。

二、加强对诉讼活动的法律监督，依法保护案件当事人诉讼权利

尊重和保障公民的诉讼权利是人权司法保障的重要内容。各级检察机关

坚持惩治犯罪与保障人权并重，实体公正与程序公正并重，既注意监督纠正有罪不究、执法不严的问题，又重视监督纠正侵犯人权、冤及无辜的问题，努力防止执法司法活动中侵犯人权问题的发生。

一是强化刑事诉讼监督，着力纠正违法办案、罚不当罪等问题。加强对立案、侦查活动的监督，及时纠正不应当立案而立案、违法采取强制措施等问题，防止侦查权滥用，保障无罪的人不受刑事追究。加强对刑事审判的法律监督，既注意监督纠正有罪判无罪、量刑畸轻的案件，又重视监督纠正无罪判有罪、量刑畸重的案件，以及因徇私枉法和严重违反法定程序影响公正审判的案件，防止罚不当罪。

二是强化刑罚执行和监管活动监督，着力纠正超期羁押、体罚被监管人员等问题。制定实施关于看守所检察、监狱检察和监外执行检察等规范性文件，强化对刑事执行活动的监督。会同有关部门开展看守所监管执法、监狱清查事故隐患等专项检查，排查解决“牢头狱霸”等问题，建立健全羁押期限告知、羁押期限届满提示、超期羁押投诉和责任追究等制度，积极推进与监管场所的执法信息联网和监控联网，向社会公布超期羁押举报电话和电子信箱，对严重超期羁押案件实行挂牌督办，逐案纠正。在监狱、看守所设立派出检察室，完善检察官接待在押人员申诉、在押人员权利告知和会见制度，保障被羁押人员合法权益。

三是强化民事、行政诉讼监督，着力纠正监督侵害当事人合法权益等问题。认真履行对民事、行政诉讼实行法律监督的职责，对认为确有错误的生效裁判、调解书依法提出抗诉或再审检察建议，对审判、民事执行活动中的违法情形及时提出检察建议，特别是对虚假诉讼、违法调解和其他显失公正、严重损害公共利益和当事人、案外人合法权益的裁判，加大监督纠正力度，维护法律尊严。

三、创新完善工作机制，努力提高保障人权工作水平

检察机关围绕更好地保障人权，积极回应群众诉求，创新工作机制，拓宽权利救济渠道，使公民权利得到充分实现。

一是加强举报信访工作。制定和完善人民检察院举报、信访工作规定，建立“一站式”受理接待中心和查询服务窗口，开设网上举报、申诉和信息查询系统，开通全国统一的12309举报电话，推行下访巡访、预约接访、视频接访、定期走访，依法保障人民群众的检举权、控告权和申诉权。推进检力下沉，在人口集中的乡镇街道设立派出检察室，开展巡回检察，就地受理控告申诉，便利群众反映诉求。

二是加强对律师执业权利的保障。最高人民检察院单独或会同有关部门，制定实施关于保障律师在刑事诉讼中依法执业的规定、加强律师执业权利保障等一系列规范性文件，完善侦查、审查逮捕、起诉等环节听取律师意见制度，保障律师的会见权、阅卷权和调查取证权。各地检察机关通过制定工作办法、实施细则，进一步规范律师接待、办理律师申请期限、回复律师申请形式等工作，建立律师预约工作机制，健全与律师沟通交流制度，进一步细化了法律和司法解释有关辩护律师诉讼权利的相关规定。

三是注重对被害人及其亲属合法权益的保护。在执法办案中，切实维护被害人及其亲属的知情权，及时接受、妥善处理被害人及其亲属的控告、申诉，依法保障被害人及其亲属的申请回避权和委托诉讼代理权等诉讼权利。为更好地保护刑事被害人权益，最高人民检察院会同有关部门联合出台了《关于开展刑事被害人救助工作的若干意见》，探索实行刑事被害人司法救助制度，明确救助范围、标准和程序，对被害人因无法获得犯罪人经济赔偿造成生活困难的，积极协调有关方面给予救助。

四是加强刑事赔偿工作。及时给予刑事赔偿是尊重和保障人权的重要体现。检察机关认真落实法律规定，完善刑事赔偿确认程序，对因错误拘留、错误逮捕，违法扣押、冻结造成财产损失等侵犯公民人身权利和财产权利的，依法给予国家赔偿。

四、强化内外部监督制约，防止自身执法不当发生侵犯人权

检察机关牢固树立监督者更要主动接受监督的意识，自觉接受人大监督、政协民主监督，特别是不断完善自身执法监督制约机制，提升严格规范

文明执法水平。

一是完善内部监督机制，确保检察权依法规范行使。规范检察机关各业务部门的职权配置，加强内部各环节的制约。成立专门的案件管理机构，研发融办案、管理、统计于一体的统一业务应用系统，全面推行执法信息网上录入、执法流程网上管理、执法活动网上监督、执法质量网上考核。建立完善查办职务犯罪工作备案、审批制度，省级以下检察院立案查办职务犯罪案件必须报上一级检察院备案审查，撤案、不起诉、采取指定居所监视居住强制措施必须报上一级检察院批准。建立案件质量评查制度，采取随机评查、重点评查、专项评查等方式，深入查找执法瑕疵和执法过错。

二是进一步深化检务公开，增强检察权运行的透明度。坚持以公开促公正，不断充实检务公开内容，除法律明确规定不公开的以外，能够公开的全部向社会公开。推进检察机关及时主动公开和依当事人申请公开制度化、规范化，建立案件流程信息查询、诉讼权利义务告知和办案结果告知等制度，不断扩大公开审查的案件范围。加强检察门户网站、“两微一端”等新媒体传播平台建设，设立检务公开大厅，实现网上网下“一站式”服务。完善新闻发布制度，及时公布司法解释、通报重大案件办理情况，为当事人和人民群众行使知情权、监督权提供便利。

三是推行人民监督员制度，强化对检察权运行的外部监督。采取随机抽选的方式，由人民监督员对检察机关拟作撤案、不起诉处理和犯罪嫌疑人不服逮捕决定的“三类案件”，以及立案不当、超期羁押、违法搜查扣押、不依法给予刑事赔偿、检察人员违法违纪办案、采取指定居所监视居住强制措施违法、阻碍律师或其他诉讼参与人依法行使诉讼权利、应当退还取保候审保证金而不退还等“八种情形”进行监督。进一步完善人民监督员知情权保障机制，探索建立人民监督员监督事项告知制度、人民监督员参与案件跟踪回访和执法检查制度，有效防止执法办案中侵犯人权现象的发生。

依法尊重和保障人权，加强对人权的司法保障，是人民检察院义不容辞的责任。检察机关将继续立足本职、完善机制，坚决打击和遏制侵犯人权犯罪活动，不断提高人权保障水平，为推进中国人权事业全面发展作出新的更大贡献。

Carrying out Procuratorial Supervision According to Law to Effectively Strengthen Judicial Protection of Human Rights

Hu Zejun, Executive Deputy Procurator-General, Supreme People's Procuratorate

In 2004, "[t]he State respects and protects human rights" was articulated in the *Constitution of the People's Republic of China,* opening a new era in which human rights are protected by law. In 2012, "respecting and protecting human rights" was listed as a key task in the *Criminal Procedure Law*, thus providing an operational guide for the judicial protection of human rights. As organs of legal supervision, procuratorates shoulder the sacred mission of ensuring unified and accurate implementation of law. To provide judicial protection for the development of human rights is part and parcel of the procuratorial functions. In the decade since the incorporation of human rights into the Constitution, procuratorates throughout the country have carried out their duties fully. They have cracked down on crimes violating human rights according to law and strengthened legal supervision over human rights violations, thus improving human rights protection. They have also proactively accepted external oversight and strengthened internal controls to guard against human rights violations within the procuratorial organs themselves. All of these contribute to the enjoyment of full human rights by all citizens and the development of the cause of human rights.

I. Punishing crimes according to law to protect the lives and property of citizens as well as their rights of the person and democratic rights.

Procuratorial organs at all levels conscientiously carry out their functions in approval of arrest, prosecution, and investigation into and prevention of work-related crimes. By cracking down on crimes and investigating into dereliction of duty, rights infringement and other work-related crimes, these organs help safeguard people's enjoyment of equal political, economic, social, and cultural rights.

First, criminal offenses are punished according to law to safeguard lives and property of citizens. Procuratorial organs engage in effort to root out terrorism, resolutely combat severe violent crimes, gang crimes, repeated crimes against property, economic crimes involving mass participation and drug-related crimes, and severely punish crimes that endanger peoples' life, health and immediate interests. They are actively involved in special food and drug safety campaigns by approving the arrest of suspects for manufacturing and selling fake or substandard drugs or toxic or hazardous food. They endeavor to strengthen judicial protection of personally identifiable information by approving the arrest of and prosecuting criminal suspects who illegally sell, make available, or obtain citizens' personally identifiable information. They seriously investigate into and deal with illegal and criminal acts of environmental pollution and develop jointly with other relevant departments judicial interpretations on the handling of offenses of environment pollution by clarifying conviction criteria and increasing penalties so as to protect people's right to enjoy a good environment.

Second, effort is redoubled to investigate into work-related crimes for the protection of civil rights. Serious efforts have been made to investigate into and deal with accordingly work-related crimes in areas closely linked to people's livelihood including social security, labor and employment, land acquisition and housing demolition, resettlement compensation, disaster relief, healthcare and recruitment examinations. The procuratorial organs also make conscientious effort to investigate into offenses that violate citizens' right of the person or democratic rights, such as illegal detention, illegal searches, interrogation by torture, evidence obtained through violence, disruption of elections and retaliation or frame-up. They focus investigation on cases of dereliction of duty in incidents such as problematic milk powder, lean meat powder, illegal cooking oil and toxic capsules. A further aspect of work is to join according to law from the very beginning investigations into serious accidents such as mine accidents, fires and explosions. Attention is also given to start in a timely manner investigations into cases involving serious dereliction of duty and leading to significant loss of life or property.

Third, more attention is paid to judicial protection of the rights and interests of special groups and people in difficulty. Strengthening judicial protection for these people is an important task in the protection of human rights. In recent years, procuratorates have increased protection for special groups and people in difficulty such as women, children, people with disabilities, migrant workers and laid-off workers. The *Rules for the People's Procuratorate's Handling of Criminal Cases Involving Minors* have been revised to include such mechanisms as social surveys, presence of appropriate adult, separate prosecution of minors and adults and sealing of minors' criminal records – all designed to help the young people who have gone astray to find their path again and remake themselves. The procuratorates are actively involved in special campaigns against trafficking in women and children and work with relevant departments to rescue and help trafficked women and children. They have worked together with relevant departments to publish opinions on strengthening legal aid to people with disability and assisted in the creation of legal aid centers for disabled persons. Civil and administrative complaints such as those of labor disputes involving migrant workers and subsidies and aid to laid-off workers are handled carefully and actions are taken to support legal actions. Efforts have also been made to explore ways to educate and support migrants involved in crimes and coordinate with competent departments to provide guarantee and boarding for migrants who have been suspects of minor offenses and granted bail, thus equally protecting their litigation rights.

II. Strengthening procuratorial supervision of litigation activities to protecting the litigation rights of parties concerned according to law.

Respecting and protecting the litigation rights of citizens is an important component of judicial protection of human rights. Procuratorial organs at all levels assign equal importance to punishing crimes and protecting human rights, value both substantive justice and procedural justice, and look for and rectify not only situations in which crimes go unpunished or laws are not strictly enforced but also cases where human rights are violated or the innocent is wrongly accused, thus preventing any violation of human rights issues in law enforcement or judicial activities.

First, procuratorial supervision over criminal proceedings is enhanced to rectify illegal handling of cases or imposition of penalties that don't fit the crimes. Supervision over case filings and investigations has been increased, redressing in a timely manner problems such as filing ineligible cases or illegal use of compulsory measures, preventing abuse of the investigation power and protecting innocent people from criminal investigation. Legal supervision over criminal trials has also been strengthened, with attention paid to imposition of penalties that don't fit the crimes, be it rendering the guilty innocent and issuing excessively light sentence, or criminalizing the innocent and giving excessively heavy sentences, or bending the law and seriously violating legal procedures to undermine the fairness of trial.

Second, procuratorial supervision over enforcement of punishment and prison management has also been strengthened, with a focus on redressing extended custody and corporal punishment of inmates. Normative documents have been developed and implemented with regard to procuratorial supervision over detention houses and prisons as well as sentences served outside prison, thus strengthening procuratorial supervision of criminal enforcement. Together with other relevant departments, the procuratorial organs have carried special inspections for enforcement activities and hidden problems in detention houses and prisons, and investigate into and address jailhouse bullying. The problem of extended custody is redressed by developing rules on notification of length of detention, reminder upon completion of detention periods, and complaints about and investigation into extended custody, actively sharing enforcement information with detention houses and prisons, obtaining access to surveillance systems in detention houses and prisons, publishing hotlines and e-mail addresses for the report of cases of extended custody, and conducting special case-by-case supervision in circumstances of severe extension. Procuratorial offices have been opened in prisons and detention houses for procurators to receive detainee complaints and mechanisms to inform detainees of their rights and to arrange meetings have been improved to protect the legitimate rights and interests of detainees.

Third, procuratorial supervision over civil and administrative litigation has been strengthened to identify and redress infringement of legitimate rights and interests parties concerned. The function of procuratorial supervision over civil and administrative litigation is also carried out conscientiously. The procuratorial organs protest against wrong judgments or mediation agreement or recommend retrial of the relevant case. Procuratorial opinions are presented upon irregularities in trials or civil enforcement. Intensified efforts have been made to guard against and redress false litigation, illegal mediation and other judgments that are obviously unjust and seriously harm public interests or the legitimate rights and interests of parties concerned or third parties to safeguard the dignity of law.

III. Innovating and improving work mechanisms to better protect human rights.

To better protect human rights, the procuratorial organs have actively responded to demands of the people, created innovative work mechanisms and broadened relief channels for the people to fully realize their civil rights.

First, work related to reporting and petitioning has been strengthened. Rules on the handling of reports, petition letters and visits by procuratorates have been developed. "One-stop" reception center and query service counter have been set up. Online portal to make a report, file a complaint and find information has been launched. A hotline (12309) has been open to public. Procuratorial organs also dispatch people on tours to hear people's complaints, receive petitioning individuals by appointment or through video conference and regularly visit petitioners to hear their needs in person so that people's rights to impeach, complain and appeal are better exercised. Efforts are made to have more procurators at the grass-roots level by setting up procuratorial offices at relatively more populous towns and villages with circuit procurators receiving complaints and appeals, making it more convenient for the people to make appeals.

Second, rights of practising lawyers have been better protected. The Supreme People's Procuratorate, working either alone or jointly with other relevant departments, have developed and implemented a series of normative documents on protecting lawyers' practices during criminal proceedings and on strengthening protection of the rights of practising lawyers. The system of legal counsel during investigation, review of arrest, and prosecution has been improved and the rights of lawyers to meet with their clients, read necessary documents, and conduct investigation and collect evidence have been better protected. Local procuratorial organs have developed detailed rules to further standardize reception of lawyers, deadlines for handling lawyers' applications and format of response to lawyers, establish mechanism of appointment with lawyers, improve communication with lawyers and further refine the relevant provisions and judicial interpretations on the litigation rights of defense lawyers.

Third, protection of the legitimate rights and interests of victims and their families has been stressed. In handling cases and law enforcement, the procuratorial organs earnestly protect the right of victims and their families to information, receive in timely fashion and properly handle accusations and complaints filed by victims and their families and protect according to law the litigation rights of victims and their families such as the right to challenge and the right to entrust. To better protect the rights and interests of victims, the Supreme People's Procuratorate and other relevant departments jointly issued *Opinions on Carrying out Rescuing and Assisting Victims of Criminal Cases*, in exploration of a system of judicial aid for crime victims with the scope, standards and procedures of such aid clarified. The procuratorates also actively coordinate relevant parties to provide assistance for victims suffering hardship without financial compensation from the criminal offenders.

Fourth, work on criminal compensation has been strengthened. Timely provision of criminal compensation is an important manifestation of respect for and protection of human rights. Prosecutorial organs earnestly implement the relevant legal provisions, improve the confirmation procedures for criminal compensation and give state compensation to victims of wrongful detention, wrongful arrest, property loss due to unlawful seizure or freezing and other violations of citizens' right of person or property rights.

IV. Strengthening external and internal controls to prevent violations of human rights by procuratorial organs in improper law enforcement.

Procuratorial organs firmly believe that as supervisors they themselves must be ready to accept supervision by the National People's Congress (NPC) and the Chinese People's Political Consultative Conference (CPPCC) and that they must continuously improve their own mechanism of controls and have more strict, standard and civilized law enforcement.

First, internal oversight is improved to ensure exercise of prosecutorial power according to law. Division of labor within procuratorial organs is standardized with strengthened internal controls. Specialized case management unit is designated. A uniform operational system combining case handling, management and statistics has been developed and law enforcement information input, process management, activity supervision and quality assessment are now all conducted online. A system of filing, reviewing and approving investigation into work-related crimes has been set up and improved. When investigating into work-related crimes, procuratorates below the provincial level must file with the higher level procuratorate for recordkeeping and review. Decisions to withdraw a case, not to prosecute or to take the coercive measures of residential surveillance at designated place must be reported to and approved by the next higher level procuratorate. A system of quality assessment has been put in place with random assessment, assessment of key arenas and special assessments to detect instances of flawed or faulty law enforcement.

Second, transparency in the exercise of prosecutorial power has been enhanced with further openness of procuratorial affairs. Bearing in mind that justice can be promoted with greater openness, all information related to procuratorial affairs is disclosed to the public except that explicitly forbidden by law. Disclosure of information by prosecutorial organs' timely initiatives or upon request of concerned parties has been institutionalized and standardized. Rules have been created on information inquiries about case processing, provision of information on litigation rights and obligations and notification of outcomes of cases, and the extent to which the public may review cases has been expanded. Procuratorates' websites and new media platforms such as Weibo, WeChat and news apps have been further developed and special rooms for enhanced procuratorial transparency have been opened, providing "one-stop service" both on- and offline. The press release system has been further improved with timely release of judicial interpretations and briefing on major cases, thus facilitating the parties concerned and the people at large to exercise their rights to know and to supervise.

Third, a system of people's supervisors has been developed to strengthen external supervision over the use of prosecutorial power. People's supervisors are randomly selected to oversee the handling of three types of cases – those procuratorial organs intend to withdraw or handle without prosecution and those involving criminal suspect refusing to accept an arrest, and in "eight situations" including improper case filings, extended custody, illegal search or seizure, failure to provide criminal compensation according to law, case handling in ways against law or disciplines, illegally taking the coercive measure of residential surveillance, obstruction of the exercise of litigation rights by lawyers or other participants in legal proceeding, or failure to refund money paid in recognizance according to law. The mechanism to protect people's supervisors' right to information has been improved and a system for people's supervisors to be informed and to participate in case follow-up and enforcement inspection has been developed so as to effectively prevent human rights violations in law enforcement.

To respect and protect human rights according to law and strengthen judicial protection of human rights are an unshirkable responsibility of the People's Procuratorates. The procuratorial organs will continue improving the mechanisms in their areas, resolutely crack down on and curb criminal activities that violate human rights, and constantly improve human rights protection, thus making new and greater contribution to the comprehensive development of human rights cause in China.

(original translation by Cynthia Yume Ning)

直挂云帆济沧海

国务院新闻办公室主任　蔡名照

“人权”是一个伟大而神圣的词语，为人类社会所不懈追求。中国共产党领导人民革命、建设和改革，其目的就是实现人民幸福。可以说，实现人民幸福是人权的真谛。十年前，“国家尊重和保障人权”被庄严载入中国《宪法》，从此中国人权事业发展迈入一个新阶段。

2013年9月12日，作者出席“第六届北京人权论坛”开幕式并致辞。

一、“人权入宪”：中国人权事业的里程碑

《宪法》是人权的保障书。人权是《宪法》的内在精神。随着中国社会主义民主法治和政治文明建设的深入发展和中国人权实践的不断进步，将人权原则写入《宪法》成为当代中国发展进步的必然。

2004年3月，第十届全国人大二次会议通过《宪法》修正案，首次将“国家尊重和保障人权”写入《宪法》，使“尊重和保障人权”由党和政府的一贯主张上升为人民和国家的意志，确立为国家根本大法的一项原则。将“国家尊重和保障人权”原则写入《宪法》，在《宪法》既有人权内容的基础上增加这一概括性、原则性条款，进一步确立、强化了《宪法》作为国家根本大法的法律价值，为党和政府实现尊重和保障人权的施政理念、为中国人权法制建设奠定了宪法保障。

“人权入宪”之后，“尊重和保障人权”等原则和内容又相继载入国家“十一五”和“十二五”的发展规划纲要、《中国共产党章程》、十八届三中全会通过的《中共中央关于全面深化改革若干重大问题的决定》等一系列党和国家重要文件之中。国家先后制定并有效实施《国家人权行动计划（2009～2010年）》和《国家人权行动计划（2012～2015年）》。

十年历程，物华阜新。十年来，中国共产党和中国政府坚持从本国国情和实际出发，以促进社会公平正义、增进人民福祉为出发点和落脚点，全面深化改革，推动经济、社会、文化各项事业的发展，保证人民平等参与、平等发展权利，让发展成果更多更公平地惠及全体人民。

十年来，中国经济保持平稳较快发展，人民生活水平稳步提高，人民的生存权和发展权得到更好的保障。社会保障事业快速发展，保障内容持续增加，保障范围不断扩大，基本公共服务均等化进一步推进。2013年，中国国内生产总值保持了7.7%的较快增长。全年农村居民人均纯收入8896元，扣除价格因素，实际增长9.3%；城镇居民人均可支配收入26955元，扣除价格因素，实际增长7.0%；居民消费价格涨幅保持在2.6%的低水平。世界上规模最大的社会保障体系初步形成。截至2014年6月，全国城乡居民养老

保险人数达 4.97 亿，其中按月领取养老待遇人数为 1.4 亿。全国失业保险人数为 1.6595 亿。参加城镇职工医疗保险、城镇居民医疗保险和新型农村合作医疗的人数超过 13.2 亿。

十年来，民主法制建设不断发展，以《宪法》为统帅的社会主义法律体系得以形成并逐步完善。国家修改《刑事诉讼法》、《国家赔偿法》、《监狱法》、《律师法》、《人民警察法》、《治安管理处罚法》等，并在新修改的《刑事诉讼法》中专门写入“尊重和保障人权”。2013 年 12 月 28 日，全国人大常委会通过了《关于废止有关劳动教养法律规定的决定》。协商民主制度化持续推进，基层直接民主健康发展，公民依法有序实现民主权利形式更加多样，国家政治生活的民主化水平进一步提高。国家治理体系和治理能力现代化建设取得新进展。政务信息更加公开，公众言论自由的权利得到合法保障。互联网成为公民表达意见和发表言论的重要渠道之一。截至 2014 年 6 月，网民规模达 6.32 亿，互联网普及率达 46.9%。

十年来，其他各项人权事业得到有效推进。国家对少数民族继续实施倾斜性政策，少数民族依法享有和行使各项权利。残疾人基本公共服务体系更加完善，残疾人平等参与社会生活的条件进一步改善，各项权利得到有效保障；加快生态文明制度建设，加大环境保护力度，依法惩治环境侵权犯罪，努力建设美丽中国；人权教育大众化、专门化并行进展。“国家人权教育与培训基地”增至八家。积极参与国际人权交流合作，认真履行《经济、社会、文化权利国际公约》等多项国际人权公约，以高度负责任的精神提交《国家人权报告》，并顺利通过两轮联合国人权理事会普遍国别人权审查。

中国人权事业的整体发展进步得到了国际上一些有识之士的认可。西班牙知名中国问题专家奥古斯都·索托最近撰文指出：“人权问题并非某一国或者世界某一地区独有的问题，而是与经济和民生发展息息相关。在人权问题上，中国正获得持续的发展和进步。这一认知既来自我和朋友的亲身经历，也来自我对中国整体发展的观察和思考。”[①]

① 《人民日报》2014 年 7 月 15 日第 2 版。

二、中国梦：谱写中国人权事业新篇章

十年征程成就辉煌。“装点此关山，今朝更好看。”中共十八大之后，习近平总书记提出中国梦重要战略思想。中国梦的提出，使“尊重和保障人权”的宪法原则更具有实践性，使中国人权事业的发展与每个人的幸福生活更加紧密地结合在一起。

中国梦的本质是国家富强、民族振兴、人民幸福。在中国人民为实现中华民族伟大复兴的中国梦而奋斗的历史进程中，“尊重和保障人权”将始终作为价值导向。“两个一百年”的奋斗目标蕴含着经济、社会、文化、公民、政治权利诉求，既是对人权的直接确认与宣示，也体现了对人权的决心和信心。“家是最小国，国是千万家。”国家富强、民族振兴、人民幸福，三位一体、有机相连。国家富强和民族振兴具体表现为经济发展、政治昌明、文化繁荣、社会和谐、生态良好，而这一切的根本使命和历史归宿则是让中国人民过上更加富裕、更有尊严的生活，使每个中国人都得到发展自我和服务社会的机会，都享有人生出彩和梦想成真的机会，最终实现每个人自由而全面的发展。中国梦归根结底是每一个中国人的梦。中国梦与中国人权事业发展进步在奋斗目标、逻辑起点和价值归宿上同源同根、同步同向、相辅相成。中国梦的目标紧紧围绕人民的利益诉求，满足不同阶层人民的生活需求，是中国人民根本利益的“最大公约数”和时代最强音，为中国人权事业树立了新起点、新愿景，注入了新内涵、新动力。

“历史是过去的现实，现实是未来的历史。”中国梦立足中国的发展实践，既是对中华民族发展状态的一种美好描述，又是一个需要脚踏实地努力实践的具体目标。站在新的起跑线上，我们比历史上任何时期都更有信心、更有能力实现“中国梦”这一蓝图。党的十八届三中全会提出的全面深化改革的总目标，即完善和发展中国特色社会主义制度、推进国家治理体系和治理能力现代化，是以“国家尊重和保障人权”和实现人民幸福为根本归宿的。2014 年 6 月 6 日，中共中央全面深化领导小组第三次会议审议通过《关于司法体制改革试点若干问题的框架意见》，对推进人权司法保障提

出了新要求。2014 年 10 月中国共产党召开十八届四中全会，研究全面推进依法治国重大问题。这是第一次在党的中央全会上专题研究依法治国基本方略，标志着中国开启人权法治保障的新阶段，必将进一步推进中国人权事业向前发展。

三、中国梦—世界梦：促进国际人权事业健康发展

中国人权事业是国际人权事业的重要组成部分。中国梦连接了过去、现在和未来，连接了当代中国与外部世界。全球维度下的中国梦，就是世界共建共享的梦，是世界和平、发展、合作、共赢的梦。

和平与安全是人权保障的前提。《世界人权宣言》开宗明义庄严宣告："对人类家庭所有成员的固有尊严及平等的和不移的权利的承认，乃是世界自由、正义与和平的基础。"有着 5000 多年历史的中华文明始终崇尚和平、和睦、和谐，这种价值追求深深溶化在中国人民的血脉之中。中国梦体现了当代中国人的理想，也蕴含着中华民族对"公"、"共"、"同"、"和"等人生哲学与社会理想的憧憬，反映了中华文化不懈追求进步的历史传统和精神实质。近年来，中国继续为维护世界和平发挥重要作用，无论是在解决国际争端还是在维护地区稳定方面中国都作出了积极贡献。目前，中国已经成为联合国常任理事国中向非洲国家派遣维和部队人数最多的国家。

中国梦是奉献世界的梦。中国在自身发展的同时，也在积极帮助其他国家共同发展，促进各国尊重和保障人权。中国的机遇就是世界的机遇，并为世界带来更多正面外溢效应。经过改革开放 35 年的发展，中国经济总量已经跃居世界第二位，占世界经济的份额已经由 10 年前的 4% 提高到 10% 左右，对世界经济增长的贡献率年均超过 20%，2013 年达近 30%。在国际金融危机阴云未散的背景下，中国克服困难，对世界经济的恢复发挥了重要作用。中国已连续五年成为非洲第一大贸易伙伴国。得益于与中国贸易的大幅增加，撒哈拉以南非洲国家近十年来取得了近 6% 的年均经济增长，中非合作对非洲经济增长的贡献率超过 20%。正如南非学者马丁·戴维斯形象指出："非洲的发展已经和中国在非洲投资贸易活动的开展呈现出一种紧密的共生

共荣关系。”①

中国不仅致力于自身发展，造福中国人民，也造福各国人民。作为世界上最大的发展中国家，中国坚持把中国人民的利益同各国人民的共同利益结合起来，向其他发展中国家提供力所能及的援助。近年来，中国对外援助规模持续增长。2010～2012年，中国对外援助金额达893.4亿元人民币。其中，对外提供无偿援助323.2亿元人民币，占对外援助总额的36.2%。多年来，中国通过项目援建、提供物资、开展技术合作和人力资源开发合作、派遣援外医疗队和志愿者、提供人道援助以及减免受援国债务等多种方式，支持和帮助发展中国家特别是最不发达国家在减贫、粮食安全、贸易发展、危机预防与重建、人口发展、妇幼保健、疾病防控、教育、环境保护等领域的发展。3年来，中国还向联合国开发计划署、儿童基金会、教育科学及文化组织、世界卫生组织以及全球抗击艾滋病、结核病和疟疾基金等国际机构累计捐款约17.6亿元人民币。2014～2017年，中国对联合国人权事务高级专员办公室的捐款也将提升至每年80万美元。

千百年来，讲信修睦、善待他人的传统思想，塑造了中华民族敦厚平和的禀性；海纳百川、兼容并包的传统哲学，孕育了中华民族推己及人的文化。世界上没有放之四海而皆准的发展道路。在国际人权领域，最重要的是要把人权普遍性与各国特殊性相结合，把国际法与国内法相结合，把尊重国家主权与维护人权相结合。中国人权事业的发展之所以能够取得巨大进步，根本原因是得益于中国自主探索、自主选择了一条符合自身实际的人权发展之路。

天人合一、世界大同的共同理想，熔铸了中华民族强不执弱、富不侮贫的精神。中国人民不接受“国强必霸”的逻辑。不管国际风云如何变幻，中国始终倡导“和而不同”、“求同存异”，倡导国与国之间、不同文明之间进行平等交流、相互借鉴、共同进步，以使各国人民都能够共享世界文明成果。中国坚决反对国际人权领域各种形式的霸权主义和强权政治，愿意同世

① 《人民日报》2014年7月25日第23版。

界各国人民和睦相处、和谐发展，共谋和平、共护和平、共享和平，促进中国梦和各国人民的梦相通相融，努力为推进国际人权事业健康发展作出积极贡献。

Hoisting the Sails to Cross the Sea

Cai Mingzhao, Minister, State Council Information Office

Human rights, being great and sacred, are pursued by mankind tirelessly. The revolutions, developments and reforms led by the Communist Party of China (CPC) are aimed at enhancing people's well-being, which is the essence of human rights. A decade ago, that "[t]he State respects and protects human rights" was solemnly articulated in the *Constitution of the People's Republic of China,* indicating a new era for China's human rights cause.

On September 12, 2013, Minister Cai Mingzhao delivered a speech at the opening ceremony of the 6th Beijing Forum on Human Rights.

I. That "[t]he State respects and protects human rights" articulated in the Constitution was a milestone in China's human rights cause.

The Constitution protects human rights and human rights are the inherent spirit of the Constitution. With progress in socialist democracy, rule of law and political civilization as well as in the human rights cause, it is a necessary step to enshrine the principle of respecting and protecting human rights into the Constitution for the further development of a modern China.

In March 2004, an amendment to the Constitution was adopted by the Second Session of the Tenth National People's Congress, which included the statement that "[t]he State respects and protects human rights" in the Constitution for the first time. By so doing, "respect for and protection of human rights" was elevated from a consistent position of the CPC and the Chinese Government to the will of the people and the state and a principle of the Constitution. The addition of this general principle to the clauses about human rights protection that had already existed in the Constitution further established and consolidated the legal value of the Constitution as the fundamental law of China. It provides constitutional guarantee for the implementation of the governance philosophy of CPC and the government to respect and protect human rights and for the development of the legal system for human rights protection.

After the principle of respecting and protecting human rights was articulated in the Constitution, it has been included in a series of important documents of the CPC and the Central Government including *Outline of the 11th Five-Year Plan for Economic and Social Development* and *12th Five-Year Plan for Economic and Social Development, The Constitution of the Communist Party of China* and *Decision of the Central Committee of the Communist Party of China on Some Major Issues Concerning Comprehensively Deepening the Reform* adopted at the Third Plenary Session of the 18th Central Committee of the CPC. We have also formulated and effectively implemented 2009-2010 and 2012-2015 *National Human Rights Action Plans.*

It is within the past decade that much progress has been achieved in many respects. During the decade, proceeding from China's national conditions and reality and bearing in mind the enhancement of social justice and improvement of people's livelihood as the starting point and ultimate goal, the CPC and the Chinese Government have deepened reform in an all-round way, promoted economic, social and cultural development and worked to ensure people's rights to equal participation and development so that more benefits of development are shared by all people in a fairer way.

The decade saw a stable and fast economic growth, a steady improvement of people's livelihood and a better protection of people's rights to subsistence and development. Social security undertakings have developed rapidly with a wider range of items, a continuously expanded coverage and further advancement of equal access to basic public services. In 2013, China maintained a relatively fast GDP growth rate of 7.7%. The per capita net income of rural residents reached 8,896 yuan last year, a 9.3% increase in real terms after adjusting for inflation; the per capita disposable income of urban residents stood at 26,955 yuan, a 7.0% increase in real terms after adjusting for inflation; CPI increase was kept a low level of 2.6%. The largest social security system around the world has been preliminarily established. As it stood in June 2014, the pension system for rural and urban residents covered around 497 million people nationwide, among which 140 million were receiving monthly pensions; unemployment insurance covered around 165.95 million people; and over 1.32 billion were covered in medical insurance for urban workers, medical insurance for urban residents or new rural cooperative medical system.

During the decade, continuous progress has been achieved in the development of democracy and legal system and a socialist legal system with the overarching Constitution has been formulated and gradually improved. A number of laws have been revised such as *Criminal Procedure Law*, in which the principle of "respecting and protecting human rights" was specially included, *State Compensation Law, Prison Law, Lawyers' Law, People's Police Law* and *Public Security Administration Punishment Law*. On December 28, 2013, the Standing Committee of the National People's Congress ratified *Decision to Repeal the Legal Provisions on Re-Education through*

Labor. With the advancement of institutionalized consultative democracy and the sound development of grass-roots democracy, there are diversified ways for people to realize their democratic rights according to law in an orderly fashion, making China's political life more democratic. Moreover, further progress has been made in the modernization of China's governance system and capacity. Government information has become more accessible to the public and citizens' right to freedom of expression has been legally protected. The Internet has become a major important channel for citizens to voice their opinions. By June 2014, the number of netizens reached 632 million and Internet penetration rate was 46.9%.

During the decade, other aspects of China's human rights cause have also moved forward. The minority ethnic groups have continued enjoying favorable and preferential policies, being entitled to and exercising various rights in accordance with the law. The basic public service system for the disabled and the conditions for them to participate in social life on an equal basis have been further improved and their various rights have been effectively protected. We have also accelerated the development of ecological civilization system by making more efforts in environmental protection and punishing environment infringement crimes for the purpose of building a beautiful China. The popularization and specialization of human rights education have made new progress and the number of national human rights education and training bases has increased to eight. We have been actively engaged in the international exchanges and cooperation on human rights and have earnestly implemented international conventions on human rights including *International Covenant on Economic, Social and Cultural Rights.* We have taken a highly responsible attitude in submitting *China's Human Rights Report* and have successfully undergone two rounds of Universal Periodic Review conducted by the United Nations Human Rights Council.

The overall progress of China's human rights cause has been recognized by men of insight in the international community. Augusto Soto, a well-known Spanish expert on the research of China, recently wrote that "[t]he issue of human rights is one that goes beyond borders; instead, it is closely bound up with the economic development and the improvement of people's livelihood. With regard to human rights protection,

China is developing continuously and making steady progress. This conclusion comes not only from experiences of mine and my friends but also my observation of and reflection on China's overall development. "①

II. The Chinese Dream: a new chapter on China's human rights cause.

The ten-year efforts have yielded many fruitful results. After the 18th CPC National Congress, General Secretary Xi Jinping put forth the important strategic thinking of the Chinese Dream. The Chinese Dream proposition renders the constitutional principle of "respecting and protecting human rights" more effectively implementable and links human rights protection more closely to the happiness of every Chinese citizen.

The essence of the Chinese Dream is to build a prosperous and strong country, to rejuvenate the nation, and to bring people a happy life. In the historical course of striving for the Chinese Dream of great national rejuvenation, the principle of "respecting and protecting human rights" will always be the value orientation. The "Two Centennial Goals" aiming at building an all-round prosperous society and achieving the great rejuvenation of the Chinese nation embody the Chinese people's demand for economic, social, cultural, civil and political rights, which not only directly confirm the commitment to human rights but also demonstrate the determination and confidence to realize human rights. "A family is a miniature of a country while the whole country is made up of millions of families." There is a close correlation among the prosperity and greatness of a country, the rejuvenation of a nation and the happiness of its people. The prosperity and greatness of a country and the rejuvenation of a nation can be achieved through a booming economy, a well-developed political environment, a thriving cultural atmosphere, a harmonious society as well as a favorable ecological environment. But the fundamental mission and the ultimate purpose are for the Chinese people to live a more prosperous and dignified

---

① *People's Daily*, July 15, 2014, page 2.

life, for each and everyone of them to have the opportunities to develop themselves, to serve the society, to lead a spectacular life and to achieve their dreams, in other words, free and comprehensive development of each individual. The Chinese Dream, in the final analysis, is the dream of every individual in China. The Chinese Dream and the progress of China's human rights cause share the same origins, move in the same direction and complement each other in goals, logical starting points and values. The Chinese Dream centers on people's demand for rights and aims at meeting the needs in life of people from all walks of life. It is the greatest "common denominator" of the fundamental interests of the Chinese people and represents the strongest voice of the times, injecting fresh contents and impetus to China's human rights cause as well as creating a new starting point and a new vision.

"History is the reality in the past, while reality will be history in the future." The Chinese Dream, based on the development of the whole country, is not only an ideal interpretation of its future but also a concrete goal to be realized only with down-to-earth efforts. Standing on a new starting point, we are more confident and capable to fulfill the blueprint of the Chinese Dream than at any time in history. The general goal of comprehensively deepening reform, set at the Third Plenary Session of the 18th CPC Central Committee, i.e., to improve and develop the socialist system with Chinese characteristics and to modernize the governance system and capacity, is proposed for the ultimate purpose of "respecting and protecting human rights" and promoting people's well-being. On June 6, 2014, the CPC Central Committee's Leading Group for Comprehensively Deepening Reform deliberated and approved in its third meeting the *Framework Opinions on Several Issues Concerning Pilot Reform of Judicial System*, which put forward new requirements for promoting judicial protection of human rights. In October, 2014, the Fourth Plenary Session of the 18th CPC Central Committee studied major issues concerning promoting rule of law in an all-round manner, the first such study by the plenum. It marked the beginning of a new phase in human rights protection according to law and will for sure accelerate the development of China's human rights cause.

Ⅲ. The Chinese Dream – a world dream: to promote sound development of international human rights cause.

China's human rights cause is an indispensable component of the international human rights cause. The Chinese Dream connects the past, present and future and links contemporary China with the outside world. From a global perspective, the Chinese Dream is a dream for peace, development, cooperation and win-win shared and pursued by people from all nations.

Peace and security are the prerequisites of protecting human rights. The *Universal Declaration of Human Rights* begins by solemnly declaring that "recognition of the inherent dignity and of the equal and inalienable rights of all members of the human family is the foundation of freedom, justice and peace in the world". The Chinese civilization of over 5,000 years has always worshiped peace, concord and harmony, which is deeply rooted in the heart of every Chinese individual. The Chinese Dream embodies not only wishes of contemporary Chinese people, but also the nation's longing for such social ideals as "fairness" (gōng, 公), "togetherness" (gòng, 共), "universality" (tóng, 同) and "harmony" (hé, 和), reflecting the relentless pursuit of progress as a tradition and spirit of the Chinese civilization. In recent years, China has continuously played an important role in protecting world peace. China has made positive contribution to both settlement of international disputes and maintaining regional stability. At present, China deploys the largest number of peacekeeping force in African countries among permanent members of the UN Security Council.

The Chinese Dream is also about bringing benefits to the whole world. China not only develops itself but also actively helps other countries to develop together and promotes respect for and protection of human rights. China's opportunities are shared by the whole world and have more positive spillover effects to other countries as well. Thirty-five years into reform and opening-up, the Chinese economy now ranks the second largest in the world, accounting for 10% of the world economy, increased from 4% ten years ago. China's contribution to world's economic growth is over 20% annually, even close to 30% in 2013. Against the backdrop of the lingering international financial crisis, China has played an important role in the recovery of the world economy despite difficulties. China has become Africa's largest trading partner for five consecutive years. Thanks to the tremendous increase in trade with China, Sub-Saharan African countries have registered an annual economic growth of almost 6% over the past decade. China-Africa cooperation contributes to more than 20% of Africa's economic growth. As South African scholar Martin Davis pointed out, "Africa's development and the trade and investment activities of China in Africa are closely related and enjoy common prosperity".①

China's commitment to its development brings benefits to people within and without China. As the world's largest developing country, China has endeavored to integrate the interests of Chinese people with those people in other countries and provided assistance for other developing countries. The recent years have witnessed a continuous increase of China's foreign aid. From 2010 to 2012, foreign aid to other countries totaled 89.34 billion yuan, among which 32.32 billion was gratuitous, accounting for 36.2% of the total. Over the years, China has supported and helped developing countries, especially those least developed ones, in poverty reduction, food security, trade development, crisis prevention and recovery, population development, maternal and child health, disease prevention and control, education and environmental protection by various ways such as construction assistance, materials and supplies, technical cooperation and human resources development, deployment of medical teams and volunteers, humanitarian assistance and debt relief. Over the past three years, China has donated a total of 1.76 billion yuan to UNDP, UNICEF, UNESCO, WHO, the Global Fund to Fight AIDS, Tuberculosis and Malaria and some other international institutions. From 2014 to 2017, China's contribution to the Office of the High Commissioner for Human Rights will also increase to 800,000 US dollars per year.

For thousands of years, traditional ideas of integrity, harmony and friendliness have shaped a good-natured and calm Chinese nation. The traditional philosophy of being tolerant and inclusive has fostered a culture that encourages people to put themselves in other's shoes. There is no universal path of development in the

---

① *People's Daily*, July 25, 2014, page 23.

world. With regard to international human rights protection, what matters most is to combine the universality of human rights with particularity of a country, the international law with national laws, and the respect for state sovereignty with protection of human rights. The fundamental reason for China to have achieved remarkable progress in human rights protection is that China has independently explored and chosen a path for human rights protection that suits its national conditions.

Bearing in mind a common ideal of cosmopolitanism and harmony between human and nature, the Chinese nation, even when it is strong and wealthy, does not oppress the weak or bully the poor. The Chinese people do not accept the logic that "a strong country is bound to seek hegemony". No matter how the international situation changes, China is always an advocate of "harmony without uniformity", "seeking common ground while reserving differences", exchanges and mutual learning among different countries and civilizations on an equal footing to make common progress for people of all nations to share the achievements of different civilizations. China resolutely opposes all forms of hegemonism and power politics in the international arena of human rights and is willing to live in harmony with people from other nations, develop hand-in-hand harmoniously, and pursue, protect and share peace together. We will promote convergence between the Chinese Dream and dreams of other countries and make positive contribution to the sound development of international human rights cause.

(original translation by Jiang Yu)

从互联网普及看中国的人权保护

国家互联网信息办公室副主任　任贤良

2004年3月14日，中华人民共和国第十届全国人民代表大会第二次会议通过《宪法》修正案，首次将“人权”概念引入《中华人民共和国宪法》，明确规定“国家尊重和保障人权”。仅仅三个多月后，中国互联网发展就迎来一个值得纪念的日子。6月30日，中国网民首次突破1亿，达到1.03亿人；不仅如此，全国宽带用户数首次超过全国所有网民用户的一半。

白驹过隙，“人权入宪”已经整整十年。2014年，中国也迎来全功能接入国际互联网的第20个年头。20年间，互联网走入中国的千家万户，网民规模也已经猛增数倍达6.32亿，网民数量世界第一，中国已成为网络大国。

在一个有着13亿多人口的最大发展中国家，互联网接入爆炸式的发展与“国家尊重和保障人权”的宪法理念之间有着什么样的联系？两者是两层皮、互不相干的关系？又或者相互契合乃至相辅相成？时至今日，有必要好好对此做一下梳理。

这样的梳理，对中国下一步发展互联网有着承前启后的重要意义。而对于渴望弥合数字鸿沟、搭乘互联网经济增长快车的众多发展中国家来说，梳理总结出来的“中国经验”或许可以提供一个可资借鉴、同时具有可操作性的“后发崛起”方案。

“以人为本”的互联网接入

有许多机构曾就“互联网接入是不是一项人权”开展全球问卷调查，毫无悬念，大多数应答者给出了肯定的回答。有意思的是，被誉为“互联网之父”的温顿·瑟夫博士却坚持认为，互联网技术是有助于实现人权保障这个目的的工具之一，其本身并非一项权利。对此，万维网的发明者蒂姆·伯纳斯—李爵士并不认同，在他看来，互联网技术以及以此为基础的万维网、电子邮件和即时通讯等通信系统、社会网络、电子商务等已经成为人们生活中不可分割的重要部分，因此，互联网不是可以随时替换的工具，业已成为人类生存、体验的有机构成之一。

综合两位互联网发展先驱的不同看法，我们可以清晰地看到，在今天，无论是言论自由、参政议政等公民和政治权利，还是劳动权、教育权等经济社会文化权利的实现，离不开互联网提供的种种便利；随着信息化一步步铺开和深入，越来越多的活动被搬到了网络上，同时，基于信息化的创新层出不穷，不断开创人类交流互动的新途径，网络空间已然是人类活动不可或缺的领域。接入互联网的权利就相当于开启网络空间大门的钥匙，使随时随地与世界相连成为现实。

中国政府在用行动实实在在推进互联网和信息化的普及，先后制定了一系列政策，规划互联网发展，明确互联网和社会信息化阶段性发展重点。1993 年，中国成立“国家经济信息化联席会议”，该会议负责领导国家公用经济信息通信网建设。1997 年，制定《国家信息化“九五”规划和 2010 年远景目标》，将互联网列入国家信息基础设施建设，提出通过大力发展互联网产业推进国民经济信息化进程。2002 年，颁布《国民经济和社会发展第十个五年计划信息化专项规划》，确定中国信息化发展的重点包括推行电子政务、振兴软件产业、加强信息资源开发利用、加快发展电子商务等。2002 年 11 月，中国共产党第十六次全国代表大会提出，以信息化带动工业化，以工业化促进信息化，走出一条新型工业化路子。

在 2004 年“人权入宪”之后的第二年，中国政府颁布了《2006 ～ 2020

年国家信息化发展战略》，将信息化上升为国家发展战略，为信息化的基础设施建设和成果普及提供了强有力的保证。在《2006～2020年国家信息化发展战略》中，中国政府将“要以人为本，惠及全民，创造广大群众用得上、用得起、用得好的信息化发展环境”规定为信息化发展的指导思想和战略方针之一。就此，“以人为本”成为中国对互联网接入权利的核心概括，“用得上、用得起、用得好”是互联网接入权利“中国化”的主要内容。

为了让广大老百姓“用得上”互联网，中国投入大量资金建设互联网基础设施，建起了覆盖全国、惠及全民的互联网基础设施，促进了互联网的普及和应用。1997～2013年，全国共完成互联网基础设施建设投资6万亿元人民币。截至2013年年底，全国通信光缆线路总长度达到1745.1万公里，已建成辐射全国的通信光缆网络。计算机拥有量从2002年3800万台增加至2011年的3亿台，中国农村居民家庭电脑拥有量也在过去10年增加了10倍。在2012年，中国就已经实现了100%的乡镇基本具备互联网接入能力，100%的乡镇和88%的行政村通宽带。中国手机网民规模增长迅速，2012年使用手机上网的网民达到4.2亿人，第一次超越使用台式电脑接入互联网的网民数量。2013年中国政府公布的《“宽带中国”战略及实施方案》，首次将宽带网络作为新时期国家经济社会发展的战略性公共基础设施，力争到2020年中国的宽带网络基础设施发展水平与发达国家之间的差距大幅缩小。届时，宽带网络将全面覆盖城乡，固定宽带家庭普及率达到70%，3G / LTE用户普及率达到85%，行政村通宽带比例超过98%。

为了让广大老百姓“用得起”互联网，中国政府加大财政资金支持力度，充分利用中央各类专项资金，引导地方相关资金投向网络研发及产业化以及农村和老少边穷地区的宽带网络发展。面对中国中西部农村地区通宽带的运维成本远高于用户能够支付的宽带使用费、企业长期运营也难以收回投资的状况，2004年中国政府启动“通信村村通工程”，让越来越多的农村通电话、通宽带；截至2013年年底，中国移动、中国电信、中国联通三家基础电信企业在农村特别是中西部地区投资超过800亿元。在《“宽带中国”战略及实施方案》中，国务院还首次提出“完善电信普遍服务补偿机制，形成支持农村和中西部地区宽带发展的长效机制”等降低互联网费用的创新举措。

为了让广大老百姓“用得好”互联网，中国政府鼓励发展有利于促进经济社会发展、提升公共服务水平、便利人们工作生活的互联网应用，努力构建结构合理、发展均衡的互联网应用格局，提高互联网整体发展和应用水平。中国政府大力推动电子商务类、教育类网站发展，积极推进电子政务建设，支持发展网络广播、网络电视等新兴媒体，倡导提供形式多样、内容丰富的互联网信息服务，以满足人们多样化、多层次的信息消费需求。截至2013年年底，中国域名总数为1844万个，网站总数为320万个，网页数量为1500亿个；全球十大互联网企业中中国有3家，2013年网络购物用户达到3亿，全国信息消费整体规模达到2.2万亿元人民币，电子商务交易规模突破10万亿元人民币；论坛用户数量为1.2亿人，博客和个人空间用户数量为4.37亿人，社交网站用户数量为2.78亿人，网络文学用户数为2.74亿人，网络视频用户数量为4.28亿人，微博用户数量为2.81亿人，即时通信用户数量为5.32亿人；手机即时通信用户为4.31亿，手机微博用户达到1.96亿。

可以说，在当下的中国，无论是偏远山区的民众，还是一线城市的精英，都或多或少地被互联网进入中国所掀起的浪潮所波及。互联网的普及，改变了中国，也改变了我们每一个人的生活。在经济领域，互联网在促进经济结构调整、转变经济发展方式等方面发挥着越来越重要的作用，成为推动中国经济发展的重要引擎。互联网促进了文化产业发展，大大增强了中国文化产业的总体实力。互联网促进了政府信息公开，在增进公众知情权、参与权、表达权、监督权等方面的作用日益凸显。

无论最终把互联网接入权归入公民和政治权利或者经济社会文化权利，不可否认的是，互联网接入权有赖于一国政府逐级、逐步的予以实现。在“国家尊重和保障人权”的宪法理念和“以人为本”的互联网接入权利观的指引下，中国政府做了大量的政策立法工作，最大限度地调用自身资源能力，保障了广大中国公民有效地享有互联网接入的权利。回顾中国互联网20年的发展历程，用“幸福网事”来概括中国人对互联网共同的记忆一点也不为过。

经验和展望

现如今，互联网已经成为中国社会运行的基本要素和基础支撑，如毛细血管般渗透到国家社会生活的各个领域，以前所未有的深度和广度深刻改变着经济发展格局和信息传播格局，给中国社会带来全新气象。从蹒跚学步到阔步前行，中国互联网接入和信息化推进速度之快让世人惊叹，在被称为人类“第三次浪潮”的信息化过程中，中国和世界第一次站上同一条起跑线。

从中国互联网 20 年的发展中，或许我们可以得出以下两点经验。

一是互联网接入权作为一项人权具有普遍意义，但权利的具体实现主要依靠各个国家自身的努力，因此具有特殊性；同时，互联网接入权又是历史的产物，它的充分实现是同每个国家经济文化水平相联系的逐渐发展的过程。换句话说，并不是把互联网接入提升到人权这样高的位阶后，互联网接入权就会自然而然实现了，更为重要的是如何为这项权利的实现找到广泛而强大的需求和社会共识以及实现这项权利的社会和物质基础。

从 20 世纪 90 年代始，中国政府就审时度势，战略性地将信息化和互联网与中国政治、经济、社会、文化发展充分紧密结合，努力使其成为中国人民生活、工作、学习不可或缺的重要工具，由此，大力发展互联网成为中国全国全社会的基本共识，互联网发展装上了强大的需求引擎。反过来，互联网发展带来的巨大经济效益显著增强中国国力，中国政府在对互联网加大投资和建设力度时游刃有余。正是这样的良性循环构成对中国互联网跨越式发展的有力支撑。

二是和许多发展中国家相仿，中国在互联网和信息技术自主创新方面还相对落后，区域和城乡差异比较明显，特别是人均带宽与国际先进水平差距较大，国内互联网发展瓶颈仍然较为突出。在这样的国情和发展阶段中，要克服初始条件不佳的权利实现困境，实现互联网接入跨越式的发展，从根本上需要一国政治统治集团发挥锐意进取的姿态，需要政治统治集团将本国人民的福祉奉为最高宗旨并做出不懈的努力，更需要一国政治秩序保持长久的稳定。

一国政治秩序稳定指的是政治体系的连续性和有序性，它包括国家政权体系的稳定、权力结构的稳定、政治过程的有序状态。政治秩序稳定能够保证政治精英克服短期利益的诱惑，为国家民族百姓的梦想作出长期规划和顶层设计，政治秩序稳定也是国家行政机关能够高效落实政治决策的基本前提。相反，如果一国政治失序乃至爆发激烈的政治冲突，其后果无外乎周而复始地发生街头骚乱、政局变更，囿于循环动荡的怪圈，国家不振、人民遭殃。

从这个角度来看，中国在保障民众互联网接入权方面取得举世瞩目成绩的最大经验，就是坚持中国共产党的坚强领导，坚持走中国特色社会主义道路。正是坚持了这两条，中国政府几十年如一日，始终坚持以经济建设为中心，又全面推进经济建设、政治建设、文化建设、社会建设、生态文明建设；既坚持四项基本原则，又坚持改革开放；既强调解放和发展社会生产力，又强调逐步实现全体人民共同富裕、促进人的全面发展。政治的稳定和道路的明确犹如定海神针，一切规划、政策、立法、行政就相应地有了指向性、稳定性、连续性；各级政府、社会各界往同一个目标着力，全国上下拧成一股绳，形成合力。这就是中国在互联网方面取得现有成绩的最大秘诀。

2012 年，在中国共产党第十八届代表大会上，以习近平为总书记的新一届中国共产党中央领导集体正式接过接力棒，并针对中国发展互联网采取了一系列强有力的举措。中国共产党十八大报告明确把“信息化水平大幅提升”纳入全面建成小康社会的目标之一，并提出了走中国特色新型工业化、信息化、城镇化、农业现代化道路，促进“四化”同步发展。十八届三中全会后，国家主席习近平提出，将中国建设成网络强国的战略部署要与“两个一百年”奋斗目标同步推进，向着网络基础设施基本普及、自主创新能力显著增强、信息经济全面发展、网络安全保障有力的目标不断前进。2014 年，中央网络安全和信息化建设领导小组成立。领导小组以规格高、力度大、立意远来统筹指导中国迈向网络强国的发展战略，体现了中国最高层全面深化改革、加强顶层设计的意志，显示出在保障网络安全、维护国家利益、推动信息化发展的决心。一个更强有力、更有权威性的机构，是中国网络安全和信息化国家战略迈出的重要一步。

“日月之行，若出其中；星汉灿烂，若出其里。”在习近平为总书记的新一届中国共产党中央领导集体带领下，拥有6亿网民的网络大国加速向网络强国挺进。实现之时，指日可待。中国人民有这个信心！

Protection of Human Rights in China from the Perspective of Internet Penetration

Ren Xianliang, Vice Director of the State Internet Information Office

On March 14, 2004, the Tenth National People's Congress adopted at its Second Session amendments to the *Constitution of the People's Republic of China,* introducing the concept of human rights in the Constitution with the statement that "[t]he State respects and protects human rights". June 30, just three months later, was a red-letter day for Internet development in China. Chinese netizens exceeded 100 million, reaching 103 million, and broadband users reached more than half of the total for the first time.

The year of 2014 marked the tenth anniversary of human rights being articulated in the Constitution. It was also the 20th year since China officially gained access to the Internet. In the two decades, thousands of Chinese households started to use the Internet and the number of netizens has multiplied to 632 million. Now China is a big country in Internet use, boasting the world's largest pool of netizens.

Is there a link between the explosive growth of Internet access and the constitutional concept of respect for and protection of human rights in this largest developing country with 1.3 billion people? Are the two separate and independent of each other? Or do they exist side-by-side and complement each other? These questions are worth our reflection today.

Answers to the above questions may be of great significance to the further development of the Internet in China. In addition, developing nations eager to close the digital gap and take an express train to Internet-driven growth are looking to the Chinese experience for lessons learnt and a feasible scheme of their own.

People-Oriented Approach to Internet Access.

Many questionnaires contain this questions: is Internet access a human right? And beyond any doubt the answer from majority is "yes". However, Dr. Vinton G. Cerf, Father of the Internet, considers the Internet an enabler of human rights instead of a human right per se. Sir Timothy John Berners-Lee, the inventor of the World Wide Web, holds that the Internet, together with the World Wide Web, communication systems such as Email and instant messaging, social networks or E-commerce that are based on this technology, have all become essential elements of human life and that in this connection rather than a tool which can be replaced anytime, the Internet is an integral part of human survival and experiences.

A conclusion to be drawn from these pioneers' viewpoints is that today the realization of both civil and political rights such as freedom of expression and political participation and economic, social and cultural rights such as the rights to work and education depend much on the conveniences offered by the Internet. With the ever-deepening reliance on information technology, more and more daily activities are now happening online. At the same time, as IT-based innovations flourish, new approaches to interpersonal communication have emerged, making cyberspace an indispensable part of people's life. The right to the Internet access is like a key to the cyberspace, making access to the world anytime and anywhere a reality.

The Chinese government has taken concrete actions to promote the widespread growth of the Internet and informatization by adopting a series of policies for Internet development and defining several phased priorities to boost Internet usage and societal informatization. In 1993, the National Economic Informatization Joint Meeting was initiated to lead the construction of a nation-wide public economic information network. In 1997, the *9th Five-Year Plan for State Informatization and the Long-Range Objective of the Year 2010* was formulated, which listed the Internet as part of the state information infrastructure and set the goal of pushing forward national economic informatization via vigorous development of the Internet industry. In 2002 the *Specialized Plan for Informatization in the Tenth Five-Year Plan for National Economic and Social Development* was promulgated, defining China's priorities in this field, including the promotion of an e-government, the vigorous development of the nation's software industry, the strengthening of development and utilization of information resources and the acceleration of e-commerce development. In November 2002, the 16th National Congress of the Communist Party of China (CPC) decided to use IT to propel industrialization, which will in turn stimulate IT application, blazing a new trail to industrialization.

In the second year after "[t]he State respects and protects human rights" was articulated in the Constitution, the *State Informatization Development Strategy (2006~2020)* was formulated. It defined informatization as a national strategy, a pledge to boost the construction of informatization infrastructure and its achievements. In the Strategy, the Chinese Government vows to provide accessible, affordable and convenient Internet services for the benefit of all people and to guide informatization development with this principle. Since then, people-oriented development has become a core concept in the right to Internet access in China and accessibility, affordability and convenience in Internet access have become the Chinese expressions of the exercise of such right.

In order that the Chinese people may access the Internet, large capital has been invested in the construction of nationwide Internet infrastructure with the aim of benefiting the whole nation as well as facilitating Internet penetration and application. From 1997 to 2013, a total of 6 trillion yuan was invested to this aim, building a nationwide optical cable network with a total length of 17.451 million km covering the whole country by late 2013. Computer ownership increased from 38 million in 2002 to 300 million in 2011. Even in rural areas, the number of households possessing computers increased by ten folds over the past decade. By 2012, all Chinese towns and townships had access to the Internet, with broadband reaching all towns and townships and 88% incorporated villages. The number of mobile Internet users surged, as 420 million people used mobile handsets to access the Internet in 2012, for the first time exceeding the number of netizens using desktop computers. In 2013, the Chinese Government drafted the "Broadband China" strategy and implementation plan and for the first time regarded broadband network as a strategic public infrastructure for national socio-economic development in the new era. The Chinese Government seeks to bridge the gap of broadband network infrastructure between China and developed countries by 2020, targeting comprehensive broadband coverage for urban and rural areas, 70% household penetration rate for fixed broadband, 85% penetration rate for 3G / LTE and broadband coverage for over 98% of incorporated towns.

In order to make the Internet affordable for our people, the Chinese Government has increased its financial support, made full use of various kinds of special funds and directed local funds to be invested into the R&D and industrialization of network capabilities and the establishment of broadband networks in rural and former revolutionary base areas, areas inhabited by minority nationalities, remote and border areas and poverty-stricken areas. As broadband operation and maintenance costs in the central and western rural areas of China are much higher than what users can afford and operators cannot recover their investment even with long-term operation, in 2004, the Chinese Government launched a campaign to extend telephone service and broadband to all villages. By the end of 2013, the three major telecom operators, namely China Mobile, China Telecom and China Unicom, had invested more than 80 billion yuan in rural areas, especially in central and western China. In "Broadband China", the State Council proposed for the first time several innovative initiatives to reduce Internet fees such as improved universal telecom service compensation and long-term mechanisms to support development of broadband in rural, central and western areas.

In order to make Internet access convenient for our people, the Chinese Government has encouraged Internet use for the promotion of economic and social progress, the enhancement of public services and the facilitation of work and life of its citizens; the government has also stepped up its efforts to build a well-structured and balanced use of the Internet so as to improve its advancement and application. The Chinese Government has vigorously promoted the development of e-commerce and education-focused websites, given impetus to e-government development, advocated the development of new media such as online radio and online television and called for the provision of varied and rich Internet information services to satisfy diversified and multi-tiered needs in information consumption. At the end of 2013, the number of domain names in China reached 18.44 million, with websites totaling 3.2 million and web pages 150 billion. Three of the top 10 Internet enterprises of the world were from China. 300 million people had shopped online. The total value of information consumption reached 2.2 trillion yuan. E-commerce transaction turnovers surged past 10 trillion. There were 120 million bulletin board system (BBS) users, 437 million blogs and personal homepages, 278 million social network sites users, 274 million online literature readers, 428 million online video viewers, 281 million microbloggers and 532 million users of instant messaging service. Cell phone instant messaging users numbered 431 million and cell phone microblog users reached 196 million.

In today's China, the lives of all people, from peasants in remote mountainous areas to elites in metropolitan cities, are influenced by the introduction of Internet access in China. The penetration of Internet has changed the panorama of the country and the life of each and every one of its citizens. The Internet is playing an increasingly important role in promoting economic restructuring and transforming mode of economic development as an engine driving growth. The Internet has also promoted development of the cultural industry, greatly increasing its overall strength. The Internet has served to facilitate disclosure of government information, playing an increasingly prominent role in satisfying people's rights to information, participation, expression and supervision.

No matter whether access to the Internet is ultimately categorized as a civil and political right or an economic, social and cultural right, there is no denying that the right to Internet access should be realized by the government in a step-by-step and progressive manner. Bearing in mind the constitutional concept of "respecting and protecting human rights" as well as the "people-oriented" approach to the right to Internet access, the Chinese Government has adopted policies and enacted laws and mobilized enormous resources to ensure that all Chinese people have access to the Internet. A review of the past 20 years of Internet development unveils a happy memory for Chinese.

Experience and Prospects.

Today, the Internet has become an essential element and underlying foundation of social interaction in China. It has penetrated all areas of social life in our country, interweaving all aspects of life much like the capillaries in our bodies. It has extensively and profoundly changed the patterns of economic development and information transmission, bringing new promises to our society. From a faltering start to forward strides, access to the Internet and informatization have developed at breath-taking speeds. In this "Third Wave" of informatization, China finally stands at the same starting line as the rest of the world.

The last 20 years of Internet development in China leave us two lessons.

First, it is of universal significance to classify the right to Internet access as a human right, but the realization of this right mainly depends on the efforts of individual countries, therefore this right remains distinct in nature. At the same time, the right to Internet access is also a product of history and its full implementation a gradual process closely related to the economy and culture of every country. In other words, the right of Internet access is not automatically realized when it is classified as a human right. More importantly, we must foster extensive and strong demands and social consensus for its realization and create a solid social and material foundation .

Since the 1990s, the Chinese Government has closely assessed its national situation, coming to the decision to strategically integrate informatization and the Internet with China's political, economic, social and cultural development so that the Internet would become an indispensable tool in the life, work and education of our people. Vigorously developing the Internet has thus become a shared view and strong demand in our society. Internet development has in turn brought China great economic benefits and enhanced its national strength, giving the Chinese Government greater capacity to invest in and further develop the Internet. It is this virtuous circle that has underpinned the leapfrog development of China's Internet.

Second, like many other developing countries, China still lags behind in proprietary innovations with regard to the Internet and information technology; obvious regional and rural-urban differences still exist; there is still big gap to advanced international level in terms of per capita bandwidth and Internet development is still confronted with apparent bottlenecks. In this national situation and phase of development, in order to overcome the poor initial conditions and achieve leapfrog development, the ruling group must forge ahead with determination and unremitting efforts with for the well-being of our people as top priority and the long-term political stability must be maintained.

A stable political order involves the continuity and order of the relevant political system, including a stable state regime, a stable power structures and an orderly political process. With stability of political order, political elites overcome temptations of short-term interests and work towards the long-term planning and institutional designs necessary for the dreams of the nation and its people to come true. Such stability is also a prerequisite for state administrative organs to effectively implement political decisions. On the contrary, political disorder and even intense political conflicts in a state may lead to repeated riots or regime changes, trapping the country in a vicious circle of turbulence, thus impeding its development and causing great harm to its people.

From this perspective, the underlying reasons for China's excellent track record in ensuring citizens' right to Internet access are that it has firmly upheld CPC leadership and firmly pursued a path of socialism with Chinese characteristics. For decades, the Chinese Government has taken economic development as its central task and sought comprehensive advancements in economic, political, cultural, social and ecological fields. In doing so, the government adheres to the Four Cardinal Principles as well as its Reform and Opening up Policy. It emphasizes both the importance to release and develop social productive forces and the long-term need to achieve common prosperity for all people and comprehensive development for each and every citizen. With political stability and a clear path, all plans, policies, legislation and administration are well motivated, stable and continuous. Governments at all levels and the whole society achieve synergy by heading towards a common goal. This is the ultimate reason behind the remarkable achievements in Internet development in

China.

In 2012, at the 18th National Congress of the CPC, the CPC Central Committee led by General Secretary Xi Jinping became the new leadership and adopted a series of powerful measures aimed at promoting Internet development. The Report to the 18th CPC National Congress clearly stated that IT application should be significantly expanded as part of the strive towards a moderately prosperous society across all aspects. The Report pointed out that we should pursue in parallel news ways of industrialization, informatization, urbanization and agricultural modernization with Chinese characteristics. After the Third Plenum of the 18th CPC Central Committee, President Xi Jinping pointed out that the strategic effort to become a cyber power should be implemented in parallel with the nation's "Two Centenary Goals." The President stressed that we should lay a strong foundation of network infrastructure, significantly enhance the nation's capacity for proprietary innovation, promote all-round development of information economy and effectively protect network security. In 2014, the Central Leading Group for Internet Security and Informatization was set up, involving senior officials. With impressive measures and high-minded goals, the leading group aims to steer China's development into a cyber-power. It demonstrates the desire of Chinese leaders to deepen reform comprehensively and improve top-level design and their determination to protect network security, ensure national interests and promote informatization. A more forceful and authoritative organization is an important step in implementing the national strategy.

"The sun and moon are reflected against the seas, and the stars are born from its depths." Under the leadership of the CPC Central Committee with Xi Jinping as General Secretary, China and its 600 million netizens are striving to be a cyber power, which will hopefully happen soon. We have full confidence in achieving this goal.

(original translation by Li Xiaoyu)

立法筑造保障人权的坚实堡垒

全国人大常委会法制工作委员会副主任　郑淑娜

2004年3月14日，第十届全国人民代表大会第二次会议通过《宪法》修正案，把“国家尊重和保障人权”正式载入了国家的根本大法。这是中国社会主义民主和法制建设达到一个新水平的标志，对推进中国的人权事业、实现社会全面进步产生重大而深远的影响。“人权入宪”十年来，全国人大及其常委会严格遵循《宪法》确立的“国家尊重和保障人权”的原则，通过立法切实建立起保障人权的坚实堡垒。

一、“人权入宪”标志着中国人权保护进入了一个新阶段

在中国，“人权入宪”是有着深刻的历史背景的。新中国成立60多年来，政府一直为维护和改善人权作着不懈的努力并且取得了显著的成就：国家的独立和统一为人民的生命和安全提供了保障；改革落后的生产关系，解放生产力，通过改革开放使经济迅速健康发展，为人民的生存和发展提供物质保障；人民实现了当家做主，享有广泛的政治权利；《宪法》和法律为行政机关管理权和司法机关司法权设定法律界限，保障公民的合法权利不受侵犯；坚持民族平等，实行民族区域自治，保障少数民族的各项权利；国家努力建立与社会经济发展水平相适应的社会保障制度，对弱势社会成员给予物质帮助。

1982年《宪法》在“总纲”之后把“公民的基本权利和义务”专列一章，体现了国家对公民权利的重视。2004年《宪法》修正案将“国家尊重和保障人权”写在“公民的基本权利和义务”一章的第一条，把人权和公民基本权利联系在一起，有利于按照“尊重和保障人权”的原则要求，进一步加强对公民基本权利的保护。随着“国家尊重和保障人权”成为一切国家机关、组织和个人遵循的宪法原则，中国人权保障的立法也进入了一个迅速发展的时期。

二、完善发展社会主义民主政治的法律，支持人民行使当家做主的权利

选举权和被选举权是《宪法》规定的首要的公民基本权利，是社会主义民主政治的直接体现。发展社会主义民主政治是中国共产党和中国政府始终不渝的奋斗目标，也是全国人大及其常委会立法的重要内容。

保障人人享有平等的选举权利，是我们党和国家一贯的政治主张和追求。2010年3月14日，第十一届全国人大三次会议通过关于修改《选举法》的决定，规定城乡按相同人口比例选举人大代表的制度，改变了过去50多年来农村和城市按不同人口比例选举人大代表的状况。从2011年起到2012年12月底，全国县、乡两级人大完成了新一轮的换届选举，这是《选举法》修改后首次实行城乡按相同人口比例选举人大代表，进一步增加了代表的广泛性，扩大了人民民主权利。9亿多选民依法参与民主选举，成为发展社会主义民主政治、保障人民当家做主的一次重要实践。

在城乡社区治理、基层公共事务和公益事业中实行群众自我管理、自我服务、自我教育、自我监督，是人民依法直接行使民主权利的重要方式。自1998年《村民委员会组织法》公布施行以来，村民自治制度已经发展成为中国特色的社会主义民主政治的重要组成部分。随着农村经济社会的发展，特别是城乡户籍制度、农村税费制度改革的深化，村民自治也遇到一些新问题。2010年10月，全国人大常委会修订了《村民委员会组织法》，进一步完善了村民委员会成员的选举程序，完善了对村民委员会成员的罢免程序、民主议事制度、民主管理和民主监督制度，对调动广大农民群众的积极性、主动

性和创造性，促进农村改革发展稳定发挥了重要作用。

三、完善刑事法律和刑事诉讼制度，打击犯罪、保护人民

尊重和保障人权是刑事立法的重要指导原则。十年来，全国人大常委会通过了《刑法修正案（六）》、《刑法修正案（七）》、《刑法修正案（八）》，尤其是《刑法修正案（八）》进一步落实宽严相济的刑事政策，取消了13个经济性非暴力犯罪的死刑，占死刑罪名总数的19.1%；对部分判处死缓的罪犯减刑后的实际执行刑期作了严格规范，对数罪并罚执行期限作了调整；加大了对累犯和黑社会性质组织犯罪的惩处力度，将醉酒驾车、飙车、拒不支付劳动报酬等严重危害群众利益的行为规定为犯罪，进一步完善了危害食品安全、生产销售假药和破坏环境资源等方面犯罪的规定。《刑法修正案（八）》强化了《刑法》对民生的保护，有利于更好地发挥《刑法》在惩治犯罪、保护人民、维护社会秩序、保障国家安全等方面的重要作用。

《刑事诉讼法》一方面保证准确及时地查明犯罪事实，惩罚犯罪分子，另一方面保障无罪的人不受刑事追究，尊重和保障人权，保护公民的诉讼权利和其他合法权利。2012年全国人大修改了《刑事诉讼法》，将“尊重和保障人权”这一宪法原则写入《刑事诉讼法》作为刑事诉讼制度的基本原则。这次修改还涉及一系列加强人权保护的内容：完善非法证据排除制度，遏制刑讯逼供和其他非法收集证据的行为；完善逮捕、监视居住的条件、程序和采取强制措施后通知家属的规定；强化辩护人在刑事诉讼中的法律地位，扩大法律援助的适用范围；完善讯问犯罪嫌疑人的程序和必要的侦查措施，强化对侦查措施的规范和监督，防止侦查权的滥用；规定未成年人刑事案件特别诉讼程序，如附条件不起诉和犯罪记录封存制度等。

为了确保死刑判决的慎重和公正，2006年10月全国人大常委会修改了《人民法院组织法》，将死刑案件核准权统一收归最高人民法院，严格控制和慎重适用死刑，充分体现了对生命权利的尊重和保障。

《国家赔偿法》是促进行政机关和刑事司法机关及其工作人员依法行使职权，保障和落实公民人身权利和财产权利的一部重要法律。2010年4月，

全国人大常委会对《国家赔偿法》进行了修改，畅通了赔偿请求渠道，完善了赔偿办理程序，明确了精神损害赔偿，保障了赔偿费用给付，体现了《宪法》规定的尊重和保障人权的精神和理念。

四、规范行政权力行使，保障公民合法权益不受侵犯

在中国，国家行政机关是实施人权保障法律的主要机关，依法行政成为尊重和保障人权的宪法原则付诸实施的关键。

为了贯彻《行政许可法》，规范行政许可事项，全国人大常委会通过了关于修改《公路法》、《公司法》、《证券法》、《票据法》、《拍卖法》、《野生动物保护法》、《渔业法》、《种子法》、《学位条例》等法律的决定，对这些法律中不符合《行政许可法》的规定，不符合转变政府职能、改革行政管理体制要求的个别条款予以调整或取消。

行政强制制度涉及行政管理的效率，也涉及对公民的人身权和财产权的处分或者限制。2011 年 6 月，全国人大常委会通过了《行政强制法》，既赋予行政机关必要的强制手段，以保障行政机关依法履行职责，维护公共利益和公共秩序，又对行政强制行为进行规范，以避免和防止行政权力的滥用，保护公民、法人和其他组织的合法权益。

社会治安管理是保障公共安全，保护公民合法权益的重要内容。2005 年 8 月，全国人大常委会制定《治安管理处罚法》，将一些新的违法行为纳入应给予治安管理处罚的范围，适当提高了罚款的数额；同时缩小了行政拘留处罚的自由裁量幅度，完善了处罚程序，强化了对公安机关和人民警察执法行为的规范和监督。

自然灾害、事故灾难给人民群众的生命财产造成巨大损失，规范突发事件的应对机制，对于保护人民生命财产有着重要意义。2007 年 8 月，全国人大常委会通过了《突发事件应对法》，规定了突发事件的预防与应急准备、监测与预警、应急处置与救援、事后恢复与重建等应对活动，有效保护人民生命财产安全，维护国家安全、公共安全、环境安全和社会秩序。

五、强化社会领域立法，保民生，保障公民权利

坚持以人为本，贯彻全面、协调、可持续的科学发展观，促进经济社会和人的全面发展，是中国经济社会发展的战略思想和指导方针，也是新时期立法工作的重要指导思想。

全国人大常委会高度重视保障劳动者就业和权益方面的立法。2007 年，审议通过了《劳动合同法》、《就业促进法》和《劳动争议调解仲裁法》三部法律；2011 年，修改了《职业病防治法》，保护劳动者的生命健康权利；2012 年，针对劳务派遣用工问题又对《劳动合同法》有关规定进行了修改，由此形成了一套比较完备的劳动法律制度，是中国社会领域立法的重要成果。

社会保障制度是改善民生的基本制度，是社会安定的重要保证。2010 年 10 月，全国人大常委会制定《社会保险法》，确立了“广覆盖、保基本、多层次、可持续”的社会保险制度，建立基本养老保险、基本医疗保险、工伤保险、失业保险、生育保险等社会保险制度，保障公民在年老、患病、工伤、失业、生育等情况下依法获得物质帮助的权利。

妇女、未成年人和残疾人是相对弱势的社会群体，需要立法对其权益予以特殊保障。修改《妇女权益保障法》，进一步完善了妇女权益的保障措施，增加了对损害妇女权益行为的处罚规定。修改《未成年人保护法》，进一步强化了家庭、学校、社会、国家对未成年人的保护责任，明确了未成年人的受教育权，保护未成年人身心健康，促进未成年人全面发展。修订《残疾人保障法》，充实了禁止歧视残疾人的有关规定，并从康复、教育、劳动就业、文化生活、社会保障和无障碍环境建设等方面强化了对残疾人权利的保障，促进残疾人平等参与社会生活、共享社会物质文化成果。

传染病是威胁人民生命健康权最严重的因素之一，精神卫生也日益成为重大的公共卫生问题和严重的社会问题。2004 年 8 月修订的《传染病防治法》，规定了及时救治、不得歧视、保护隐私、保障生活、合理报酬、依法补偿等原则和制度，充分体现了对人的生命权、健康权、隐私权和财产权的尊重和保护。2012 年 10 月制定的《精神卫生法》，切实保障精神障碍患者

的合法权益，保证其人格尊严和人身安全不受侵犯，保证公民的合法权益不因滥用非自愿住院治疗措施而受到侵害，努力实现保护个人权利与维护他人安全之间的平衡。

食品安全与人民群众的身体健康和生命安全息息相关，全国人大常委会制定《食品安全法》和《农产品质量法》，保障食品和农产品安全，维护人民群众的身体健康和生命安全。

环境问题已经成为全面建成小康社会的重要制约、人的全面发展的重要威胁。2014 年 4 月新修订的《环境保护法》，突出了民生思想，对重点污染物排放总量控制作出明确规定，对组织开展环境质量对公众健康影响的研究提出了积极鼓励，从信息公开、公益诉讼等方面明确提出保障公众环境权益，为解决提出环境问题、有效改善环境质量、满足公众环境诉求、保障人民身心健康提供了法律支撑，充分体现了改善民生的思想和以人为本的核心要求。

十年来，在“尊重和保障人权”这一宪法原则的指导下，中国的立法工作取得了极大的成就，形成了一整套包含《宪法》相关法、行政法、社会法、刑法、诉讼法等多个法律部门的人权保障法律体系。从这些法律贯彻实施的效果来看，确实发挥了立法对中国特色社会主义事业和社会生活的引领和推动作用，切实为国家尊重和保障人权提供了强有力的法律支撑。2010 年，中国特色社会主义法律体系已经建成。未来一个阶段内，中国全国人大及其常委会的一项重要工作，就是要根据社会发展的需求不断完善中国特色社会主义法律体系。按照中国共产党十八大提出的要求，我们要更加注重健全民主制度、丰富民主形式，保证人民依法实行民主选举、民主决策、民主管理、民主监督；更加注重发挥法治在国家治理和社会管理中的重要作用，维护国家法制统一、尊严、权威，保证人民依法享有广泛权利和自由。可以预见，在中国共产党的领导下，在《宪法》“尊重和保障人权”的指导下，中国的立法事业必将继续丰富和完善人权保障的相关制度，必将继续闪耀着人性和人权的光芒。

Fortifying Legislation for Human Rights Protection

Zheng Shu'na, Vice Chairperson, Legislative Affairs Commission of the Standing Committee of the National People's Congress

On March 14, 2004, the Second Session of the Tenth National People's Congress adopted an amendment to the Constitution, declaring that "[t]he State respects and protects human rights". It marked a new high in China's socialist democracy and legal construction and had important and far-reaching influence for the better protection of human rights and comprehensive social progress. In the 10 years since then, the National People's Congress and its standing committee have acted in strict observance of the constitutional principle of "respecting and protecting human rights" and turned legislations into a fortress for the protection of human rights.

I. Incorporation of "human rights" in the Constitution marked the beginning of a new stage for human rights protection in China.

It is worth noting the profound historical background for the incorporation of "human rights" in the Constitution. In the more than 60 years since the founding of New China, the government has made great efforts to protect and improve human rights and gained prominent achievements. Its independence and unity protects

people's life and security. China reformed the backward productive relations, liberated productivity and advanced economic development through reform and opening-up, which help secure people's subsistence and development. The people are now masters of their own country and enjoy extensive political rights. The Constitution and laws set legal boundary for the power of administrative and judicial organs respectively to protect citizens' lawful rights from infringement. China insists on the equality between different ethnic groups and implements regional autonomy of ethnic minorities to protect ethnic minorities' rights. China strives to build a social security system commensurate with its level of social and economic development and provides material support to the vulnerable members of the society.

In 1982, a chapter devoted "the fundamental rights and duties of rights and citizens" was inserted after the "general principle" of the Constitution, reflecting the importance attached to citizens' rights. The 2004 amendment put "[t]he State respects and protects human rights" clause before all other articles in the chapter on the fundamental rights and duties of citizens. The linkage thus established between human rights and citizens' fundamental rights serves to enhance the protection of citizens' fundamental rights according to the principle that "[t]he State respects and protects human rights". As the principle that "[t]he State respects and protects human rights" became constitutional, binding all state organs, organizations and individuals, legislation for human rights protection entered a fast developing era.

II. Improving and developing laws on socialist democracy to support the people in exercise of their right as masters of the country.

The right to vote and stand for election is a primary fundamental right of citizens and a direct embodiment of socialist democracy. Developing socialist democracy is a consistent goal of the CPC and the Chinese Government and an important content of legislation by the National People's Congress and its standing committee.

Ensuring equal right to vote for all has been a consistent political view and pursuit of the CPC and the government. On March 14, 2010, the Third Session of the 11th National People's Congress adopted the decision to amend the *Electoral Law,* which provides that election of NPC deputies shall be elected on the basis of the same population ratio in both urban and rural areas, changing the practice of different population ratios in the previous 50 years. From 2011 to the end of 2012, people's congresses at the county and township levels completed a new round of election. It was the first time to apply this new rule contained in the amendment to the *Electoral Law,* which increased the representativeness of people's deputies and expanded people's democratic rights. More than 900 million voters participated in the voting and the event was an important practice of socialist democracy and effort to make sure that people exercise the right to manage their own affairs.

In urban and rural community governance, public affairs at the grass-roots level and programs for public good, the people practice self-management, self-service, self-education and self-supervision as an important way to exercise directly their democratic rights. Since the promulgation of the *Organic Law of Villagers' Committees* in 1998, village self-governance system has developed into an important part of socialist democracy with Chinese characteristics. Along with the development of rural economy and society, especially with deepened reform of the urban and rural household registration system and the rural tax and fee institutions, village self-governance has run into some new problems. In October 2010, the NPC Standing Committee amended the *Organic Law of Villagers' Committees* by further improving the electoral and dismissal procedures of village committee members as well as the rules on democratic discussions, management and supervision. The amendment plays an important role in motivating the villagers to fully tap their initiative and creativity and in promoting rural reform, development and stability.

III. Refining the criminal laws and criminal procedures to crack down on crimes and protect the people.

Respecting and protecting human rights is an important principle guiding criminal legislation. In the past 10 years, the NPC Standing Committee adopted the 6th, 7th, and 8th *Amendments to the Criminal Law* in further elaboration of the criminal principle of combining punishment with leniency, the 8th one in particular. The death penalty was dropped for 13 economic and non-violent crimes, accounting for 19.1% of all crimes punishable by death. Strict standards were set on the actual prison term to be served by criminals sentenced to death with a two-year reprieve and then commuted to a long prison term. Readjustment was made to the quantification of concurrent punishment for several crimes. Punishment was increased for recidivists and crimes by mafia-style gangs. Behaviors that severely endanger people's interests such as drunk driving, drag racing and non-payment of labor remuneration were criminalized. Regulations on crimes of endangering food safety, producing and selling fake medicines and destroying environment and resources were further improved. The 8th Amendment serves to strengthen protection of people's livelihood and give better play to the role of the *Criminal Law* in punishing crimes, protecting people, maintaining social order and safeguarding national security.

The *Criminal Procedure Law* ensures prompt investigation into and correct revelation of crime facts and punishment of criminals on one hand and on the other hand protects the innocent from criminal liability, respects and protects human rights and protects citizens' litigation rights and other lawful rights. In 2012, the NPC amended the *Criminal Procedure Law*, introducing the constitutional principle of "respecting and protecting human rights" in it as a basic principle in criminal procedures. The amendment also involved a series of provisions on strengthening human rights protection as follows. Illegal evidence exclusion system was improved to curb the practice of extorting confessions by torture and other illegal evidence gatherings. Provisions on the conditions and procedures of arrest and residential surveillance and on notification of family members after adoption of coercive measures were further refined. The legal status of the defenders in criminal procedures were consolidated and the scope of the legal aid scheme was expanded. Procedures for questioning criminal suspects and taking necessary means of investigation were detailed and standardization of and supervision over means of investigation were strengthened to prevent abuse of the power of investigation. Special procedures were provided for the handling of criminal offenses by minors such as conditional non-prosecution and criminal record sealing.

To ensure caution and justice in death sentences, in October 2006, the NPC Standing Committee amended the *Organic Law of the People's Courts* to withdraw the death penalty approval power to the Supreme People's Court. The strict control and cautious application of death penalty reflects respect for and protection of right to life.

The *State Compensation Law* was an important law to promote the exercise of power according to law by the administrative and judicial organs and their personnel so as to protect and fulfill citizens' right of the person and property rights. In April 2010, the NPC Standing Committee amended the *State Compensation Law* to clarify the compensation request channel, improve the compensation procedure, provide for moral damage compensation and offer guarantee for payment of compensation, reflecting the spirit and idea of respecting and protecting human rights as enshrined in the Constitution.

IV. Standardizing the exercise of administrative power to protect citizens' lawful rights and interests from infringement.

In China, the administrative organs are the main body to implement human rights protection laws. Therefore, the practice of law-based administration is key to implementing the constitutional principle of respecting and protecting human rights.

In order to implement the *Administrative Permission Law* and normalize administrative licensing, the NPC Standing Committee passed the decision to modify *Highway Act, Company Law, Securities Law, Negotiable Instrument Law, Auction Law, Wildlife Conservation Law, Fisheries Law, Seed Law* and *Regulations of Academic Degrees*. Provisions that had been inconsistent with the *Administrative Permission Law* and those that had not served the need for transforming government functions and reforming the administrative system were either revised or cancelled.

The administrative compulsory system bears on the efficiency of administration and the suspension or limitation of citizens' right of person and property rights. In June 2011, the NPC Standing Committee adopted the *Administrative Compulsion Law,* conferring the necessary compulsory measures to the administrative organs for them to fulfill duties according to law to protect public interests and order, and at the same time setting the norms governing administrative compulsory behaviors so as to prevent abuse of administrative power and protect the lawful rights and interests of citizens, legal persons and other organizations.

Administration of public security is an important part of maintaining public security and protecting citizens' lawful rights and interests. In August 2005, the NPC Standing Committee enacted the *Public Security Administration Punishment Law* to identify some additional illegal acts punishable under this law, increased the amount of fines, reduce range of discretion with regard to administrative detention, improve punishment procedure and strengthen control and supervision over law enforcement by public security organs and the police.

Natural disasters and accidents bring great losses to people's lives and property. Creating and regulating emergency response mechanisms is of great significance to protecting people's lives and property. In August 2007, the NPC Standing Committee passed the *Emergency Response Law,* which provides for emergency prevention and preparedness, surveillance and early warning, emergency response and relief, recovery and reconstruction so as to effectively protect people's lives and property and safeguard national security, public security, environmental security and social order.

V. Strengthening legislation in and the relevant fields to improve people's livelihood and protect citizens' rights.

It is the strategy and guideline for China's socio-economic development and also an important principle guiding legislation in this new era to implement with a people-oriented approach the scientific outlook on comprehensive, coordinated and sustainable development to promote socio-economic and man's overall development .

The NPC Standing Committee attaches great importance to legislation that protects employment and laborers' rights. In 2007, it reviewed and adopted the *Labor Contract Law, Law on Promotion of Employment* and *Law on Mediation and Arbitration of Labor Disputes;* in 2011, it amended the *Law on the Prevention and Control of Occupational Diseases* to protect laborers' right to life and health; in 2012, to address problems in labor dispatching, it amended the *Labor Contract Law.* These laws form a relatively full-fledged labor law system and are important results of legislation in the relevant field.

The social security system is the basic system to improve people's livelihood and an important guarantee of social stability. In October 2010, the NPC Standing Committee enacted the *Social Insurance Law.* The law established a social insurance system with wide and multi-leveled coverage and affordable and sustainable services and created such schemes as basic endowment insurance, basic medical insurance, work-related injury insurance, unemployment insurance and maternity insurance to make sure that citizens receive material help according to law when they are old, ill or unemployed, have work-related injury or give birth.

Women, minors and disabled persons are relatively vulnerable social groups and need special legislative protection for their rights and interests. The amended *Law on the Protection of the Rights and Interests of Women* furthered improved protection measures and added punishments on infringements. The amended *Law on Protection of Minors* strengthened the duties of families, schools, the society and the state to protect the minors and explicitly provided for minors' right to education with a view to protecting their physical and mental health and promoting their overall development. The amended *Law on Protection of the Disabled Persons* substantiated clauses that prohibited discrimination against persons with disability and strengthened protection of their rights in areas including rehabilitation, education, employment, cultural life, social security and accessible facilities to facilitate equal participation in social life and sharing of fruits of social development.

Infectious diseases are among the most severe factors endangering people's right to life and health and mental health is increasingly an important public health problem and serious social problems. The *Law on Prevention and Control of Infectious Diseases* amended in August 2004 includes such principles as timely treatment, non discrimination, privacy protection, living support, reasonable remuneration and lawful compensation, which fully reflects the respect for and protection of rights to life, health, privacy and property. In October 2012, the *Mental Health Law* was enacted to effectively protect the legitimate rights and interests of people with mental disorders, protect their dignity and personal security from infringement, protect citizens' lawful rights and interests from infringement as a result of the abuse of involuntary hospitalization measures and strive to balance protection of personal rights and protection of other people's security.

Food safety is linked closely to people's health and life safety. The NPC Standing Committee enacted *Food Safety Law* and *Law on Quality and Safety of Agricultural Products* to make sure that food and agricultural products are safe so as to protecting people's health and life safety.

Environmental problems have become an important constraint to comprehensively building a moderately prosperous society and a severe threat to man's overall development. In April 2014, the modified *Environmental Protection Law* was promulgated with people's livelihood in mind by explicitly providing for aggregate controls over discharge of key pollutants, encouraging researches on assessment of environmental impact on the public health, and supporting the protection of environmental rights and interests of the public through information disclosure and public interest litigation. The law lends legal support to solve environmental problems, improve environmental quality, satisfying people's environmental appeals and protecting their physical and mental health, reflecting the thought of improving people's livelihood and a people-oriented approach.

In the past 10 years, guided by the constitutional principle of respecting and protecting human rights, great achievement has been made in legislation, creating a legal system for human rights protection including constitution-related laws, administrative laws, social laws, criminal laws, litigation laws and other laws. Judging from the implementation of these laws, legislation has led and promoted the cause of socialism and social life with Chinese characteristics and provided strong legal support for the respect for and protection of human rights. By 2010, the socialist legal system with Chinese characteristics had been put in place. In the future, an important job of the NPC and its standing committee is to constantly improve the socialist legal system with Chinese characteristics in light of the needs of social development. According to the requirements set forth at the 18th CPC National Congress, we will pay more attention to improving the democratic system and developing diverse forms of democracy so that people practise democratic election, democratic decision-making, democratic management and democratic supervision according to law. We will also make greater effort to tap the important role of rule of law in national governance and social management, safeguard the unity, dignity and authority of the country's legal system and ensure that people enjoy extensive rights and freedoms according to law. It can be predicted that under the leadership of the CPC and the auspice of the Constitution's respect for and protection of human rights, China will continue enriching and improving institutions for human rights protection through legislation with the glory of humanity and human rights.

(original translation by Niu Ya'nan)

努力为每个公民提供更好更公平的教育

教育部部长　袁贵仁

受教育权利是人的基本权利。中国政府一直高度重视保障公民的受教育权，切实履行《宪法》、法律及《儿童权利公约》《残疾人权利公约》等重要国际公约，坚持教育优先发展，大力促进教育公平，全面提高教育质量，努力为每个孩子提供平等接受教育的机会，为每个公民提供更好更公平的教育，为每个人平等参与、平等发展奠定坚实基础。

一、坚持优先发展教育，切实保障公民的受教育权

一是坚持“三个优先”。经济社会发展规划优先安排教育发展、财政资金优先保障教育投入、公共资源优先满足教育和人力资源开发需要。通过制定中长期教育改革和发展规划纲要、编制教育事业发展五年规划、出台有关教育改革决定等，不断明确教育事业改革发展的指导方针、目标任务和政策措施。

二是切实加大教育投入。金融危机以来，在全球经济复苏乏力、国内经济增速放缓、财政收入增速回落的情况下，千方百计保证财政教育投入。公共财政教育投入年均增长速度高于同期财政收入年均增长幅度，教育支出已

成为公共财政的第一大支出。2012年财政性教育经费支出2.2万亿元，占国内生产总值的比例达到4.28%，为教育事业改革发展奠定了坚实基础。

三是保障公民受教育权的法律法规进一步健全。“人权入宪”后，在有关教育法律修订工作中，保障公民受教育权放在了突出位置。2006年发布实施新的《义务教育法》，着力维护适龄儿童、少年平等接受义务教育的权利，对残疾儿童、流动人口子女、边远贫困地区或家庭经济困难的儿童少年、有不良行为少年等特殊群体接受义务教育权利的保障机制做了专门、具体的规定。针对实践中突出问题，出台《校车安全管理条例》、《教育督导条例》等行政法规，着力解决学生安全、学校教育监管等问题。各级教育部门积极推动各级各类学校运用法律的手段治理学校，确保办学宗旨、教育活动与制度规范符合法治要求。同时，公民受教育权的救济渠道进一步完善，特别是高等学校普遍建立了学生申诉机制，各级司法机关不断重视和加强对公民受教育权的司法保护，建立形成了多渠道、多层次的权利保障机制。

二、不断扩大教育规模，保障公民享有更多受教育机会

2006年2月，宁夏银川市金凤区良田镇光彩回民小学的老师在给学生发免费教科书。

一是九年免费义务教育全面实现。经过不懈努力，2011 年年底中国所有县级行政单位全面实现普及九年义务教育和扫除青少年文盲目标。2008 年起在全国范围内实施免费义务教育，免费为农村学生和城市家庭经济困难学生提供教科书，对农村家庭经济困难的寄宿学生提供生活补助。

二是高中阶段教育基本普及。2013 年，高中阶段毛入学率达到 86%，这意味着中国目前新增劳动力绝大部分接受过高中阶段及以上教育。

三是高等教育进入大众化发展阶段。1999 年中国加快了高等教育发展步伐，2002 年毛入学率达到 15%，进入大众化阶段。2013 年，毛入学率提高到 34.5%，在学总规模 3460 万名，稳居世界第一。

四是学前教育快速发展。近年来实施了学前教育三年行动计划，2013 年毛入园率达到 67.5%，更多孩子特别是农村孩子有了接受学前教育的机会。

三、加大资源倾斜力度，提高农村和中西部地区教育水平

受经济社会发展影响以及自然条件、历史等原因，长期以来中国农村和中西部地区教育水平相对落后。近年来，中国政府大力推动教育资源向农村和中西部地区倾斜，保障这些地区的学生同样能够接受到有质量的教育。

一是推进义务教育均衡发展。通过与各省区市签订备忘录，确定各地义务教育均衡发展的时间表、路线图和任务书。启动省级政府推进义务教育均衡发展考核评估和义务教育基本均衡县验收认定工作。实施农村义务教育薄弱学校改造计划、中西部农村初中校舍改造工程、农村寄宿制学校建设工程等一系列工程，大力改善农村边远地区学校办学条件。2014 年 1 月发布《关于全面改善贫困地区义务教育薄弱学校基本办学条件的意见》，按照“缺什么补什么”的原则，用 3 ～ 5 年的时间，使这些地区的学校达到基本办学标准，满足基本办学需要。

如今，贵州省雷山县桃江小学的苗家孩子最高兴的事儿就是到学校去上学。

二是加强农村教师队伍建设。通过一系列措施，不断改善教师的工作、学习和生活条件，鼓励优秀教师以多种方式到农村和中西部任教。2006年起，实施“农村义务教育阶段学校教师特设岗位计划”，截至2013年年底共招聘36万名特岗教师。2007年起，6所部属师范大学共招收免费师范生7万余名，其中90%以上学生毕业后到中西部中小学任教。2010年起，实施“中小学教师国家级培训计划”，实施边远艰苦地区农村学校教师周转宿舍建设，改善农村教师安居条件。2013年起，在连片特困地区实施乡村教师生活补助，惠及14个省区的近40万乡村教师。

三是提升中西部地区高等教育水平。2013年起，实施“中西部高等教育振兴计划”，启动“中西部高校基础能力建设工程规划（一期）”，重点支持24个中西部省份100所地方本科高校基础能力建设；启动中西部高校综合实力提升工程，重点支持在13个没有教育部直属高校的中西部省份和新疆生产建设兵团各建设一所有特色、高水平的地方大学。

2007 年 6 月，即将毕业离校的广西工学院 2007 届毕业生身着学士服装，在校园里合影留念。

四是促进高等教育入学机会公平。 从 2008 年起，实施“支援中西部地区招生协作计划”，由高等教育资源丰富的东部省市高校招收升学率相对偏低的中西部省份学生，规模由 2008 年的 3.5 万人扩大到 2014 年的 20 万人，相当于在中西部地区建设了 80 所年招生 2500 人的公办高校。2012 年起连续三年实施“农村贫困地区定向招生专项计划”，招生数由最初的 1 万名增至 5 万名，不断提高贫困地区农村学生上重点高校的比例。

五是通过教育信息化推进优质教育资源共享。 把信息技术作为促进公平、提高质量的重要手段，加快建设“三通两平台”，即宽带网络校校通、优质资源班班通、网络学习空间人人通和教育资源公共服务平台、教育管理公共服务平台，让更多孩子特别是贫困地区孩子共享优质教育资源。

四、健全政策扶持体系，保障特殊群体受教育权益

一是认真解决农民工子女受教育问题。 2003 年，中国政府明确了“以流

入地政府管理为主、以全日制公办中小学为主”的“两为主”政策，确保随迁子女平等受教育权利。截至 2013 年年底，全国义务教育阶段 1277 万名随迁子女在公办学校就学，比例达到了 80.41%。如将上海和浙江等地政府购买民办学校的 39 万个学额计算在内，国家财政性教育经费保障随迁子女就学的比例已达到 83.46%。2012 年 8 月，中国政府着手解决随迁子女接受义务教育后在当地参加升学考试问题，目前有 28 个省份放开了异地高考。切实关心和解决农村留守儿童上学问题，构建政府、社区、学校、家庭多维联动的留守儿童教育、关爱与服务体系。

2013 年 11 月，浙江省绍兴市第一所进城务工人员子女学校——绍兴县蓝天实验学校学生在上计算机课。

二是家庭经济困难学生资助体系实现全覆盖。2007 年开始，中国逐步建立起覆盖学前教育到研究生教育，全新、完整、立体的家庭经济困难学生资助政策体系，确保每一个学生不因家庭经济困难而失学。2006 ～ 2012 年，资助人次从 2700 万增加到 8400 万，增长近 3 倍；资助金额从 200 亿元增加到 1100 亿元，增长了近 5 倍。此外，2012 年开始实施农村免费中等职业教育。

2011 年 9 月，江苏连云港赣榆县 109 名家庭困难大学生新生每人领取了 3000 元的爱心助学金。

2011 年 11 月，湖南省隆回县万和实验学校小学生正在有滋有味地吃午餐。

三是全面改善贫困地区农村义务教育学生营养状况。2011 年秋季学期开始，启动集中连片特殊困难地区“农村义务教育学生营养改善计划”，为农村学生提供膳食补助。目前覆盖3000多万学生，全国超过1/3的县实施了营养改善计划，超过1/4的农村义务教育阶段学生享受补助政策。这是中国第一次大规模的营养干预计划，受到各方面好评。

四是大力发展特殊教育。高度重视残疾儿童教育工作，目前残疾儿童少年接受义务教育比例为72.7%，超过一半的残疾学生在普通学校随班就读。2014年1月，出台“特殊教育提升计划”（2014～2016年），计划用3年时间，初步建立“布局合理、学段衔接、普职融通、医教结合”的特殊教育体系，全国基本普及残疾儿童少年义务教育，视力、听力、智力残疾儿童少年义务教育入学率达到90%以上。

五是大力发展民族地区教育。在政策、资金、项目等方面给予民族地区大力支持。中央财政安排专项资金，补助人口较少民族农村义务教育阶段寄宿生生活费，对西藏农牧区中小学生实行“三包”政策，即包吃、包住、包学习。加大对口支援力度，实行教育援疆、援藏和支援四川、云南、甘肃、青海四省藏区。在民族地区中小学大力推进双语教育，目前共有1万多所学校使用21个民族的29种文字开展双语教学。

东乌旗蒙古族第二小学是一所马背小学成长起来的蒙语授课小学，2001年以来，全旗14所苏木学校的孩子们都在这优美的学校中学习、生活。

五、拓宽接受教育渠道，满足公民多样化、个性化需求

努力为公民创造人人可学、时时可学、处处可学的条件。

一是大力发展职业教育，为不同类型学生提供不同选择。中等、高等职业教育招生规模已分别占了高中阶段教育和高等教育的半壁江山。2014 年 5 月，出台《国务院关于加快发展现代职业教育的决定》，加快构建以就业为导向的现代职业教育体系，培养培训大批中高级技能型人才，增强就业创业能力。

二是加快发展民办教育，提供更加多样的教育服务。目前全国民办学校近 15 万所、在校生 4000 多万，其中民办学前教育在园幼儿占总数的 51%、小学生占 7%、初中生占 10%、普通高中生占 10%、中职学生占 11%、高校学生占 11%。社会力量办学成为中国教育事业的重要组成部分。

三是加强继续教育，创造更加灵活方便的学习条件。随着知识经济时代的到来，教育正在从一次性学校教育向终身教育转变。2012 年，中国政府以广播电视大学为基础，成立了国家开放大学等 6 所开放大学，探索将高校的优质教育资源免费向社会开放，推动学习型社会建设，全面提高公民素质。

四是开展中外合作办学，引进国外优质教育资源。近年来举办中外合作办学机构和项目 2000 余个，一批高起点的中外合作办学机构相继成立，为学生开辟了一条“不出国留学”的途径。

保障每个人平等接受教育、成就人生梦想，既是中国梦的重要内容，也是中国梦的有力支撑。面向未来，中国政府将坚定不移地实施科教兴国和人才强国战略，坚持教育优先发展，不断深化教育改革，持续推进学习型社会建设，努力为每个人的自由、全面发展创造良好条件。

Working for Better and More Equitable Education for All

Yuan Guiren, Minister of Education

The right to education is a fundamental right. The Chinese Government has always attached great importance to the right to education and earnestly implemented its Constitution and laws as well as important international conventions such as *Convention on the Rights of the Child* and *Convention on the Rights of Persons with Disabilities.* It regards education as a top priority, makes great efforts to promote educational equity and enhance education quality, and strives to provide equal access to education for every child and better and more equitable education for every citizen so as to lay down a solid foundation for equal participation and equitable development for everyone.

I. Prioritizing the development of education and protecting citizens' right to education.

First, China insists that education should be developed as a priority in plans on socio-economic development, that investment in education should be provided as a priority in public finance and that the needs of education and human resources development should be satisfied as a priority with public resources. The guiding principles, targets and policy measures for the reform and development of education have been constantly reaffirmed through the formulation of short-term and long-term plans, the conduct of five-year planning and the decisions on education reforms.

Second, more money has been invested in education. Since the outbreak of the financial crisis, while recovery in the outside world and economic growth in China have both been slow and growth of fiscal revenue have slowed down, various measures have been taken to guarantee investment in education. The annual growth rate of government spending on education is higher than that of fiscal revenue. Education has become the largest expenditure item of the government. In 2012, the public finance expenditure on education amounted to 2.2 trillion yuan, accounting for 4.28% of GDP. The investments have laid down a solid foundation for the reform and development of education.

Third, laws and regulations on the right to education are further strengthened. After the human rights clause was articulated in the Constitution, protecting the right to education has been placed in a very important position in the revision of the relevant laws. In 2006, the new *Compulsory Education Law* was issued. The law protects the right of school-aged children and young people to equal access to education. The law contains specific regulations on the protection of the right to education of special populations such as disabled children, children of migrant workers, children in poor and remote areas, children of families with economic difficulties and mischievous children. In view of some outstanding problems in reality, the Chinese Government issued *Regulations on the Management of School Buses, Regulations on Education Supervision* and other administrative regulations to address the issue of students' safety and school supervision. Departments of education at all levels actively advocate school governance by legal means and make sure that the school's mission, education activities and rules align with rule of law. In the meantime, the relief channels for right to education are further improved. In particular, universities have put in place student appeal mechanisms. Judicial organs at all levels attach importance to and have take action to consolidate the judicial protection of people's right to education. A multi-channel and multi-level scheme to protect this right has been established.

II. Further expanding the scale of education to provide more education opportunities for citizens.

First, nine-year free and compulsory education is extended to all children in China. With unswerving effort, by the end of 2011, all counties in China had achieved the targets in providing nine-year compulsory education and eliminating illiteracy among young people. Free and compulsory education has been provided throughout the country since 2008. Free textbooks are provided for rural students and urban students from poor families. Living allowances are provided for boarding students from poor rural families.

In February 2006, teachers were handing out free textbooks to students in Guangcai Huimin Primary School in Liangtian, Jinfeng district of Yinchuan, Ningxia.

Second, almost all young people at appropriate ages receive senior secondary school education. In 2013, the gross enrollment rate of senior secondary schools was 86%, which means that the majority of the new labor force have received senior secondary school education or above.

Third, higher education has entered into a phase of greater popularization.

In 1999, China quickened its step to develop higher education. In 2002, the gross enrollment rate reached 15%, which set China into the mass higher education phase. In 2013, the gross enrollment rate increased to 34.5% and the number of enrolled students totaled 34.6 million. These figures safely put China in the first place in the world.

Fourth, pre-school education has developed very fast. In recent years, a three-year pre-school education program has been adopted. In 2013, the gross enrollment rate of kindergartners was 67.5%. More children have the opportunity to receive pre-school education, especially in rural areas.

III. Providing more resources to improve education in rural areas and in central and western regions.

Due to levels of socio-economic development, natural conditions, history and other reasons, the level of education in rural areas and the central and western regions has lagged behind. In recent years, more resources have been provided to make sure that students in these areas also receive quality education.

First, efforts have been made to promote balanced development of compulsory education. The Central Government has signed memorandums with all provinces including the time table, road map and task description for the achievement of this objective. Provincial governments have launched programs to evaluate the progress in balanced development of compulsory education and to certify the counties that have achieved the objective. A series of projects have been undertaken to improve the weak compulsory education schools in rural areas, renovate junior secondary school premises in rural areas in central and western China and the construction of boarding schools in rural areas so as to improve schooling conditions in remote rural areas. In January 2014, *Opinions on Comprehensively Improving Conditions of Weak Compulsory Education Schools in Poverty-Stricken Areas* were issued. In line with the principle of "supplying what is needed", schools in these areas will be helped to reach the basic education standards and satisfy the basic needs of students in the next 3~5 years.

Now, going to school is the happiest thing for these children of Miao ethnic group in Taojiang Primary School, Leishan County, Guizhou.

Second, measures have been taken to build up the capacity of teachers in rural areas. The working, learning and living conditions of teachers have been improved through a series of measures. Good teachers are incentivized to work in the rural areas and the central and western regions. Since 2006, *Rural Compulsory Education School Teacher Recruitment Ad Hoc Post Plan* has been implemented and 360,000 teachers had been recruited by the end of 2013. Over 70,000 students have been enrolled for free in the six normal universities affiliated to the Ministry of Education since 2007 and more than 90% of them will after graduation teach at primary schools in the central and western regions. Since 2010, *National Primary and Secondary School Teachers Training Program* has been implemented. Temporary dormitories have been built for teachers in remote and poor rural areas to improve the living conditions. Since 2013, living allowances have been provided to teachers in contiguous poverty-stricken areas, benefiting 400,000 teachers in 14 provinces.

In June 2007, students graduating from Guangxi University of Science and Technology are taking pictures in baccalaureate gowns on the campus.

Third, quality of higher education in the central and western regions has been improved. In 2013, the *Central and Western Regions Higher Education Revitalization Plan* and the *Program on Capacity Building of Higher Education Institutions in Central and Western China (Phase I)* were launched to support 100 universities in 24 central and western provinces to build up basic capacities. A overall capacity-building project has also been launched to support the development of one distinctive and high-level university in each of the 13 central and western provinces that had no university affiliated to the Ministry of Education, and one for Xinjiang Production and Construction Corps.

Fourth, the equality of opportunity for higher education has been promoted. Since 2008, the *Plan on Collaborative Enrollment to Support the Central and Western Regions* has been implemented. According to that plan, universities in eastern regions with rich higher education resources enroll students from western regions with low enrollment rates. The size of admissions has increased from 35,000 students in 2008 to 200,000 in 2014. This figure is equal to the construction in the western regions of 80 public universities, each with a capacity of 2,500 admissions annually. A *Special Plan for Enrollment Targeting Students from Poverty-Stricken Rural Areas* has been implemented for three years in a row since 2012. The number of students enrolled increased from 10,000 in 2012 to 50,000 in 2014. More and more students from poor rural areas are now able to enter top universities.

Fifth, quality education resources are shared through application of information technology. The information technology is used as an important means to promote equity and improve quality. Measures have been taken so that every school has access to broadband, every class has access to education resources and every student has access to the internet as a learning space. Public service platforms providing education resources and enabling education management have also been built at accelerated speed. These measures have enabled and will continue to enable more children in poverty-stricken areas to enjoy access to more education resources.

IV. Improving policy support to protect the right to education of special populations.

First, serious effort has been made to address education for children of migrant workers. In 2003, the Chinese Government made it clear that these migrant workers' children's right to education should be guaranteed with the government of the locality where their parents work taking primary responsibility and through enrollment in full-time public primary and secondary schools. At the end of 2013, 12.77 million such children were receiving compulsory education in public schools, accounting for 80.41% of the total. If the government-purchased 390,000 private-school places in Shanghai and Zhejiang were included, the schooling of 83.46% migrant workers' children living with their parents were financially guaranteed in public finance. In August 2012, the Chinese Government started to tackle the problems facing these children with regard to taking examinations at the locality where they have received compulsory education after the compulsory education phase. Now, 28 provinces allow students of migrant workers to sit college entrance examination locally. The education of the left-behind children in rural areas is addressed through an education, care and service system involving the government, communities, schools and families.

In November 2013, students at Shaoxing Lantian Experiment School are having their computer lesson. This school is the first school especially for migrant workers' children in Shaoxing.

Second, the funding system for students from poor families has full coverage. Since 2007, China has gradually established a new, comprehensive and multi-dimensional funding system for students of poor families. The system extends from pre-school education to postgraduate programs so that no student drops out due to family hardships. From 2006 to 2012, the number of students receiving grant increased three-fold, from 27 million to 84 million. The funding increased by nearly 5 times, from 20 billion yuan to 110 billion. In addition, free vocational education has been provided in rural areas since 2012.

In September 2011, 109 university students from poor families received an education grant of 3,000 yuan each in Ganyu county, Lianyungang, Jiangsu Province.

Third, effort has been taken to comprehensively improve the nutritional status of students receiving compulsory education in poverty-stricken rural areas. A project was launched in the autumn semester of 2011 to improve nutrition for rural compulsory education students in contiguous poor rural areas by providing food allowances. The project now covers over 30 million rural students. Over one third of the counties have been implementing this project and more than one fourth of the rural compulsory education students enjoy the benefits. This first large-scale nutrition intervention program in China wins high acclaim from the whole society.

In November 2011, students at Wanhe Experiment Primary School of Longhui county, Hunan were happily having lunch.

Fourth, special education is vigorously developed. The education of disabled children is given high attention. Now, 72.7% of children with disabilities receive compulsory education and more than half of them are in regular schools. In January 2014, the *Special Education Promotion Plan (2014-2016)* was launched. According to the plan, in the next 3 years, a special education with reasonable layout, smooth linkage between different levels of education, convergence between general and vocational education, and combined medical service with education will be initially put in place. By then, compulsory education will be provided to all disabled children and more than 90% of children with visual, hearing or intelligent disabilities will be enrolled in compulsory education.

Fifth, efforts have been redoubled to develop education in areas mainly inhabited by ethnic minorities. Enormous policy, financial and project support has been given to these areas. The Central Government makes earmarked transfers to subsidize living expenses for rural boarding students of ethnic minorities with relatively fewer population. Primary and secondary school students in the farming and pastoral areas in Tibet enjoy guaranteed food, board and education for free. The counterpart aid has been strengthened, with targeted education support for Xinjiang, Tibet as well as Tibetan areas in Sichuan, Yunnan, Gansu and Qinghai. Bilingual education is promoted in primary and secondary schools and now more than 10,000 schools offer bilingual education in 29 languages of 21 ethnic groups.

Dongwu Banner No.2 Mongolian Primary School is a primary school developed from a horseback school. At school, courses are taught in the Mongolian language. Since 2001, students of all the 14 Sumus of Dongwu Banner have been studying and living on the beautiful campus of this school.

V. Broadening channels of education to satisfy citizens' various personalized needs.

The Chinese Government makes efforts to create conditions for everyone to study at anytime and any place.

First, vocational education is promoted to offer different options for different types of students. The number of students in vocational education makes up half of the students receiving secondary and higher education. In May 2014, *Decision of the State Council on the Promotion of Modern Vocational Education* was issued to speed up the creation of an employment-oriented modern vocational education system and to bring out a large number of middle and senior level skilled workers with enhanced skills to take jobs or start businesses.

Second, private education is promoted to provide a variety of education services. There are nearly 150,000 private schools with 40 million enrolled students. 51% of children are receiving pre-school education in private kindergartens, 7% of students are in private primary schools, 10% of students in private junior secondary schools, 10% of students in private general senior secondary schools, 11% in private vocational secondary schools, and 11% in private universities. These private schools and universities become important education providers in China.

Third, continuing education is strengthened to create more flexible and convenient learning conditions. As the era of knowledge economy comes, education evolves from one-off schooling to life-long education. In 2012, the Chinese Government established the Open University of China on the basis of China Central Radio and TV University and 5 other open universities, which are designed to explore the provision of higher education resources for the society free of charge so as to enable the development of a learning society and comprehensively improve the quality of citizens.

Fourth, education institutions jointly operated by Chinese and foreign entities are encouraged to introduce foreign education resources. There have been more than 2,000 such institutions and projects in recent years. With the appearance of more quality cooperative education agencies, it is possible for students to receive good foreign education without leaving China.

That all people enjoy equal opportunity in education and realize their dreams in life not only constitutes an important element of but also underpins the Chinese Dream. The Chinese Government will stick to the strategy of invigorating the country through science and technology and with talented people. Education will always be given a top priority and education reform will be deepened. Further efforts will be made to advance the development of a learning society and favorable conditions will be created for everyone to achieve free and comprehensive development.

(original translation by Yang Ji)

通信业助力中国人权发展

工业和信息化部部长　苗　圩

2004年，“国家尊重和保障人权”首次被写入中国《宪法》，引起了国际社会的广泛关注，成为中国人权发展的重要里程碑。通信权是人权的重要组成部分之一，信息和通信伴随整个人类的发展进程，记录并推动文明的演进，也是人权文化价值演进的重要载体和工具。“人权入宪”的十年间，通信业高速发展，基础设施建设日益完善，用户规模不断扩大，在经济社会各领域、各环节的影响力显著提高，为改善民生和提升社会公共服务能力作出了重要贡献，在保障公民权益、服务弱势群体、提供普遍服务、保障信息安全等方面，取得了突出成就，有效地推动了中国人权发展。

一、保障公民权益

十年来，中国通信业产品供给数量和服务水平持续提高，通信运营企业加快转型，不断创新，业务种类日益丰富，用户权益保护措施日趋完善，用户满意度稳步提升。2004～2013年，每用户电信业务总量[①]从1425元增长至2627元(以2000年电信不变单价折算)，年度复合增长率6.3%。与此同时，电信服务价格水平不断下降，电信资费综合价格水平下降了50%，广大民众切实享受到了电信发展改革的成果。

① 每用户电信业务总量=电信业务总量/用户数。

（一）基础设施日趋完善

信息基础设施是国家战略性公共基础设施，是经济社会发展的重要基础。中国大力支持信息基础设施建设，2004 年至 2013 年，先后实施了“村村通电话”工程，电信网、互联网、广播电视网“三网融合”，“宽带中国”战略等，有力地推动了信息基础设施的完善，建成了覆盖全国、惠及全民的信息基础设施。

十年间，全国光缆线路长度从 274 万公里增加到 1745 万公里，其中长途光缆线路从 59 万公里增加到 90 万公里，单波长 100G 波分复用系统广泛应用，已经覆盖了全国大部分省份城市；固定长途电话交换机容量从 869 万路端增加到 1270 万路端，局用交换机容量从 35083 万门增加到 41052 万门；移动电话交换机容量从 33698 万户增加到 196545 万户；移动基站达到 241 万个，其中 3G 基站达到 109 万个；互联网宽带接入端口数从 1802 万个增加到 35972 万个，光纤到户网络已经覆盖家庭超过 16700 万户，建成了全球最大用户规模的互联网。

（二）电话用户快速发展

十年间，中国信息通信服务和应用水平普遍提高，发展成果更多地惠及全民。截至 2013 年，全国电话用户总数达到 15 亿户，其中移动电话用户总数 12.3 亿户，移动电话普及率从 2004 年的 24.9 部 / 百人达到 90.3 部 / 百人，增长了 262.7%。

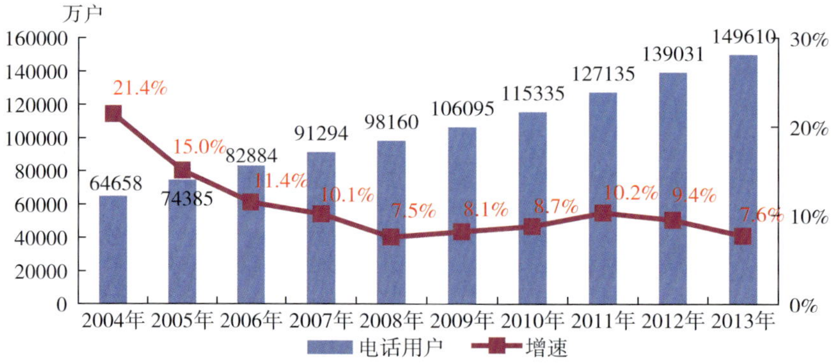

2004 ～ 2013 年中国电话用户发展情况

资料来源：《2013 中国通信统计年度报告》。

（三）宽带接入大幅提速

互联网是公众获取信息、发表言论的重要途径，中国一直高度重视互联网基础设施的发展，通过普及推广卫星通信、光纤通信、计算机网络等技术，实施“宽带中国”战略，构建起覆盖全国、惠及全民的互联网基础设施，有效推动了中国人权事业建设和发展。

十年间，互联网宽带接入用户总规模从 0.11 亿户增长到 1.89 亿户。宽带接入速率得到明显提升，4M 以上宽带用户占比已达到 78.8%，高速光纤接入（FTTH / O）用户达到 4082 万户，用户占比达到 21.7%。

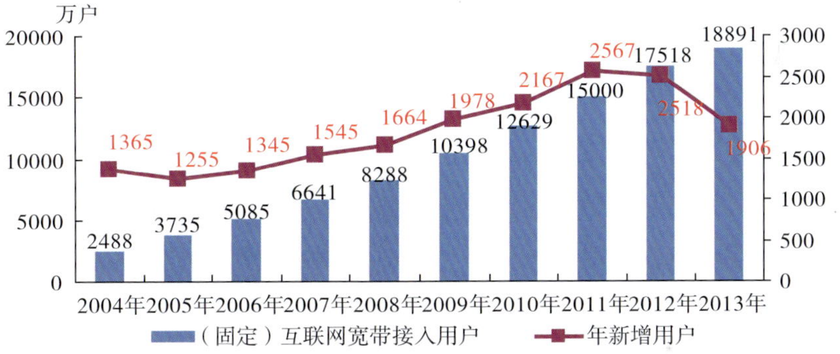

2004 ～ 2013 年中国（固定）互联网宽带接入用户发展情况

资料来源：《2013 中国通信统计年度报告》。

2004 ～ 2013 年中国互联网网民人数及普及率发展情况

资料来源：《2013 中国通信统计年度报告》。

十年间，中国互联网网民规模从0.8亿增加到6.18亿，互联网普及率从6.2%增长到45.8%。截至2013年年底，手机网民规模已达5.0亿，占手机用户的81%，移动互联网流量保持迅猛增长态势，全年累计达到132138.1万GB，月户均移动接入流量超过139MB。

互联网的普及和完善，极大地扩展了言论自由空间。网络论坛、网络新闻、博客/个人空间、社交网站、网络文学、网络视频、微博、即时通信等多种互联网平台及应用极大地提升了中国网民的用户体验。

（四）民生领域深度渗透

随着物联网、云计算、移动互联网、电子商务等新兴业态的快速兴起，通信业在教育、医疗、社保、文化等诸多民生领域实现了深度渗透，通过低成本、高效率、广覆盖、快传播的信息通信技术服务社会管理，便捷人民生活，助力中国人权体系建设和发展。

社会管理方面，电子政务大幅提升政府公共服务和管理能力，完善运行机制，强化政务公开，简化办事程序，提高工作效率，助力阳光政府、效能政府、廉洁政府、服务政府的建设。充分运用物联网、云计算、移动互联网等通信和信息技术手段建设智慧城市，通过感测、传送、整合和分析城市运行核心系统的各项关键数据，对工作服务、社会管理、产业运作等活动作出智能响应，构建城市发展的智能环境，实现了集应急指挥、治安监管、交通管控、城管执法等于一体的城市管理模式，为居民重塑了生活环境，构建了全新的城市形态。

服务生活方面，医疗、教育、文化、金融等多领域的信息化产品和服务手段促进上述社会资源分配更加公平、服务更为便捷、监管更加透明，有效助推了多领域内的体制改革，全面服务人民生活、学习和发展。

二、服务弱势群体

信息无障碍是中国信息化发展规划中的重要组成部分，也是中国社会主义现代化建设事业进程中的主要内容，中国一直积极促进信息传播公平、保障弱势人群的信息权利、关注消除数字鸿沟、帮助残障人士等弱势群体跟上信息社会发展步伐，并在推动全体社会成员平等共享社会文明进步和社会发展带来的机会与福祉等方面做了大量有益的工作。

目前，中国已制定了信息无障碍标准体系框架和无障碍建设“十二五”实施方案，大力推进信息无障碍标准的制定和无障碍设施的建设，推动相关产品和服务的研发、应用和创新，开展形式多样的扶残、助残活动。已成功发布了《手柄电话助听器耦合技术要求和测量方法》、《信息终端设备信息无障碍辅助技术的要求和评测方法》、《信息无障碍　呼叫中心服务系统技术要求》、《信息无障碍　语音上网技术要求》、《信息无障碍　公众场所内听力障碍人群辅助系统技术要求》、《网站设计无障碍技术要求》等多项信息无障碍标准，涵盖了辅助设备、通信终端、无障碍网站、语音上网和环境评估等多个方面。

为实现信息普遍服务，2012 年中国成立了国家信息无障碍公共服务平台，深入探索研究符合中国网站特色的信息无障碍解决方案。从 2013 年 5 月 19 日（第 23 个全国助残日）至 2014 年 5 月 18 日（第 24 个全国助残日）的一年时间内，中国业已完成近 300 个政务和主流网络媒体系统的无障碍建设工作，实现无障碍服务的网站达到 10000 多个，占全国政务和主流媒体网站总数的 15%。为 100 所农村特殊教育学校建成宽带基础设施，并提供三年免费上网服务，国家信息无障碍服务体系已逐步成型。

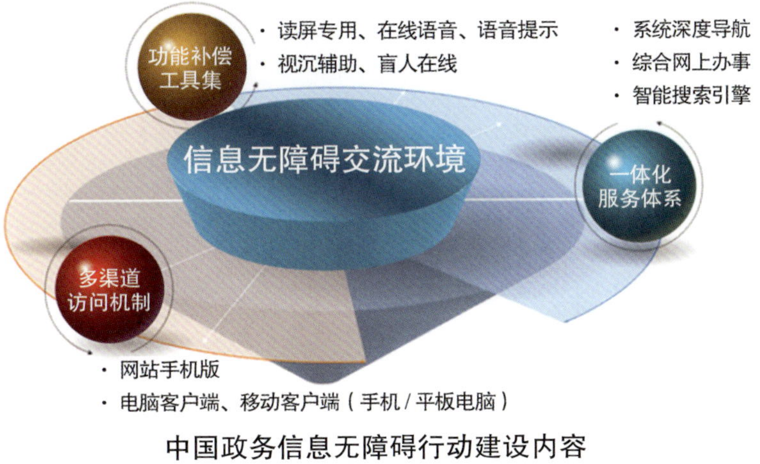

中国政务信息无障碍行动建设内容

资料来源：“美丽中国——中国政务信息无障碍行动”推进工作小组。

三、提供普遍服务

为了贯彻落实中国农村改革发展的一系列战略部署，从2004年起，原信息产业部、工业和信息化部实施农村电信普遍服务——村村通工程（简称“村通工程”）。

按照《电信条例》等相关规定，三家基础电信企业采取“分片包干”方式承担电信普遍服务义务，从行政村通电话、自然村通电话、乡镇互联网接入、信息下乡四个方面，持续深入开展村通工程建设。村通工程整体按照“三个三步走”推进：（1）基础网络建设方面，按乡镇、行政村、自然村进行网络覆盖的逐级延伸；（2）业务提供方面，按照通电话、通宽带、通信息层层推进；（3）服务能力方面，从建设基础设施、构建信息平台到推广适合农民特点的业务分步实施。

村通工程“三个三步走”战略示意

资料来源：工业和信息化部电信研究院。

到2013年年底，村通工程已经实施了十年，这十年间累计投入870亿元，使农村地区信息通信设施和应用推广都取得了显著成效，已经实现了全国“村村通电话，乡乡能上网”。在行政村通电话方面，10年共新增7.6万个行政村通电话，通电话行政村比例从88%提高到100%；在自然村通电话方面，10年共新增12.8万个20户以上自然村通电话，自然村通电话比例从90%提高到95.6%；在乡村通互联网方面，10年共新增近4000个乡镇和13.7万个行政村通宽带，基本实现全国100%乡镇通宽带，通宽带行政村的比例从67%提升到91%；在信息下乡方面，全国开展信息下乡活动的乡镇覆盖率达到85%，建成“农信通”、“信息田园”、“金农通”等全国性农村综合信息服务平台，涉农互联网站近2万个，建成乡镇信息服务站3万多个、村信息服务点近30万个、乡镇网上信息库近3万个、村信息栏目近27.8万个。2012年开始与教育部、扶贫办、残联合作开展了“农村中小学通宽带”、“残校通宽带”等项目，实现了5300所贫困农村中小学开通宽带，200所残校和中小学获得3年免费上网。

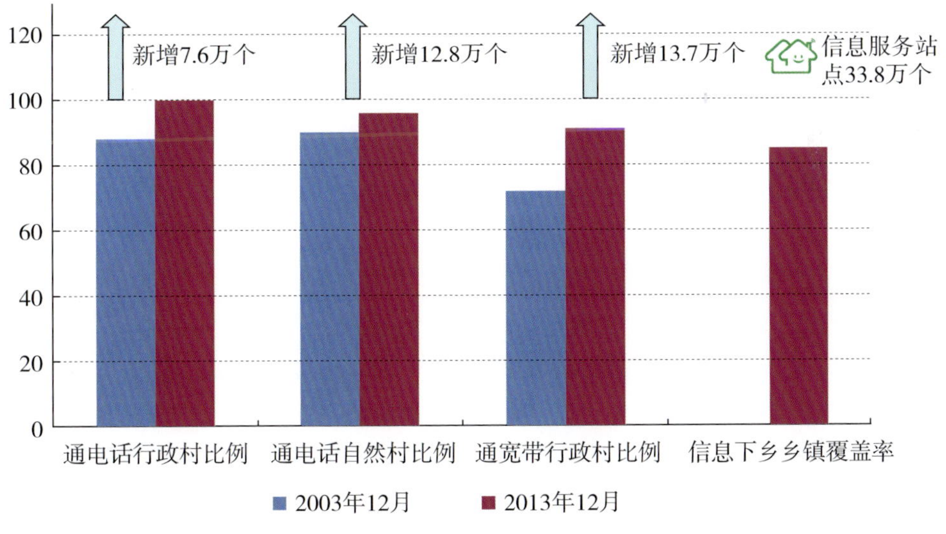

2004～2013年村通工程实施成果

资料来源：工业和信息化部。

村通工程的实施使农村通信基础设施得到跨越式发展，农村信息化整体水平大幅提升，为农业增产、农民增收、农村繁荣和农民生活质量的提高发挥了积极作用，主要体现在以下几个方面：（1）村通工程为改善民生作出了积极贡献。现代通信手段结束了偏僻农村与外界隔绝的历史，为广大农牧民脱贫致富、农副产品销售、外出就业、治病救急和文化教育带来极大便利，为改善少数民族地区生产生活条件、维护民族团结稳定发挥了积极作用。（2）村通工程对防灾减灾提供极大帮助。在汶川和玉树大地震以及冰雪、洪涝、泥石流等灾害中，村通工程成为抢险救灾的“生命线”和“保障线”。（3）村通工程促进了农村信息化和农业生产的进步。中国自主研制的低成本信息化终端如固定无线接入系统、宽带机顶盒、农村信息机、电视宽带手写板、经济型电脑和手机等大量进入农村，第三代移动通信、高速宽带、物联网、动植物溯源、大棚监控等高科技应用正在农村地区推广应用，信息化成果正实实在在地转化为农业发展、农民增收的手段和能力，为传统农业生产和农村管理带来了新的变革。

根据 2013 年 8 月发布的《“宽带中国”战略及实施方案》，到 2020 年，行政村通宽带比例超过 98%、宽带接入能力达到 12Mbps，中国的宽带普遍服务将得到进一步提升。目前，中国政府正在研究完善电信普遍服务补偿机制，引导企业进一步加快农村地区宽带基础设施建设和宽带信息应用的推广普及，为全面提升信息化水平而努力。

四、保障信息安全

信息化已成为推动经济社会发展和变革的重要力量。信息安全是信息化进程中不可或缺的重要内容。随着电子政务、电子商务和社交网络等经济和社会活动信息化的发展，信息安全已成为国家安全、社会安全、经济安全的重要组成部分，也是保障公民相关权利的重要方面。中国十分重视信息网络安全，推出了一系列的政策、法律法规和标准来保障信息安全。

在政策方面，《国家中长期科学和技术发展规划纲要（2006 ～ 2020 年）》中将信息安全作为优先发展的前沿技术列入其中。“十二五”规划中强调了信息安全在信息化发展中的重要性，从产业政策完善、创新能力建设、骨干企业培育、应用推广力度、标准体系建设、产品规范认证、人才队伍建设等方面提出了既具有宏观指导性又具有实际可操作性的政策措施。从 2006 年起，原信息产业部与工业和信息化部启动和持续推动“绿色上网”工程，建设绿色健康的网络环境，保护公民特别是青少年的身心健康。

在法律法规方面，通过实施了《中华人民共和国电子签名法》、《全国人大常委会关于加强网络信息保护的决定》、《通信网络安全防护管理办法》、《电信和互联网用户个人信息保护规定》等一系列与信息安全相关的法律法规和部门规章，在网络与信息系统安全、电子签名认证、保密及密码管理、计算机病毒防治、金融及打击网络违法犯罪行为等领域，初步形成了信息安全法律制度框架，为保障信息安全创造了良好的法律环境。

在信息安全标准方面，10 年间，国家标准化管理委员会批准了超过 130 多项现行的信息安全相关国家标准，使现行的信息安全相关国家标准超过了 150 项；工信部制定并发布了通信行业相关信息安全标准 200 余项。这些标准的发布和实施，对于完善中国信息安全标准体系、规范和指导信息安全保障体系建设具有重要意义。

2014 年年初，中国成立了中央网络安全和信息化领导小组，由中共中央总书记习近平亲自担任组长。该小组的成立标志着中国将网络信息安全和信息化上升到了国家高度，必将极大推动信息化发展，加强信息安全保障能力。

Telecommunication Industry Contributes to Human Rights Protection in China

Miao Wei, Minister of Industry and Information Technology

In 2004, that "[t]he State respects and protects human rights" was articulated in the *Constitution of the People's Republic of China* for the first time. This was considered a milestone in the development of China's human rights cause and attracted wide attention from the international community. The right to communication is an important component of human rights. Information and communication, throughout the history of mankind, not only helps record and promote the advancement of civilizations but also serves as an important vehicle and tool for the evolution of the cultural value of human rights. In the decade since articulation of human rights in the Constitution, the telecommunication industry has experienced rapid development with its infrastructure being improved continuously, its users skyrocketing and its influence markedly increased in all economic and service sectors. The rapid development of the telecommunication industry has made a remarkable contribution to the improvement of people's livelihood and public services with impressive achievements in protecting people's rights and interests, serving vulnerable groups, providing universal services, protecting information security and many other aspects, thus effectively advancing human rights protection in China.

I. Protecting citizen's rights and interests.

Over the past decade, the supply of products and services in the telecommunication industry has continuously improved. Communication operators offer an increasingly wide range of services by speeding up transformation and making innovations. User satisfaction has risen steadily as their rights and interests are increasingly better protected. From 2004 to 2013, the per-user business volume of telecommunication services① increased from 1,425 yuan to 2,627 (assuming a flat price for telecommunication in 2000) with a compound annual growth rate of 6.3%. Meanwhile, the price of telecommunication services continued to drop with a 50% decrease in the comprehensive price level of telecommunication charges. As a result, all people have shared the fruits of telecommunication reform.

1. Gradual infrastructural improvement

Information infrastructure is a public infrastructure of strategic importance to national development and an important foundation for economic and social development. The Chinese Government has strongly supported the development of information infrastructure. From 2004 to 2013, special campaigns have been conducted to extend telephone service to all villages in China, promote triple play service and implement the "Broadband China" strategy, vastly improving the information infrastructure, which now covers the whole nation and benefits all citizens.

During the past decade, the total length of optical fiber cable in China increased from 2.74 million kilometers to 17.45 million kilometers, among which the length of long distance optical cable lines increased from 590,000 kilometers to 900,000 kilometers. In addition, a 100G wavelength division multiplexing system has been widely applied, covering a majority of provinces and cities in China. The capacity of fixed and long-distance telephone exchange has increased from 8.69 million lines to

① Per user business volume of telecommunication services is the business volume of telecommunication services divided by the number of users.

12.7 million lines and office telephone exchange capacity from 350.83 million lines to 410.52 million lines. The capacity of mobile telephone exchanges has increased from 336.98 million lines to 1,965.45 million lines. The number of base stations of mobile telephones has reached 2.41 million, including 1.09 million 3G base stations. Broadband Internet access ports have increased from 18.02 million to 359.72 million and over 167 million households have "fiber to the home" (FTTH), making China the largest country in Internet use.

2. Rapid expansion of phone subscription

Over the past decade, with better information and telecommunication service and applications, people are able to reap further benefits from the country's development. By 2013, the number of telephone subscribers reached 1.5 billion, among which 1.23 billion were mobile telephone subscribers and mobile phone penetration increasing by 262.7% from 24.9 handsets per hundred people in 2004 to 90.3 sets per hundred in 2013.

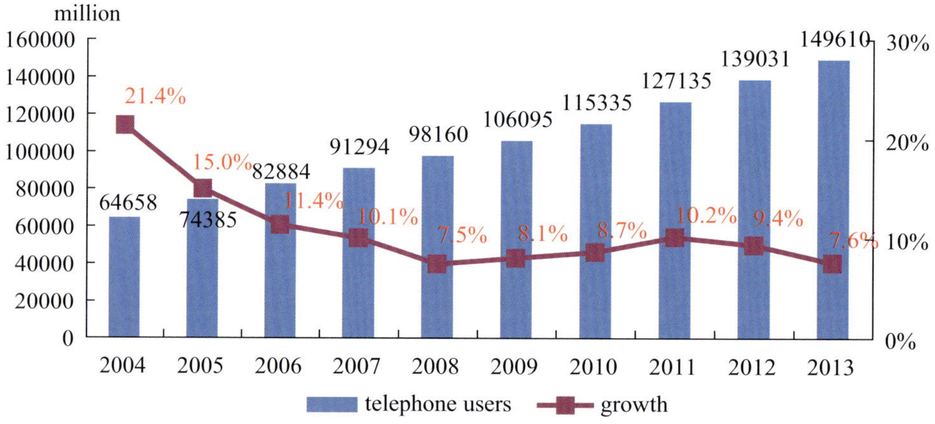

Growth of telephone subscription in China (2004~2013)

Source: *Annual Report of China's Communication Industry Statistics in 2013.*

3. Accelerated increase of broadband access

The Internet is an important way for the public to access information and voice their opinions. China has always attached great importance to the development of Internet infrastructure. Through the popularization of technologies such as satellite communication, optical fiber communications and computer networks, and the implementation of the "Broadband China" strategy, China has built an Internet infrastructure that covers the whole country, benefiting everyone and effectively promoting the development of China's human rights cause.

In the past decade, the total number of broadband users has grown from 11 million to 189 million and the speed of broadband access has improved significantly. Users enjoying a bandwidth of 4M and above accounted for more than 78.8% and Fiber to the Home (FTTH / O) subscribers numbered 40.82 million, accounting for 21.7% of all subscribers.

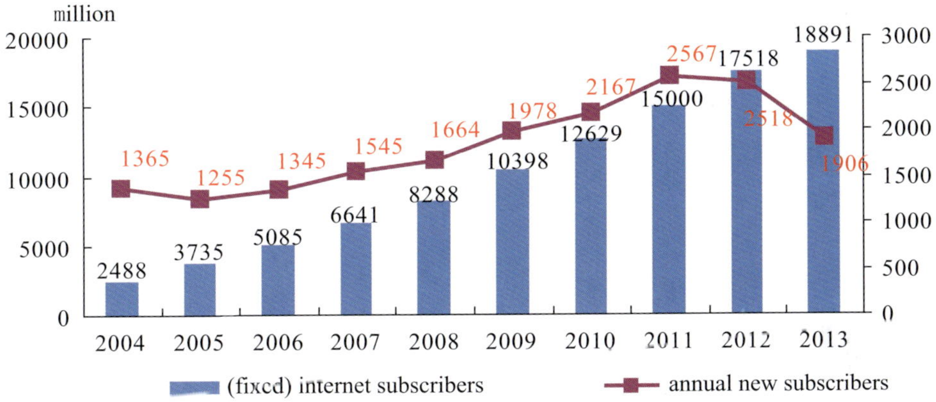

Development of (fixed) Internet broadband access users (2004~2013)

Source: *Annual Report of China's Communication Industry Statistics in 2013.*

In the ten years, Chinese netizens increased from 80 million to 618 million. Internet penetration increased from 6.2% to 45.8%. By the end of 2013, there were 500 million users accessing the Internet by mobile phone, accounting for 81% of mobile phone users. Mobile Internet traffic has been continuously growing by leaps and bounds, reaching a total of 1,321,381,000 GB in the whole year. Average monthly mobile Internet traffic has risen above 139 MB per mobile phone user.

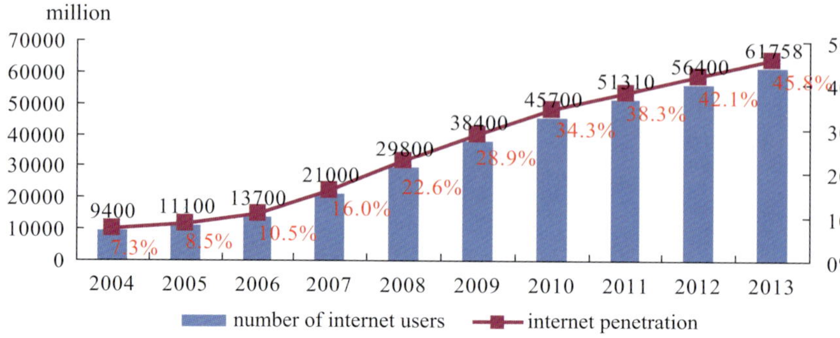

Internet user population and the development of Internet penetration (2004~2013)

Source: *Annual Report of China's Communication Industry Statistics in 2013.*

The popularity and improvement of the Internet has tremendously contributed to the freedom of expression. A variety of Internet platforms and applications such as online forums, online news, blogs, personal webpages, social networks, online literature, online videos, microblogs and instant messaging have greatly enhanced the user experience of Chinese netizens.

4. Deep involvement in people's livelihood

Since the appearance of various new formats of Internet businesses such as the Internet of Things, cloud computing, mobile Internet and e-commerce, the telecommunication industry has become deeply involved in education, health care, social security, culture and other areas of people's livelihood. Telecommunication technology's low cost, high efficiency, wide coverage and fast spread features have been applied in social management and used to facilitate people's lives, helping in the development of China's human rights protection system.

In regard to social management, e-government has significantly enhanced the government's capacity to provide public services and administration by improving operational mechanisms, strengthening the transparency of governmental affairs, simplifying procedures and increasing efficiency in order to build a transparent, efficient, clean and service-oriented government. The government has made full use of the Internet of Things, cloud computing, mobile Internet and other information and communication means to build smart cities. Through the detection, transmission, integration and analysis of key data in the core city operation systems, the government has been able to make smart responses to work services, social management, industrial operations and other activities as well as create a smart environment for urban development. This has resulted in the construction of an urban management system that integrates emergency command, public security supervision, traffic control, and urban management law enforcement, reshaping the local environment into a new city that better fits the people.

In regard to facilitating people's lives, IT products and services in areas such as healthcare, education, culture and finance have contributed to a fairer distribution of the social resources listed above as well as more convenient services and more transparent regulations. These products and services have also effectively facilitated institutional reforms in various fields, thus better serving people in life, study and personal development.

II. Serving vulnerable groups.

Information accessibility plays a key role in China's informatization development plan and is the main force behind China's socialist modernization drive. China has done much to promote fair dissemination of information, support the information rights of vulnerable groups, and eliminate the digital divide. The government has also assisted the disabled persons and other vulnerable groups in keeping up with the pace of development for this information society and sharing as equals the opportunities and well-being created in the process of social progress and development.

At present, China has developed a systematic framework of information accessibility standards and the 12th Five-Year Plan for the development of accessibility, vigorously promoting the formulation of information accessibility standards and the construction of accessible facilities. China has also promoted the R&D, application and innovation of products and services for the disabled and coordinated various relevant activities for their benefit. Several information accessibility standards have been successfully issued, such as *Requirements of Hearing Aids Compatibility and Measurement Methods for Telephone Handset, Technical Requirements and Evaluation Methods for Assistive Technology of Information Accessibility in Information Terminals,*

Information Accessibility Technical Requirement for Call Center, Information Accessibility Technical Requirement of Voice-Enabled Web Service, Information Accessibility Technical Requirements for Deaf Assistant System in Public Place, and *Information Accessibility for People with Physical Disabilities Technical Requirements for Web Accessibility.* These standards cover many aspects including assistive equipment, communication terminals, accessible websites, voice-enabled web services and environmental assessment.

In order to achieve universal access to information services, China established in 2012 a national public service platform for information accessibility to thoroughly explore accessible information solutions for Chinese websites. Between May 19, 2013 (the 23rd National Day to Help the Disabled) and May 18, 2014 (the 24th National Day to Help the Disabled), China effectively promoted accessibility in close to 300 government sites and mainstream web media sites and more than 10,000 websites (15% of all government and mainstream media sites) began to provide accessible services. Broadband infrastructure as well as a three-years internet access for free are provided for 100 special education schools in rural areas. A national accessible information service system has gradually taken shape.

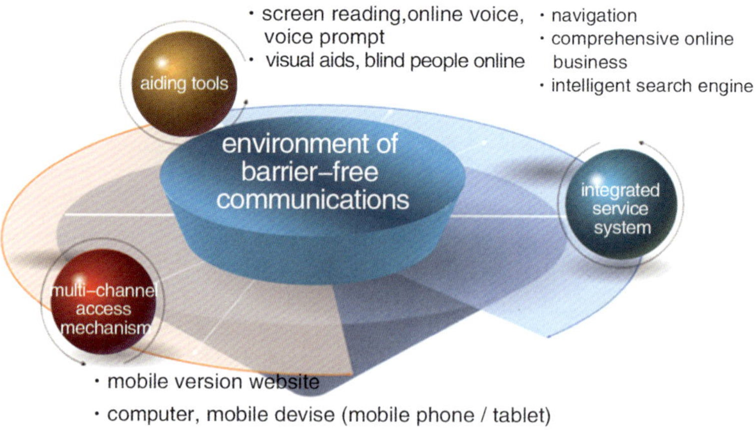

Government information accessibility campaign

Source: The working group of "Beautiful China – government information accessibility campaign in China".

III. Providing universal service.

To implement a series of strategic arrangements in China's rural reform and development, the Ministry of Information Industry (predecessor of Ministry of Industry and Information Technology) started to push for the extension of telecommunication services to all villages.

In accordance with the *Telecommunications Regulations,* the three main telecom operators took up the responsibility for providing universal telecom service. Efforts were made to extend phone services to all incorporated and then natural villages, Internet access to townships and towns and then universal information access in rural areas. The project was implemented in triple three-steps: (a) the basic network infrastructure was extended to townships and towns first, then to incorporated villages and finally natural villages; (b) in service provision, telephone, broadband and information accesses were offered one after another; and (c) service capabilities were gradually scaled up from infrastructure construction to information platforms and then farmer-specific services.

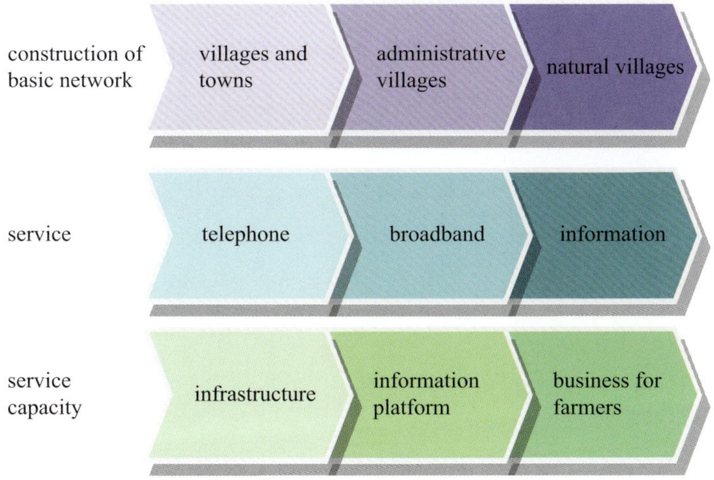

Triple three-steps to extend telecommunication services to all villages

Source: China Academy of Telecommunication Research (CATR).

By the end of 2013, the Project had been successfully implemented for ten years, boasting a total investment of 87 billion yuan with telecommunications facilities and applications across extensive rural areas, and providing every village with phone service and every township with Internet access. The past decade saw 76,000 additional villages gaining access to phone services, thus all incorporated villages now have phone services as compared with the previous proportion of 88%. An additional 128,000 natural villages of over 20 households had telephones installed over the past decade and telephony coverage of natural villages increased to 95.6% from 90%. Over the 10 years, nearly 4,000 more towns and townships and 137,000 more incorporated villages gained access to broadband, covering almost 100% of towns and townships nationwide and 91% of all incorporated villages (of the figure was 67% when the project was launched). The "Bringing Information to the Countryside" program now covers 85% of towns and township. Comprehensive information service platforms, such as Nongxintong, Info Village and Jinnongtong, have been created. There are nearly 20,000 agriculture-related websites, over 31,000 information service stations, nearly 300,000 village information service points, 30,000 online information libraries, and 278,000 village information columns. In 2012, in cooperation with the Ministry of Education, State Council Leading Group of Poverty Alleviation and Development and China Disabled Persons' Federation, programs such as "Broadband Access in Rural Primary and Secondary Schools" and "Broadband Access in Schools for Disabled Students" were successfully launched. And now 5,300 primary and secondary schools in impoverished areas have access to broadband and 200 schools for the disabled as well as many primary and middle schools have been granted free Internet access for three years.

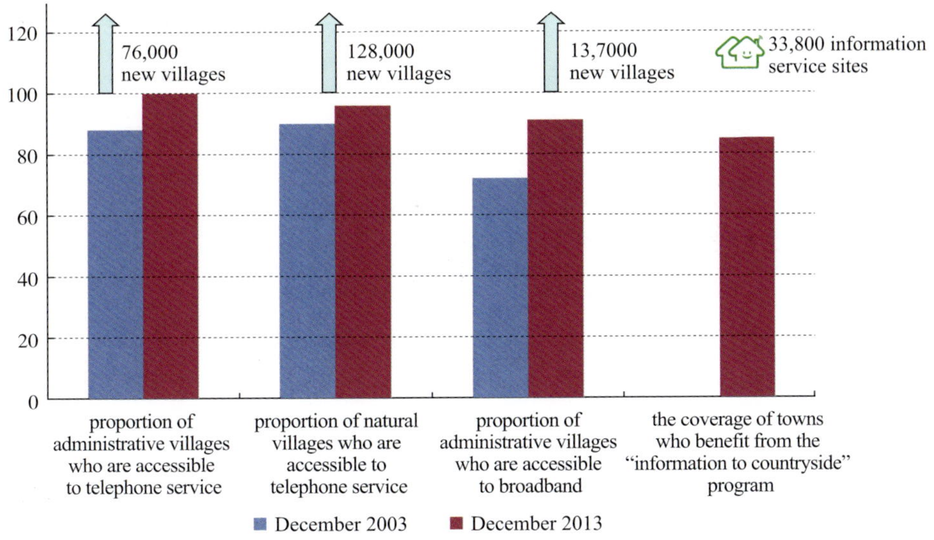

The achievements of project to extend telecommunication services to all villages (2004~2013)

Source: MIIT.

Thanks to the project, telecommunication infrastructure and the application of telecommunication technologies in rural areas have developed by leaps and bounds, greatly benefiting agricultural output, development of rural areas, as well as the income and living standard of rural residents. More specifically the project has:

Improved people's livelihood. With modern telecommunications tools, remote villages have bidden farewell to isolation from outside world and enjoyed great convenience in poverty alleviation, agricultural and sideline product sales, employment, health care and first aid, culture and education. Modern communication has also played a positive role in improving the lives of ethnic minorities and promoting solidarity among ethnic groups.

Aided disaster prevention and mitigation. In the massive Wenchuan and Yushu earthquakes as well as major snowstorms, floods and mudslides, the project served as a lifeline and a guarantee.

Promoted the application of information technology and progress in agricultural production. China's home-grown low-cost information terminals such as fixed wireless access systems, broadband set-top box, information machines,

TV broadband handwriting board, low-cost computers and cell phones have been widely used in rural areas. Hi-tech applications such as the third generation mobile communications (3G), high speed broadband, Internet of Things, traceability of animals and plants, and greenhouse monitoring have also been rolled out in rural areas. Telecommunication technologies have been translated into tools for agricultural development and rural residents' income growth, changing the traditional agricultural production and rural area administration.

According to *Broadband China Strategy and Implementation Plan* issued in August 2013, 98% incorporated villages will have broadband access by 2020 with an access speed of 12 Mbps. The universal coverage of broadband service will be furthered. At present, the Chinese Government is doing research on improving compensation mechanisms for universal telecom services so as to guide the enterprises to speed up promotion of broadband infrastructure and information application in rural areas and to comprehensively expand the extent of use of information technologies.

IV. Ensuring information security.

The application of information technology has become a key driver in promoting socio-economic development and changes. Information security is essential to applying information technologies. With the development of economic and social information-based tools such as e-government, e-commerce and social networks, information security has become an integral part of national, social and economic security and plays a key role in the protection of citizens' rights. China attaches great importance to cyber security and has released a series of policies, laws, regulations and standards to ensure information security.

On policy side, information security has been listed in *National Outlines for Medium and Long-term Planning for Scientific and Technological Development (2006-2020)* as a priority and a cutting-edge technology. It has also been highlighted in the 12th Five-Year Plan, which includes some instructive and practical policy measures such as improving industrial policy, enhancing innovation capabilities, fostering key enterprises, strengthening promotion, building a system of standards, engaging in product certification, and building up human resources. The Ministry of Information Industry (predecessor of MIIT) launched in 2006 and has continuously promoted the "Green Internet" program with a view to building a healthy network environment and protecting citizens' physical and mental health, young people in particular.

Furthermore, by adopting and implementing a series of laws, regulations and department rules relevant to information security, such as *Law of the People's Republic of China on Electronic Signature, Decision of the Standing Committee of the National People's Congress on Strengthening Information Protection on Networks, Measures for the Administration of Communication Network Security Protection, Provisions on Protecting the Personal Information of Telecommunications and Internet Users,* a legal framework for the protection of information security has basically taken shape, covering network and information system security, e-signature identification, confidentiality and password management, computer virus prevention, finance and cracking down on online crimes, creating a healthy legal environment for information security.

Additionally, over the past decade, the Standardization Administration of China (SAC) has approved more than 130 national standards on information security, bumping the number of existing information security standards to over 150. The Ministry of Industry and Information Technology has formulated and released over 200 telecommunication industry-related information security standards. The publication and implementation of these standards are conducive to improving China's information security standard system and guiding the development of an information security protection system.

In early 2004, the Central Leading Group for Internet Security and Informatization was established, headed by Xi Jinping, General Secretary of the CPC Central Committee. The creation of this group highlighted the prioritization of network information security and informatization and will greatly facilitate the application of information technologies and build up the capacity to protect information security.

(original translation by Jiang Yu and Li Xiaoyu)

发挥司法行政职能作用
促进中国人权事业发展

司法部部长　吴爱英

中国共产党和中国政府历来高度重视尊重和保障人权。2004 年 3 月 14 日，第十届全国人民代表大会第二次会议通过《宪法》修正案，将“国家尊重和保障人权”写入《宪法》。“人权入宪”十年来，司法部和地方各级司法行政机关认真贯彻落实《宪法》法律，依法履行职责，改革完善体制机制，为中国人权事业发展进步做出了积极贡献。

一、开展人权法治宣传教育，增强全社会人权保护意识

开展人权法治宣传教育，在全社会树立尊重和保障人权的法治意识，是中国政府推动人权事业发展的一大创举。“人权入宪”十年来，中国政府持之以恒地开展人权法治宣传教育，为尊重和保障人权奠定了坚实基础。

（一）在全社会普遍开展宪法教育

《宪法》是国家的根本法，也是保护人权的根本法。司法部和地方各级司法行政机关坚持把《宪法》宣传教育作为全民普法的首要任务，突出宣传《宪法》，宣传“人权入宪”的重大意义，宣传《宪法》关于尊重和保障人

权的规定。把每年的12月4日即中国现行宪法实施日作为全国法制宣传日，在全社会组织开展《宪法》集中宣传活动。通过开展《宪法》学习报告会、主题宣讲、知识竞赛等，推动《宪法》宣传教育深入开展，增强全社会人权保护意识，使尊重和保障人权成为全社会的自觉行动。

（二）把人权法治宣传作为全民普法的重要内容

坚持以人为本，大力宣传与公民生产生活密切相关的就业、就学、就医等法律法规，增强全社会依法保障公民的受教育权和健康权等基本权利的意识。围绕社会改革和城市化进程，大力宣传物权保护、城市拆迁、土地征用、土地承包流转等法律法规，增强全社会依法保障财产权等基本权利的意识。围绕社会特殊群体保护，大力宣传妇女儿童、老年人、残疾人权益保护等法律法规，增强全社会依法保障生存权、平等权和人身权等相关权利的意识。围绕司法人权的保护，大力宣传民事、刑事、行政诉讼法律制度，增强全社会依法保障被告人、在押人员和服刑人员等的辩护权、人身权和获得赔偿权的意识。同时，大力宣传公民行使权利时应当履行相应义务，增强全社会权利义务相统一的意识。通过广泛开展人权法治宣传，使人权保护法治观念深入人心，为人权保护营造了良好法治氛围。

（三）切实提高人权法治宣传的针对性和实效性

坚持把领导干部和国家工作人员作为人权法治宣传教育的关键，切实增强其人权保护意识，在推进经济社会发展、服务和改善民生、增进社会福祉中，自觉坚持以人为本，维护公民合法权益。坚持以法律进机关、进乡村、进社区、进学校、进企业、进单位的“法律六进”活动为载体，大力推进人权法治宣传向社会面上拓展、向社会基层延伸，努力扩大人权法治宣传的覆盖面和影响力。大力推动人权法治宣传创新，充分利用大众媒体和新媒体开展人权法治宣传，运用涉及人权保障的正、反面典型案例开展以案释法，增强人权法治宣传的吸引力和感染力，提高了人权法治宣传的针对性和实效性。

二、严格刑罚执行，依法保障人权

司法行政机关是监禁刑和非监禁刑的刑罚执行机关，在依法保障人权中承担重要职责。全国各级司法行政机关坚持依法严格公正文明执法，切实保障人权，有力推动了人权事业的发展。

（一）认真做好监禁刑刑罚执行工作

监狱是国家监禁刑刑罚执行机关。司法行政机关认真贯彻落实《监狱法》，严格执行刑罚，依法保障人权。

一是加强罪犯教育改造工作。确立了把教育改造罪犯作为监狱工作中心任务的指导思想，出台了《监狱教育改造工作规定》等一系列制度，形成了对罪犯的思想、法制、文化、管理、劳动教育等一系列教育矫正措施，普遍开展罪犯的心理咨询、心理矫治和个别化教育、个案矫治等活动，2008 年以来，100 多万名罪犯获得职业技术资格证书，6000 多名罪犯获得国家承认的大专及以上毕业证书，提高了罪犯回归融入社会的能力。根据女犯和未成年罪犯的特点有针对性地采取教育改造措施，教育改造质量不断提高。

二是加强执法规范化建设。持续开展了“规范执法行为，促进执法公正”、“规范化管理年”等活动。建立了集教育、管理、执法、劳动、罪犯权益保障、监督等于一体的监狱执法标准和程序，实现了执法规范化、制度化。依法切实保障罪犯享有辩护、申诉、控告、检举及通讯、会见等权利，严禁监狱人民警察体罚、虐待、侮辱、殴打罪犯或指使他人殴打、体罚罪犯。深化狱务公开，接受罪犯及其家属以及社会的监督，增强监狱执法透明度和公信力。健全警务督察制度，切实加强执法监督。

三是加强罪犯安全生产和生活卫生保障。改善生产条件，优化劳动环境。加强罪犯医疗保障，医疗纳入所在地卫生、防疫计划。

四是深化监狱体制改革。推进监狱布局调整，推行监狱信息化建设，努力改善执法和监管改造条件，为保障罪犯合法权益奠定了基础。

（二）做好社区矫正工作

中国的社区矫正是将被判处管制、缓刑、假释、暂予监外执行的罪犯置于社区内进行矫正的非监禁刑刑罚执行制度。这一刑罚执行制度的重大改革集中体现了国家尊重和保障人权的宪法原则，是在刑罚执行中落实宽严相济刑事政策的重要举措，也是“人权入宪”十年来中国在人权司法保障上取得的重要成果之一。中国的社区矫正从 2003 年开始，经过试点、扩大试点和全面试行两个阶段，目前已进入全面推进阶段。截至 2014 年 9 月底，全国累计接收社区服刑人员 211.3 万人，累计解除 138.2 万人，在册 73.1 万人，在矫正期间的重新犯罪率一直保持在 0.2% 的较低水平。各级司法行政机关认真落实社区矫正任务，切实加强监督管理，落实社区服刑人员报告、居住地变更、外出请销假等制度，有效防止了脱管漏管。切实加强教育矫正，深入开展思想教育、法制教育、社会公德教育、个案矫正、心理辅导和社区服务，不断提高教育矫正质量。切实加强社会适应性帮扶，帮助解决社区服刑人员就业、就学、临时救助、最低生活保障等问题，为有困难的社区服刑人员提供过渡性食宿、技能培训和就业指导等，有力促进了社区服刑人员顺利融入社会。

同时，各级司法行政机关积极做好刑满释放人员安置帮教工作，建立衔接工作机制，实现对刑满释放人员无缝衔接。积极推动以政府投入为主的刑满释放人员过渡性安置基地建设，全国共建设过渡性安置基地 141 个，为无家可归、无亲可投、无业可就的刑满释放人员提供 3 ～ 6 个月的免费食宿、心理辅导、技能培训和推荐就业等服务。做好教育帮扶工作，加强对刑满释放人员的思想政治、法制、道德和文化教育，推动落实刑满释放人员就业扶持、社会保障等政策，解决他们的实际困难，提高他们适应社会的能力，有力促进了刑满释放人员顺利回归社会。

三、做好法律服务工作，保障公民合法权益

让公民获得有效的法律帮助，是保障人权的基本要求。多年来，各级司法行政机关认真履行职责，不断完善律师法律服务和法律援助制度，推动建立公共法律服务体系，在维护法律正确实施、维护社会公平正义、保障公民合法权益方面发挥了重要作用。

（一）充分发挥律师在保障人权中的积极作用

律师是维护和保障人权的重要力量，各级司法行政机关积极采取有效措施，推动律师在人权保护中依法履行职责，充分发挥职能作用。

一是大力发展律师事业。将发展律师行业纳入经济社会发展规划，推动

律师事业不断发展，努力满足人民群众对法律服务的需求。截至2013年年底，全国共有律师事务所2.04万家，比2004年的1.45万家增长了41%。律师总数达25.24万人，比2004年初的14.51万人增长了74%。广大律师积极开展刑事辩护和民事代理活动，为公众提供优质高效的法律服务。2013年，全国律师办理诉讼案件250多万件，非诉讼法律事务81万多件，为维护社会公平正义、保障人权做出了积极贡献。

二是改革完善律师制度。2012年修改后的《刑事诉讼法》进一步明确了律师在整个诉讼过程中的地位、权利和责任。2007年对《律师法》进行了修订，以立法形式肯定了律师制度改革发展取得的成果。每一轮的中国司法体制和工作机制改革都把律师制度改革作为重要内容，专门做出安排部署。司法部先后制定、修订出台了《律师执业管理办法》等16件部颁规章或规范性文件，健全完善了律师制度体系，为律师依法尽职履责提供了根本保障。

三是依法保障律师执业权利。《刑事诉讼法》和新修订的《律师法》，对律师参与诉讼活动特别是刑事诉讼活动中享有的会见权、阅卷权、调查取证权等做了补充、强化。各级司法行政机关和律师协会协调有关部门，建立健全制度，制定保障律师诉讼权利的措施，严格依法落实法律赋予律师在刑事诉讼中会见、阅卷、收集证据和发问、质证、辩论等方面的执业权利。推动完善律师会见、阅卷等接待服务设施，便于律师办理立案、会见、阅卷、参与庭审等事务。建立健全律师执业权利救济机制，对妨碍律师行使诉讼权利的，启动相应程序予以纠正。全国律协和各地律师协会积极履行职责，依法维护律师执业权利。

（二）大力推进法律援助工作

法律援助是国家建立的为经济困难公民和特殊案件当事人提供免费法律服务、保障其平等实现合法权益的一项重要法律制度，是保障社会困难群体人权的重要途径。

一是健全完善法律援助制度。2003年国务院颁布实施《法律援助条例》和修订后的《刑事诉讼法》，扩大了法律援助在刑事诉讼中的适用范围，将法律援助从审判阶段延伸到侦查和审查起诉阶段。司法部先后与有关部门联合下发了《关于民事诉讼法律援助工作的规定》和《关于刑事诉讼法律援助工作的规定》，进一步完善了民事诉讼中法律援助与司法救助衔接机制，健全了刑事诉讼法律援助公检法司衔接配合机制，形成了完整的法律援助工作制度体系。

二是不断扩大法律援助覆盖面。各地普遍将就医、就业、就学、劳动报酬、社会保障等与民生紧密相关的权益保护事项纳入法律援助补充事项范围，努力使法律援助惠及更多困难群众。十年来，全国法律援助机构共组织办理法律援助案件 685 万件，为 8655 万人提供法律援助，有效维护了困难群众合法权益。

三是深化法律援助便民服务。部署开展了“法律援助便民服务”主题活动，在全国推行十项便民措施。加强基层服务网络、便民服务窗口和工作站点建设，推进法律援助向社区、乡村延伸，目前共设立法律援助工作站 6.5 万余个。健全完善便民服务措施，畅通申请渠道，简化受理审查程序。加强农民工、妇女、儿童、老年人、残疾人等重点人群法律援助工作，切实维护其合法权益。

四是增强法律援助保障能力。建立了中央和地方共同分担的法律援助经费保障体制。十年来，法律援助财政投入实现了年均增长 16.6%，2013 年法律援助经费总额是 2004 年的 6.6 倍。

（三）切实加强公共法律服务体系建设

建立公共法律服务体系，满足人民群众基本法律服务需求，是推进人权保障工作的重要措施。司法部制定了《关于推进公共法律服务体系建设的意见》，加快建立健全符合国情、覆盖城乡、惠及全民的公共法律服务体系。

一是健全完善公共法律服务网络。整合律师、公证、基层法律服务、司法鉴定等法律服务资源，建立健全县、乡、村司法行政法律服务中心、站点，方便群众及时获得法律帮助。

二是大力拓展公共法律服务领域。积极推动法律服务向民生领域延伸，不断满足群众的基本法律需求。

三是加大政策扶持力度。各地普遍将公共法律服务纳入政府公共服务体系，纳入政府购买项目，为公共法律服务体系建设提供了有力保障。

Advancing Human Rights Protection in China Through Judicial Administration

Wu Aiying, Minister of Justice

The Communist Party of China and the Chinese Government have always attached much importance to respect for and protection of human rights. On March 14, 2004, the Second Session of the Tenth National People's Congress adopted an amendment to the Constitution, stating that "[t]he State respects and protects human rights". During the ten years since then, the Ministry of Justice and judicial administrative organs at all levels have earnestly implemented the Constitution, fulfilled their duties according to law, and reformed and improved the system and mechanisms, thus contributing greatly to the development of China's human rights cause.

I. Publicity and education campaigns have been conducted for human rights and rule of law to increase social awareness of human rights protection.

It is a great creation of the Chinese Government to increase society's awareness of human rights protection and rule of law through publicity and education campaigns with a view to advancing human rights protection. Since the concept of human rights was articulated in the Constitution ten years ago, the Chinese Government has consistently carried out such campaigns, laying down a solid foundation for the respect for and protection of human rights.

1. Extensive constitutional education

The Constitution is the basic law of the country and also the basic law to protect human rights. The Ministry of Justice and judicial administrative organs at all levels prioritize the publicity and education on the constitution in the national effort to popularize legal knowledge. They have focused on publicity of the Constitution, the significance of putting human rights in the Constitution, and provisions on respect for and protection of human rights in the Constitution. December 4, the date of entry into force of the current Constitution, was made a National Legal Publicity Day. Activities such as lectures, themed speeches and knowledge contests are organized on the day and help increase people's awareness of human rights protection and translate respect for and protection of human rights into conscious actions.

2. Human rights protection and rule of law as important contents in national effort to popularize legal knowledge

The government insists on a people-oriented approach and has increased publicity of regulations closely linked to people's life and work such as employment, education and healthcare so as to enhance social awareness of such basic rights as education and health. In the process of social reform and urbanization, the government has enhanced publicity of regulations and laws on property rights protection, urban housing demolition and relocation, land expropriation and transfer of land use rights in order to increase awareness for the protection of property and other basic rights according to law. With regard to special populations, the government has increased publicity of regulations and laws on the protection of women, children, senior citizens and the disabled so as to increase awareness for the protection of the rights to subsistence and equality as well as the right of person. To protect human rights in the judicial process, the government has increased publicity of legal institutions with regard to civil, criminal and administrative procedures, thus enhancing awareness of the protection according to law of the right of person and right to defense and compensation for the defendants, detainees and prisoners. At the same time, the idea of unity of rights and obligations is planted by advocating that citizens should meet corresponding obligations while exercising their rights. With extensive publicity campaign, human rights protection and rule of law have taken deep root in people's minds and a sound environment has been created for human rights protection.

3. More targeted and effective communication

As government officials and civil servants are key to human rights and rule of law publicity and education, actions have been taken to increase their awareness of human rights protection and enable them to pursue a people-oriented approach and protect citizens' lawful rights and interests in their effort to promote economic and social development, serve and improve people's livelihood and increase social welfare. Through activities of the "six entries of law" that spread legal knowledge in government agencies, rural areas, communities, schools, enterprises and work units, human rights and rule of law is also promoted both extensively to all sectors of the society and vertically to grass-roots so as to expand its coverage and influence. New and innovative means of publicity have been used for example messages for mass media and new media and use of typical cases to explain legal provisions, making the campaign more attractive and convincing and the communication more targeted and effective.

II. Conducting punishment strictly and protecting human rights according to law.

The judicial administrative organs are the implementers of custodial and non-custodial penalties and shoulder important duties in human rights protection. Judicial administrative organs at all levels conduct strict, just and civilized law enforcement, thus protecting and advancing the protection of human rights.

1. Good implementation of custodial penalties

Prisons are where imprisonment is implemented. Judicial administrative organs protect human rights according to law by seriously implementing the *Prison Law* and strictly carrying out punishments.

First, work to educate and reform criminals has been strengthened. It is the central task of prisons to educate and reform criminals. With this in mind, a series of rules have been developed, such as *Provisions on Education and Reformation Work of Prison,* containing various education and corrective measures including ideological, legal, cultural, administrative and labor education. Psychological counselling and treatment for inmates and personalized education and individual case treatment are conducted extensively. Since 2008, more than one million inmates have received vocational qualification certificates and more than 6,000 have got junior college degrees or above, increasing their ability to return to society. Special education and reformation measures have been taken towards female and juvenile prisoners, resulting in better results from education and reformation.

Second, law enforcement has been further standardized. Campaigns such as "Standardizing Law Enforcement and Advancing Impartial Law Enforcement" and "Year of Standardized Management" have been conducted on a continuous basis. Law enforcement standards and procedures for prisons have been set, covering education, management, enforcement, labor, protection of criminals' rights and supervision, thus standardizing and institutionalizing law enforcement. The rights of inmates to defense, appeal, accusation, impeachment, communication and meeting are protected according to law. The prison police are strictly prohibited to corporally punish, abuse, insult or beat up inmates or instigate others to do so. Prison affairs have become more transparent and subject to supervision from inmates, their families and the rest of the society to make law enforcement in prisons more transparent and credible. The system of superintendence has been make more robust to oversee law enforcement.

Third, safety at work and living and medical security of inmates have been improved. Actions have been taken to improve their working conditions and working environment. Medical security is ensured by placing inmates also under local health and immunization programs.

Fourth, prison reforms have been deepened to adjust prison layout, advance informatization of prison and improve conditions for law enforcement and reformation, thus laying down the foundation for the protection of inmates' legitimate rights and interests.

2. Improved community correction

In China, community correction is an implementation system for non-custodial penalties that put convicts who have been sentenced to control, probation, release on parole or temporary service outside in community for correction. It is a major reform embodying the constitutional principle to respect and protect human rights, an important measure to implement the criminal policy of combining punishment with leniency and an important achievement in judicial protection of human rights since the concept was articulated in the Constitution. Community correction was started in 2003 and is now rolled out after pilot, expanded pilot and comprehensive trial implementation. By the end of September 2014, there had been 2,113,000 convicts serving their sentences under community correction across the country, among whom 1,382,000 had been relieved and 731,000 are still registered. The rate of recidivism during the period of correction has been at a relatively low level of 0.2%. Judicial administrative organs at all levels have seriously implemented community correction tasks, strengthened supervision and management and implemented rules of reporting, address changing and leave of absence, thus effectively avoided miss-out and drop-out. Education and correction are constantly strengthened and improved with the provision of ideological education, legal education, social morality education, personalized correction, psychological counselling and community service. Concrete actions are taken to help those serving sentences in community solve problems in employment, education, temporary aid and subsistence allowances so that they are better enabled to adapt to the society. Temporary boarding, skill training and employment guidance are provided for those in difficulty. These measures help people serving sentences in community to return to society.

At the same time, judicial administrative organs at all levels take proactive actions to help people who have been released upon completion of their terms to settle down. Work mechanisms have been established to facilitate transfer from prison back to the society. Efforts are made to advance with mainly government investment the construction of transitional settlement base for those released and set up 141 such bases in the country, providing released former prisoners who have no family or relatives or job with free boarding for three to six months plus psychological counseling, skills training and employment service. Such assistance as well as continued ideological, political, legal, moral and cultural education and efforts to push for the implementation of policies of employment support and social security for the former prisoners are useful in solving their problems and improving their ability to adapt, thus greatly facilitating their return to the society.

III. Providing legal services to protect the legitimate rights and interests of citizens.

Making sure that citizens receive effective legal aid is a basic requirement in human rights protection. Over the years, judicial administrative organs at all levels have earnestly performed their duties, improved institutions of legal counsel and legal aid, and advanced the establishment of a public legal service system, playing an important role in ensuring correct implementation of law, safeguarding social fairness and justice and protecting citizens' legitimate rights and interests.

1. Ensuring lawyer's positive role in human rights protection

Lawyers play an important role in protecting human rights. Judicial administrative organs at all levels have carried out effective measures to make sure that lawyers fully perform their duties in human rights protection according to law.

First, the lawyer profession is vigorously promoted. The profession is also covered in social and economic development plans and actions are taken to advanced its development so as to meet people's needs for legal services. Between 2004 and 2013, the number of law firms increased by 41%, from 14,500 to 20,400; the number of lawyers increased by 74%, from 145,100 to 252,400. Lawyers provide efficient and high-quality legal service for the public in criminal defense and civil actions. In 2013, lawyers handled more than 2.5 million lawsuits and 810,000 non-litigation legal affairs, making positive contribution to maintaining social justice and protecting human rights.

Second, the lawyer system has been reformed and improved. The 2012 revised *Criminal Procedure Law* clarified lawyer's position as well as their rights and duties in litigation procedures. The *Lawyers Law* was revised in 2007. It affirmed the achievement of the reform and development of the lawyer system. In all rounds of reforms of the judicial system and its work mechanisms, the lawyer system reform has been an important part, with specific targeted measures. The Ministry of Justice has formulated or revised 16 department rules and normative documents such as *Administrative Measures for the Practice of Law by Lawyers,* which have contributed to the improvement of the lawyer system and provided basic guarantee for lawyers to perform their duties according to law.

Third, lawyer's right to practise law is protected according to law. The *Criminal Procedure Law* and the newly revised *Lawyers Law* added and strengthened lawyer's rights to meeting, access to documents and investigation and evidence gathering during a lawsuit, especially for criminal litigation. Judicial administrative organs at various levels and lawyers associations consulted related government departments to establish and improve work mechanisms to protect lawyers' litigation rights and strictly implement according to law lawyers' rights to meeting, reading documents, gathering evidence, questioning, cross-examination and debate in practice of law in criminal lawsuits. Service facility for lawyers' meeting and access to case files has been established to facilitate their practices. Relief mechanism has been developed with procedures to rectify situations in which the exercise of lawyers' litigation rights have been obstructed. The All China Lawyers Association and local lawyers associations actively perform their duties to safeguard the rights of practising lawyers according to law.

2. Vigorously advancing work related to legal aid

Legal aid is an important legal system by which the state provides free legal service for citizens with financial hardships and parties in special cases so as to ensure equal realization of their legitimate rights and interests. It is an important way to protect the human rights of vulnerable social groups.

First, the legal aid system has been improved. In 2003, the State Council enacted *Regulations on Legal Aid* and revised the *Criminal Procedure Law,* which expanded the scope of application of legal aid in criminal proceedings and extended the assistance from the trial phase to investigation, review and prosecution phases. The Ministry of Justice and other relevant departments issued *Provisions for the Work on Legal Aid in Civil Actions* and *Provisions for the Work on Legal Aid in Criminal Actions,* which improved the connection between legal aid and judicial relief in civil actions and the legal aid coordination mechanism in criminal actions involving public security organs, procuratorial organs, people's courts and judicial administrative organs, thus creating a complete system of work on legal aid.

Second, the coverage of legal aid has been expanded. The protection of rights and interests closely related to people's livelihood such as healthcare, employment, education, labor remuneration and social security are included as items for the consideration of legal aid so as to benefit more people in strained circumstances. During the last ten years, legal aid organizations all over the country handled 6.85 million legal aid cases and provided legal aid to 86.55 million people, effectively protecting the legitimate rights and interests of people in strained circumstances.

Third, convenience services are provided in legal aid. Campaigns to enhance the convenience of legal aid have been conducted with ten convenience measures adopted all over the country. Grass-roots service network, convenience counters and service stations have been developed to extend legal aid to grass-roots communities and villages. There are now 65,000 legal aid service stations. Measures have also been taken to open application channels and simplify acceptance and examination procedures. Legal aid work concerning vulnerable groups such as migrant workers, women, children, senior citizens and the disabled has been strengthened to protect their legitimate rights and interests.

Fourth, the ability to fund legal aid has been strengthened. A system of legal aid funds shared between central and local governments is in place. In the last ten years, fiscal input in legal aid has increased on average by 16.6% annually. The total input in 2013 was 6.6 times of that in 2004.

3. Developing a public legal service system with concrete actions

To establish a public legal service system so as to meet people's basic needs is an important measure to advance human rights protection. The Ministry of Justice formulated *Opinions on Advancing the Building of Public Legal Service System* to speed up the building of a public legal service system that is suited to the national conditions, covers both urban and rural areas and benefits all people.

First, a public legal service network is developed. Legal service resources including lawyers, notarization, grass-roots legal service and judicial expertise have been mobilized and judicial administrative legal service centers and stations have been established at the county, township and village levels for people to get legal service conveniently.

Second, scope of public legal service is vigorously expanded to areas closely linked to people's livelihood so as to meet people's basic needs.

Third, policy support has been increased. Public legal service has been integrated into government public services and as items for government procurement, thus providing strong support for the development of the public legal service system.

(original translation by Niu Ya'nan)

坚决向污染宣战　切实保障公众健康

环境保护部部长　周生贤

健康权是公众的一项基本权利，保护环境的基本目的就是保障公众健康。中国政府坚持以人为本、执政为民，高度重视环境与健康问题，把环境保护作为重大民心工程、民生工程和德政工程，坚决向污染宣战，以大气、水、土壤污染治理为主战场，持续推进生态环境质量改善，切实维护广大公众健康权益。

一、控制污染减少排放改善生态环境质量

（一）强力推进主要污染物减排工作

把节能减排作为经济社会发展规划的约束性指标，强化目标责任考核，狠抓工程减排、结构减排、管理减排。全国城市污水处理率由 2005 年的 52%提高到 2013 年的 87.9%，燃煤电厂脱硫机组比例由 14%提高到 90%以上，脱硝机组和新型干法水泥脱硝从无到有，脱硝比例均达到 50%。“十一五”期间，二氧化硫、化学需氧量排放量分别下降 14.29%和 12.45%，均超额完成下降 10% 的约束性目标。2013 年，全国化学需氧量、氨氮、二氧化硫、氮氧化物排放总量分别比 2010 年下降 7.8%、7.1%、9.9% 和 2.0%。

（二）制定实施《大气污染防治行动计划》

针对雾霾污染问题，2013年9月中国政府印发实施《大气污染防治行动计划》（以下简称“大气十条”），着重强化以细颗粒物（PM2.5）为重点的大气污染防治工作，从深化污染治理、优化产业结构、调整能源结构、严格环境准入、建立区域协作机制、应对重污染天气等十方面提出具体防治措施。实施《大气十条》以来，环境保护部联合发展改革委等五部门印发《京津冀及周边地区落实大气污染防治行动计划实施细则》，制定《大气十条》重点工作部门分工方案，与31个省（区、市）人民政府签订《大气污染防治目标责任书》；提出22项配套政策，已出台环保电价、新能源汽车补贴、大气专项资金、油品质量升级价格、考核办法等11项政策；2013年安排50亿元支持京津冀及周边地区大气污染治理，2014年将安排100亿元，继续支持重点地区治理大气污染；严格大气污染防治执法监管，在全国重点地区组织开展大气污染防治专项检查，狠抓重污染天气环境应急和特殊时段专项执法督查；完善监测预警应急体系，印发《空气质量新标准第三阶段监测实施方案》，采取飞行检查，保证环境监测数据质量。截至2014年1月，全国已有161个地级以上城市共884个监测点位符合空气质量新标准监测要求。2014年1~6月，中国74个重点城市PM2.5平均浓度比上年同期下降7.9%，重污染天气影响范围、持续时间和污染强度均有所减轻。

（三）发挥环境保护优化经济发展的综合作用

严格建设项目环评，2008年以来，拒批332个、总投资1.1万亿元涉及“两高一资”、低水平重复建设和产能过剩项目。制定实施环境经济政策，初步建立包括绿色信贷、保险、贸易、价格、证券、税收等在内的环境政策框架体系。完善环境标准体系，现行有效国家环保标准超过1500项，对重点控制区火电、钢铁、石化、水泥、有色、化工等六大行业以及燃煤锅炉项目执行大气污染物特别排放限值，进一步促进经济发展和环境保护相协调相融合。

大气 PM2.5 监测。

（四）深化重点流域污染防治

发布实施《重点流域水污染防治规划（2011 ～ 2015 年）》，建立重点流域跨省界断面水质考核制度，持续完善考核指标体系。全国七大水系好于Ⅲ类水质比例由 2005 年的 41% 提高到 2013 年的 66.7%；劣Ⅴ类水质比例由 27% 下降到 10.8%。按照“保护优先，自然恢复为主”原则，编制实施《水质较好湖泊生态环境保护总体规划（2013 ～ 2020 年）》，完善水环境治理体系，建立健全水质较好湖泊生态环境保护长效机制。截至目前，中央财政已下达专项资金 95 亿元，支持 92 个省、区、市的 62 个湖泊开展生态环境保护。

（五）加强生态保护和农村环境保护

国务院成立中国生物多样性保护国家委员会，批准《中国生物多样性保护战略与行动计划（2011 ～ 2030 年）》，制订《联合国生物多样性十年中国行动（2011 ～ 2020）》。国务院办公厅印发《关于加强农村环境保护工作的意见》、《关于做好自然保护区管理有关工作的通知》、《国家级自然保护区调整管理规定》、《近期土壤环境保护和综合治理工作安排》。开展全国生态环境十年变化（2000～2010年）遥感调查与评估，全面掌握全国生态系统状况及其变化情况。积极推进全国生态保护红线划定工作。2008～2013年，中央财政共安排农村环保专项资金195亿元，实施“以奖促治、以奖代补”政策措施，支持4.6万个村庄开展环境综合整治，8700多万农村人口受益。

（六）全面推进生态文明建设示范区创建

经中央批准，环境保护部组织开展的“生态建设示范区”正式更名为“生态文明建设示范区”。环保部门先后发布了《关于大力推进生态文明建设示范区工作的意见》、《生态文明建设试点示范区指标》等一系列管理规范文件。截至目前，全国已有浙江、江苏、福建、辽宁、宁夏等16个省（区）开展生态省（区）建设，1000多个市（县）开展生态文明建设示范区建设，建成92个国家生态文明建设示范区和3815个国家级生态乡镇。

二、着力解决损害群众健康的突出环境问题

（一）环境与健康工作取得突破

保护环境归根结底是为了保障群众健康。2014年4月新修订的《中华人民共和国环境保护法》（以下简称“环境保护法”）进一步突出了保障公众健康的目标指向，专门增加环境与健康内容，要求“国家建立、健全环境与健康监测、调查和风险评估制度；鼓励和组织开展环境质量对公众健康影响的研究，采取措施预防和控制与环境污染有关的疾病”，为更好开展环境与健康工作奠定了法律基础。目前，中国已成立国家层面的环境与健康工作领导小组，发布实施《国家环境与健康行动计划（2007～2015）》、《国家环境保护“十二五”环境与健康工作规划》和《关于“十二五”期间加强环境与健康工作的指导意见》等一系列规划措施，全国重点地区环境与健康专项调查等工作正有序推进。

第四届国家环境与健康论坛在广州召开。

（二）优先解决关系民生的突出环境问题

把大气、水、土壤污染防治作为重点，进一步强化PM2.5为重点的大气污染防治，开展重点区域PM2.5来源解析工作，协调有关部门保障油品供应，完善燃煤锅炉综合整治政策和标准，实行严格考核，确保2014年淘汰黄标车和老旧车600万辆。深入开展饮用水水源保护和地下水污染防治。组织评估了全国328个地级及以上城市844个集中式饮用水水源环境状况，印发《华北平原地下水污染防治工作方案》，积极落实《全国地下水污染防治规划》。积极推进土壤污染治理。印发《土壤环境保护和综合治理方案编制指南》，制定目标责任书和考核办法。发布《关于加强工业企业关停、搬迁及原址场地再开发利用过程中污染防治工作的通知》，对关停搬迁企业制定实施环境无害化搬迁方案和履行企业场地环境调查、风险评估和治理修复责任提出具体要求。此外，深入推进化学品、持久性有机物、重金属等领域污染防治，积极落实《化学品风险防控“十二五”规划》、《全国主要行业持久性有机污染物污染防治“十二五”规划》，开展危险化学品环境管理登记，推动《关于汞的水俣公约》批约工作。中央财政增设重金属污染防治专项，截至2013年已安排116亿元支持重金属污染防治。全国堆存数十年的670万吨铬渣基本处置完毕。

（三）铁腕开展环境执法监管

保持执法检查高压态势，不打招呼、不定时间、不听汇报、直奔现场、直接查处、直接曝光，对环境违法行为"零容忍"。2013 年以来，累计出动 2085 万人次，检查企业 860 万家次，发现环境违法问题 18 万件，取缔关闭违法排污企业 2.5 万家，停产治理 1.6 万家，挂牌督办 3.5 万件。创新监管手段，采用卫星遥感及无人机进行大气污染源检查，有力惩戒违法排污行为。各级环保部门 2013 年共向公安机关移送涉嫌环境犯罪案件 700 多件，超过以往十年的总和。公安机关以污染环境罪判决近 110 件，抓捕犯罪分子 180 多人。

（四）全面推进环境信息公开

及时公开环境质量监测、建设项目环境影响评价、环境违法案件及查处等方面的环境信息，主动向社会通报环境状况、重要政策措施和突发环境事件及其应急处置信息，印发《关于当前环境保护信息公开重点工作安排的通知》、《建设项目环境影响评价政府信息公开指南（试行）》、《关于加强污染源环境监管信息公开工作的通知》和《污染源环境监管信息公开目录（第一批）》，出台国家重点监控企业污染源监督性监测、自行监测及信息公开办法。

三、着力构建生态文明建设和环境保护的"四梁八柱"[①]

构建生态文明建设和环境保护的"四梁八柱"，是全国环保系统贯彻落实习近平总书记重要讲话精神的集中体现，是推进国家生态环境治理体系和治理能力现代化的重要内容，是一段时期以来中国生态环境保护实践探索的

① "四梁八柱"是一个形象说法，用来描述生态文明建设和环境保护的宏观性、系统性、轮廓性的整体架构。它既是党中央、国务院决策部署的具体化，也是各地区和环保部门一段时期以来探索实践的总结概括，主要包括四个方面：（1）以积极探索环境保护新路为实践主体，进一步丰富环境保护的理论体系，这是推进生态文明建设的有效路径。（2）以新修订的《环境保护法》实施为龙头，形成保护生态环境的法律法规体系。（3）以深化生态环保体制改革为契机，建立严格监管所有污染物的环境保护组织制度体系。（4）以打好大气、水、土壤污染防治三大战役为抓手，构建改善环境质量的工作体系。

认识升华，是坚持整体推进、重点突破工作思路的创新举措，也是坚决向污染宣战、解决损害群众健康突出环境问题的有力保障。

（一）以积极探索环境保护新路为实践主体，进一步丰富环境保护的理论体系

正确处理经济发展与环境保护关系，牢固树立保护生态环境就是保护生产力、改善生态环境就是发展生产力的理念，更加自觉地推动绿色发展、循环发展、低碳发展。加快推进环境管理战略转型，以改善生态环境质量为目标导向，统筹协调污染治理、总量减排、环境风险防范和环境质量改善的关系。

（二）以新修订的《环境保护法》实施为龙头，形成有力保护生态环境的法律法规体系

新修订的《环境保护法》在基本理念、公众参与、法律责任等方面实现了诸多突破。在做好新《环境保护法》宣传工作的同时，组织制定执法解释、指导意见等相关配套文件，做好行政拘留、行政问责、环境刑事案件办理等工作的协调和衔接，确保新《环境保护法》得到有力实施。加快推进大气污染防治、水污染防治、土壤环境保护、生物遗传资源获取与惠益分享、核安全等专项法律法规的制修订。

（三）以深化生态环保体制改革为契机，建立严格监管所有污染物排放的环境保护组织制度体系

从再生产全过程着手，从形成山顶到海洋、天上到地下的所有污染物严格监管制度和一体化污染防治管理模式着力，增强生态环境监管的统一性和有效性。通过体制创新，建立统一监管所有污染物排放的环境保护管理制度，对所有污染物、污染源、污染介质实行统一监管，探索建立化学品全生命周期风险防控模式。独立进行环境监管和行政执法，加强对有关部门和地方政府执行国家环境法律法规和政策的监督。

（四）以打好大气、水、土壤污染防治三大战役为抓手，构建改善环境质量的工作体系

继续把大气污染防治作为重中之重，深入实施《大气十条》。进一步强化水污染防治，全力抓好土壤污染治理，抓紧编制实施《水污染防治行动计划》和《土壤污染防治行动计划》。以“六厂（场）一车”（火电厂、钢铁厂、水泥厂、造纸厂、城镇污水处理厂、畜禽养殖场和机动车）为重点，严格落实减排任务和责任考核，强化环境执法监管，加大环境信息公开力度，保障公众的环境知情权、参与权和监督权。

良好生态环境是最公平的公共产品，是最普惠的民生福祉。我们将以对人民群众、对子孙后代高度负责的态度和责任感，积极构建和主动实践“四梁八柱”，坚决向污染宣战，用铁规铁腕强化大气、水、土壤污染防治，以生态环境质量改善的实际成效维护公众健康权益。

Resolutely Declaring War on Pollution to Effectively Protect Public Health

Zhou Shengxian, Minister of Environmental Protection

The right to health is among the fundamental rights of the people. The ultimate goal of environmental protection is to protect public health. Sticking to the principle of "putting people first and governing for the people", the Chinese Government attaches great importance to environment and health, and recognizes environmental protection as an important project supported by common people, closely linked to the improvement of people's livelihood and demonstrating good governance. As such it has resolutely declared war on pollution, focusing on treatment of air, water and soil pollutions with a view to continuously improving the ecological environment quality and effectively protect the health rights and interests of the general public.

I. Controlling pollution and reducing emission to improve ecological environment.

1. Forging ahead to reduce the emission of major pollutants

Energy conservation and emission reduction are obligatory targets when planning for the economic and social development. They are achieved by intensifying performance evaluation against set targets and responsibilities and by making an extraordinary effort on emission reduction through improving pollution treatment techniques, reducing the number of heavily polluted companies and strengthening management measures. The treatment rate of urban wastewater increased to 87.9% in 2013 from 52% in 2005 and the percentage of desulfurization units in coal-fired power plants increased to over 90% from the previous 14%. Denitrification units and the new-type denitrification in the drying process of cement have been developed from scratch and the denitrification percentage of both methods reach 50%. During the 11th Five-Year Plan period, the emissions of sulfur dioxide and chemical oxygen demand decreased by 14.29% and 12.45% respectively, both exceeding the obligatory target of a 10% decrease. In 2013, the total emissions of chemical oxygen demand, ammonia nitrogen, sulfur dioxide, and nitrogen oxide all across China decreased by 7.8%, 7.1%, 9.9% and 2.0% compared with that of 2010.

2. Formulating and implementing Action Plan for Air Pollution Prevention and Control

The Chinese Government released and began to implement the *Action Plan for Air Pollution Prevention and Control* (hereinafter referred to as "the Action Plan") in September 2013 to tackle smog pollution. It proposes concrete measures for air pollution prevention and control on ten aspects including strengthening pollution treatment, optimizing the industrial structure, adjusting the energy structure, setting stricter standards on environment access, establishing a mechanism of regional collaboration, and responding to days of heavy pollution with emphasis on combating PM2.5. Since the implementation of the Action Plan, the Ministry of Environmental Protection has joined hands with five departments including the National Development and Reform Commission to release *Rules for the Implementation of the Action Plan for Air Pollution Prevention and Control in Beijing, Tianjin, Hebei and Surrounding Areas;* formulated and distributed the division scheme of the work involving key departments; and signed *Liability Agreements on Air Pollution Prevention and Control Targets* with 31 provinces (autonomous regions and municipalities). We have come up with 22 supporting measures and adopted 11 polices including environmental protection power tariff, subsidies for new energy cars, a special fund for air, gasoline and diesel price rise along with fuel quality enhancement and evaluation methods. In 2013, 5 billion yuan was allocated to support the air pollution abatement in Beijing,

Tianjin, Hebei and surrounding areas and in 2014, 10 billion yuan was allocated in continued support. We have reinforced compliance supervision and law enforcement in air pollution prevention and control. Special enforcement inspections have been carried out in key areas. We have made an extraordinary effort in emergency response to heavily polluted days and supervision over targeted enforcement missions in special periods. We have improved the systems of monitoring, early warning and emergency response. The *Implementation Plan for the Third Phase of Monitoring in Terms of the Revised Ambient Air Quality Standards* was released and distributed. Flight inspection has been adopted to ensure the quality of environmental monitoring data. By January 2014, 884 monitoring sites in 161 cities at prefecture level or above were carrying out environmental monitoring based on the revised ambient air quality standards. In the first half of 2014, the average concentration of PM2.5 in 74 key cities dropped by 7.9% compared with that of the previous year. Fewer areas were affected by heavy pollution weather for a shorter period with lower severity.

3. Optimizing economic development through environmental protection

We have set stricter standards of environmental impact assessment for construction projects. Since 2008, we have rejected 332 projects featuring "high energy consumption, heavy pollution and resource-dependent", low-level redundant development and excess production capacity with a total investment of 1.1 trillion yuan. We have formulated and implemented environmental economic policies and preliminarily established a framework system of environment policies comprised of green credit, insurance, trade, price, securities, and taxation. We have optimized the system of environment standards. There are over 1,500 national environmental protection standards in force in China. By applying the special emission limits of air pollutants to industries and projects including thermal power generation, steel and iron, petrochemicals, cement, nonferrous metals, chemical engineering and coal-fired boilers in key control areas, we have further promoted the coordination and integration between economic development and environmental protection.

The monitoring of PM2.5 in the air.

4. Deepening pollution prevention and control in key watersheds

We have released and implemented the *Plan on Prevention and Control of Water Pollution in Key River Basins (2011-2015)*. An evaluation system on the quality of water sections at provincial borders in key areas has been established and the indicators of this system have been continuously optimized. The percentage of water better than grade III water quality has increased to 66.7% in 2013 from 41% in 2005 in seven major rivers while the percentage of water with quality worse than grade V has dropped to 10.8% from 27%. According to the principle of "prioritizing protection and relying on natural recovery", we have formulated and implemented the *General Plan on the Ecological Environment Protection of Lakes with Better Water Quality (2013-2020)*. We are optimizing the water environment management system and instituting a long-term mechanism for the ecological environment protection of lakes with better water quality accordingly. Up to now, China's central finance has allocated earmarked funds totaling 9.5 billion yuan to support the ecological environment protection of 62 lakes in 92 provinces, autonomous regions and municipalities.

5. Strengthening ecological protection and rural environment protection

The State Council has set up China's National Committee of Biodiversity Conservation, ratified the *National Biodiversity Conservation Strategy and Action Plan (2011-2030)*, and formulated *China's Actions for UN Decade on Biodiversity (2011-2020)*. The General Office of the State Council has released and distributed documents including *Opinions on Strengthening the Rural Environment Protection, Notice on Better Management of Nature Reserves, Regulations on the Adjustment and Management of National Nature Reserves,* and *Arrangement for Soil Environment Protection and Comprehensive Treatment Work in Near Future.* A remote sensing survey and evaluation for changes of ecological environment all across China in the past ten years (2000-2010) was conducted to fully grasp the situation and changes of China's ecological system. We also actively promoted the designation of national ecological protection red line. From 2008 to 2013, 19.5 billion yuan was transferred from central government budget to support the comprehensive treatment of rural environment in 46,000 villages with pollution treatment incentivized with bonus instead of subsidies. The project has benefited over 87 million rural population.

6. Comprehensively advancing the development of Ecological Civilization Construction Demonstration Area

With the approval of the CPC Central Committee, the "Ecological Construction Demonstration Area" program sponsored by the Ministry of Environmental Protection was renamed as "Ecological Civilization Construction Demonstration Area". The Ministry has released a series of normative documents including *Opinions on Vigorously Promoting the Ecological Civilization Construction Demonstration Area* and *Indicators for the Pilot Ecological Civilization Construction Demonstration Area.* Up to now, 16 provinces (autonomous regions) including Zhejiang, Jiangsu, Fujian, Liaoning and Ningxia have been undertaking Ecological Province (Autonomous Region) construction. More than 1,000 cities (counties) have been carrying out ecological city (county) construction. The construction of 92 National Ecological Civilization Construction Demonstration Areas and 3,851 National Ecological Towns have already been completed.

II. Sparing no efforts to resolve outstanding environmental problems that harm people's health.

1. Breakthroughs in work on environment and health

The ultimate goal of protecting environment is to protect people's health. The *Environmental Protection Law* newly revised in April 2014 further highlights the goal of protecting people's health and has new contents about environment and health. The law stipulates that "the State shall establish and improve environment and health monitoring, investigation and risk assessment systems; encourage and organize researches on environmental quality impacts on public health, and adopt measures to prevent and control diseases related to environmental pollution", laying down a solid foundation of law for better results of the environment and health undertaking. China has already established a leading group on environment and health work at the national level, released and implemented a series of plans and programs including the *Action Plan on Environment and Health (2007-2015)*, the *12th Five-Year Plan for Work in Environment and Health*, and *Guiding Opinions on Strengthening the Work on Environment and Health during the 12th Five-Year Plan Period.* Orderly progress is made in the special survey on environment and health in key areas of China.

The Fourth National Forum on Environment and Health was held in Guangzhou.

2. Prioritizing resolution of outstanding environmental problems that bear on people's livelihood

We emphasize the prevention and control of air, water and soil pollution, and further endeavor to prevent and control air pollution with PM2.5 as its focus by exploring the sources of PM2.5 in key areas, ensuring the supplies of quality oil products through coordination with relevant departments, and improving policies and standards on the comprehensive improvement of coal-fired boilers. A strict evaluation was conducted to ensure that 6 million yellow-label vehicles and old scrapped automobiles be phased out in 2014. We also intensify our efforts in the drinking water source protection and the prevention and control of underground water pollution. We have organized an evaluation on the environmental conditions of 844 centralized drinking water sources in 328 cities at the prefecture level or above. *Work Plan on Groundwater Pollution Prevention and Control in North China Plain* has been released and distributed. *National Plan on Groundwater Pollution Control* is in implementation. We vigorously carry out treatment of soil contamination by releasing *Guide for the Compilation of Soil Environment Protection and Comprehensive Treatment Plan* and devising liability agreements and assessment methods. We promulgated *Notice on Strengthening the Pollution Prevention and Control during the Shutdown and Relocation of Industrial Companies and the Re-Use of Their Original Sites*, which listed specific requirements with regard to the formulation and implementation of environmental hazard-free relocation plans by the enterprises to be shut down or relocated, and their fulfillment of responsibilities in environmental survey, risk assessment and treatment and restoration of their original sites. In addition, we deepen the prevention and control of pollutions of chemicals, Persistent Organic Pollutants (POPs) and heavy metals. We are vigorously implementing the *12th Five-Year Plan for Prevention and Control of Risk of Chemicals* and the *12th Five-year Plan on Prevention and Control of POPs Pollution in Major Sectors*. The environmental management and registration of hazardous chemicals are in progress and our efforts to promote the ratification of *Minamata Convention on Mercury* are underway. The central government has added a special budget line on the prevention and control of heavy metal pollution and 11.6 billion yuan had been allocated by the end of 2013. The 6.7 million tons of chromium slag that have been deposited for dozens of years have been disposed properly.

3. Conducting environmental law enforcement and regulation with an iron fist

We maintain high-handed posture on the enforcement of laws and bear zero tolerance to environmental violations by direct and on-spot inspections, handling and exposure without prior notice or debriefing. Since 2013, 20.85 million person-times have been involved in the inspection of 8.6 million enterprises among which 180,000 cases of environmental violations have been found; 25,000 enterprises that illegally discharged wastewater have been prohibited and shut down; 16,000 enterprises were required to suspend production and reform; and the handling of 35,000 cases has been directly supervised by environmental protection authorities at different levels. We have innovated methods of supervision by adopting satellite remote sensing and unmanned aerial vehicle in the examination of sources of air pollution and severely punished illegal emissions. In 2013, over 700 cases suspected of environmental crimes were transferred to public security organs by environmental protection authorities at various levels, exceeding the total number in the previous ten years. About 110 cases were convicted as environmental crimes and over 180 criminals were arrested.

4. Comprehensively advancing the disclosure of environmental information

We disclose environmental information about environmental quality surveillance, environmental impact assessment on construction projects, cases of environmental violations and their handling in a timely fashion. We also take the initiative to disclose information about environmental situation, important policies and measures, unexpected environmental incidents and relevant emergency responses. We released documents including *Notice on Arrangement of Key Tasks on Current Disclosure of Environmental Protection Information, Guidelines on Disclosure of Government Information on Environmental Impact Assessment on Construction Projects (for trial implementation), Notice on Promoting Information Disclosure on the Environmental Supervision of Pollution Sources,* and *Information Disclosure Content of the Environmental Supervision on Pollution Sources (1st batch).* We unveiled methods of the supervisory monitoring and self-monitoring of pollution sources for key enterprises under surveillance and ways of information disclosure.

III. Striving to build the "Four Beams and Eight Pillars" ① for ecological civilization construction and environmental protection.

To build the "Four Beams and Eight Pillars" for ecological civilization construction and environmental protection is a summary of environmental protection agencies' effort to implement the important remarks delivered by CPC General Secretary Xi Jinping. It is an important content in the development of national ecological governance system and the modernization of governance capabilities, a refinement of thoughts based on the practical explorations in ecological environmental protection, an innovative initiative to the approach of advancing as a whole and making breakthroughs in key areas, and a strong guarantee to resolve outstanding environmental problems that harm people's health in the war on pollution.

1. Further enriching the theoretical system for environmental protection on the basis of actively exploring new ways of environmental protection

We will properly handle the relationship between economic development and environmental protection, firmly establish the concept that protecting the ecological environment equals maintaining productivity and improving the ecological

① "Four Beams and Eight Pillars" is a metaphor used to describe the whole framework of ecological civilization construction and environmental protection in a macroscopic, systematic and generalized fashion. It represents the concrete contents of the decisions and deployment made by the CPC Central Committee and the State Council, and it is also a generalization on the previous practices and explorations done by departments of environmental protection in various regions. Generally speaking, it covers efforts in four areas. (1) We are further enriching the theories of environmental protection by actively exploring new ways for environmental protection as an effective path towards ecological civilization. (2) We are formulating a system of laws and regulations that can effectively protect the ecological environment with the implementation of the newly revised *Environmental Protection Law* as the flagship. (3) We are establishing an environmental protection system that strictly monitors the discharge of all pollutants with the deepening reform of ecological environment protection system as the catalyst. (4) We are building a working system towards improving the environmental quality by winning the war against air, water and soil pollution determinedly.

environment equals boosting productivity, and promote green development, circular development and low-carbon development more conscientiously. We will accelerate the transformation of environment management strategies and coordinate the relationship of pollution management, aggregate emission reduction, environmental risk prevention and environmental quality improvement so as to enhance ecological environmental quality.

2. Formulating a system of laws and regulations that centers on the newly revised *Environmental Protection Law* and effectively protect the ecological environment

The newly revised *Environmental Protection Law* contains numerous breakthroughs in terms of basic concepts, public participation and legal responsibilities. In order to ensure the full implementation of the law, we will publicize it as widely as possible. Meanwhile, we will formulate supporting documents such as law enforcement interpretations and guiding opinions, and coordinate work related to administrative detention, administrative accountability and the handling of environmental crimes so as to ensure robust implementation of the law. We will step up to advance the making or revision of specialized laws and regulations on prevention and control of air and water pollution, soil environment protection, access to and benefit sharing of biological genetic resources and nuclear security.

3. Establishing an environmental protection system that strictly monitors the discharge of all pollutants by way of deepening reform of ecological environment protection system

We will improve the consistency and effectiveness of ecological environment supervision in the whole process of reproduction by formulating strict monitoring regulations and a unified management mode of pollution prevention and control on all pollutants from those discharged to the air or mountain tops to those discharged to the sea or underground. With institutional innovation, we will put in place an environmental protection management system with unified supervision over the discharge of all pollutants, through which all pollutants, sources and media of pollution are under unified surveillance and control. We will also explore to establish a pattern of risk prevention targeting chemicals in the whole life cycles. We will carry out environmental surveillance and administrative law enforcement independently and strengthen the supervision over the implementation of environment laws, regulations and policies by relevant departments and local governments.

4. Building a working system for improving the environment by winning the war against air, water and soil pollution determinedly

We will continue to take the prevention and control of air pollution as top priority and fully implement the Action Plan. We will further strengthen the prevention and control of water pollution and spare no effort to prevent and control soil pollution by formulating and implementing the *Action Plan for Water Pollution Prevention and Control* and *Action Plan for Soil Pollution Prevention and Control.* With our focus on coal-fired power plants, steel and iron works, cement factories, paper-making mills, urban wastewater treatment plants, livestock farms and vehicles, we will fully implement emission reduction plans, conduct strict evaluation on the outcomes, intensify supervision over enforcement of environmental laws, put more efforts into information disclosure and protect the public's rights to information, participation and supervision.

A good ecological environment, being the fairest public good, has benefits for the greatest number of people. With the attitude and sense of responsibility for the public and future generations, we will actively formulate and implement the "Four Beams and Eight Pillars" and resolutely declare war on pollution. We will intensify the prevention and control of air, water and soil pollution with strict regulations and an iron fist and safeguard public health with concrete achievements in improving ecological environment.

(original translation by Jiang Yu)

中国宗教人权事业取得新进展

国家宗教事务局局长　王作安

2004年，“国家尊重和保障人权”写入《中华人民共和国宪法》，这既是对新中国建立以来人权事业取得重要进步的充分肯定，也为进一步促进和完善中国人权事业提供了宪法保障。宗教信仰自由是一项基本人权，这是国际社会的普遍共识，也是中国政府对待宗教的基本态度。“人权入宪”后，中国政府从尊重人权、维护宪法权威的高度保障公民的宗教信仰自由权利，树立“保护、管理、引导、服务”的宗教工作理念，重视宗教立法，维护宗教界合法权益，促进宗教关系和谐，发挥宗教界人士和信教群众在促进经济社会发展中的积极作用，取得了显著成效，成为中国人权事业发展的一个重要体现。

一、保障公民宗教信仰自由权利

这十年来，中国的宗教活动场所数量由10万余处增加到14万处，宗教教职人员由约30万人增加到36万人，宗教团体由3000多个增加到5500多个，宗教院校由74所增加到81所。

支持和组织相关专家学者和宗教界人士，整理出版了《中华大藏经》、《中华道藏》、《老子集成》等大型宗教古籍文献。出版多种汉文版《古兰经》，重新翻译出版维吾尔文版《古兰经》。《圣经》印刷数量超过1亿册，成为世界上印刷《圣经》最多的国家之一。宗教界根据各自传统举办宗教节日活动，国家宗教事务局在门户网站刊发贺信，各地党政领导深入宗教活动场所致以节日祝贺，政府相关部门为大型宗教节日活动提供交通、安保方面的便利。超过1.7万名宗教界人士担任各级人大、政协的代表、委员，参与国家事务和社会事务的讨论和协商，反映宗教界的诉求，维护宗教界合法权益。

中国天主教举行主教祝圣典礼。

二、推进国内宗教立法进程

2004年，国务院颁布《宗教事务条例》(以下简称“条例”)，这是新中国第一部宗教方面的综合性行政法规。《条例》赋予了宗教团体、宗教活动场所和信教公民在设立宗教活动场所、举行宗教活动、开办宗教院校、出版发行宗教书刊、接受宗教捐献、管理宗教财产、兴办公益慈善事业和开展对外交流活动等方面的权利，同时规范了政府相关行政管理部门的行政行为，确保严格依照法定权限和程序行使权力。

自《条例》实施以来，国家宗教事务局制定实施了配套的 11 个部门规章，各省、自治区、直辖市颁布了 60 多个地方性法规和政府规章，各全国性宗教团体制定和完善了 32 项规章制度，初步形成了较为完善的法规、规章和制度体系，为公民宗教信仰自由权利提供了法律保障。

为了进一步发挥宗教团体的积极作用，推进宗教事务行政审批制度改革，国家宗教事务局取消和调整了 16 项行政审批项目，加快了简政放权步伐。在宗教教职人员和信教公民中开展法制宣传，提高他们的法律意识和公民意识，引导他们自觉在法律范围内开展活动，运用法律手段维护自身合法权益。对打着旗号进行的违法犯罪活动，严格依法处理。

三、为宗教界提供公共服务

在法律许可范围内，中国政府尽可能帮助各宗教解决实际困难。

近十年来，中央财政累计投入 8 亿多元，改善全国性宗教团体办公会所条件、重建或修缮 6 所宗教院校。2008 年，国务院下发《关于促进节约集约用地的通知》，明确宗教用地作为特殊用地可以继续通过划拨方式取得。2011 年，住房和城乡建设部制定《城市用地分类与规划建设用地标准》，明确宗教设施用地是城市公共服务设施用地的重要类型。中央财政投入寺观教堂维修款累计已超过 2 亿元，并从 2011 年起增加至每年 3000 万元。

各地政府帮助宗教活动场所通电、通水、通路，进行危旧房维修改造，整治周边环境。2010 年，青海省玉树地震发生后，国务院把受到损毁的藏传佛教寺庙和僧舍纳入灾后恢复重建总体规划，总计投入近 10 亿元。2013 年，国务院又将 29 所宗教活动场所纳入四川省芦山地震灾后重建总体规划。2009 年伊斯兰教朝觐期间，甲型 H1N1 流感疫情严峻，为朝觐穆斯林免费接种疫苗，派遣疫情防控专家赴沙特，并配备充足防控药品和器材，保障了中国赴麦加朝觐穆斯林的人身安全。2010 年和 2011 年，国家宗教事务局、人力资源和社会保障部、财政部、民政部、卫生部先后制定《关于妥善解决宗教教职人员社会保障问题的意见》和《关于进一步解决宗教教职人员社会保障问题的通知》，推动将宗教教职人员纳入社保。截至2013年年底，宗教教职人员在自愿基础上医疗保险参保率达到96.5%，养老保险参保率达到89.6%，符合条件的全部纳入低保，基本实现了社保体系全覆盖。

新落成的南京金陵协和神学院。

四、维护宗教界的合法权益

通过不懈努力，一批寺庙、宫观、清真寺、教堂交还宗教界作为宗教活动场所开放。各地政府依法处理数十起伤害宗教感情、损害宗教界合法权益的事件。各级政府宗教事务部门帮助宗教界协调解决与社会有关方面的利益纠纷，参与处理城市建设中涉及拆迁宗教团体、宗教活动场所房产的问题，防止宗教界利益受损。2006年，国务院修订出台《风景名胜区条例》，要求风景名胜区内宗教活动场所的管理依照国家有关宗教活动场所管理的规定执行。2008年，国家发展改革委发文规定，与宗教活动场所有关的游览参观点，要对宗教教职人员和参加宗教活动的信教群众给予门票优惠。2011年，国家宗教事务局与中国人民银行联合发文，允许宗教活动场所和宗教院校按照银行结算账户管理规定，向银行业金融机构申请开立单位银行结算账户。2012

年，国家宗教事务局颁布《宗教院校教师资格认定和职称评审聘任办法（试行）》、《宗教院校学位授予办法（试行）》，解决了宗教院校教师资格、职称和学生学位问题。2012 年，国家宗教事务局联合中央统战部、国家发展改革委、公安部、住房和城乡建设部、文化部、工商总局、旅游局、证监会、文物局等制定《关于处理涉及佛教寺庙、道教宫观管理有关问题的意见》，切实纠正佛教寺庙、道教宫观“被承包”、“被经营”与“被上市”等现象，维护宗教界合法权益。2013 年，国家发展改革委发文规定，宗教活动场所用电执行居民生活用电价格，减轻了宗教活动场所的经济负担。

五、支持宗教界从事公益慈善活动

中国政府支持宗教界开展灾害救助、扶助残疾人、养老、托幼、扶贫助困、捐资助学、医疗卫生服务、环境保护、社会公共设施建设等领域的非营利活动，为促进社会公平正义发挥积极作用。2010 年，中共中央、国务院、中央军委表彰玉树地震抗震救灾先进集体和个人，将表现突出的宗教活动场所和宗教界人士纳入表彰范围，这是新中国成立以来的第一次。2012 年，国家宗教事务局会同中央统战部、国家发展改革委、财政部、民政部和税务总局制定《关于鼓励和规范宗教界从事公益慈善活动的意见》，为宗教界从事公益慈善活动提供了良好的制度环境和政策空间。2014 年，国家宗教事务局联合民政部下发《关于规范宗教界收留孤儿、弃婴活动的通知》，切实保障宗教界开展孤儿弃婴救助活动。从 2012 年开始，中国宗教界每年开展以“慈爱人间・五教同行”为主题的“宗教慈善周”活动，仅捐款数额就达 5.6 亿元，提升了宗教公益慈善的形象。中国政府支持宗教界参与生态文明建设，中国道教界提出“生态道观”项目，制定《中国道教界保护环境的八年规划（2010 ～ 2017）纲要意见》，此举得到联合国开发署的关注，并得到有关国际环境组织的支持。

中国道教界为青海玉树地震灾区捐款。

六、保护少数民族宗教信仰自由

中国政府特别重视保护少数民族的宗教信仰。西藏现有寺庙1700多处，住寺僧尼4.6万余人，活佛358名。藏传佛教活佛转世传承方式得到充分尊重，寺庙学经、辩经、受戒、灌顶、修行等传统宗教活动和寺庙学经考核晋升学位活动正常进行，每逢重大宗教节日都循例举行各种宗教活动。信教群众家中普遍设有经堂或佛龛，转经、朝佛、请寺庙僧尼做法事等活动得到尊重，每年到拉萨朝佛进香的藏族群众达百万人次以上。中央政府拨巨资修缮寺庙，保护寺庙的壁画、雕刻、塑像、唐卡、经卷、法器、佛龛等宗教文化载体，支持整理出版藏传佛教文献典籍。2000年以来，中央政府先后投入20.4亿元在西藏实施一系列文物保护工程。各寺庙的传统印经院得到继承和发展，西藏现有木如寺印经院、布达拉宫印经院等大型传统印经院近60家，年印经卷6.3万种，民间经书销售摊点20家。中国政府尊重穆斯林群众的宗教信仰和风俗习惯，为穆斯林赴麦加朝觐活动提供各种便利条件，从2007年起，每年参加朝觐人数均在1万人以上。在新疆，现有清真寺2.4万多座，教职人员2.9万多人，穆斯林在饮食、衣饰、年节、婚姻、丧葬等方面的风俗习惯得到充分尊重。近年来，新疆连续发生严重暴力恐怖事件，中国政府在依法严厉打击暴力恐怖活动的同时，特别注意防止把暴力恐怖活动与某一民族和某个宗教联系在一起，更加注意尊重和保护穆斯林群众的宗教信仰，满足穆斯林群众的正常宗教需求。中国政府支持伊斯兰教界人士阐释伊斯兰教爱国、和平、团结、中道、仁慈等主张，揭露宗教极端思想反人类、反社会和反宗教的实质，帮助穆斯林树立正信正行，自觉反对和抵制一切暴力恐怖活动。

藏传佛教信众点酥油灯。

中国穆斯林欢度开斋节。

七、鼓励宗教界开展对外友好交往

中国政府支持各宗教坚持独立自主自办原则，在平等友好、相互尊重基础上同各国宗教界开展交流和合作。十年来，中国宗教对外交流日趋活跃，已经与超过 80 个国家的宗教组织建立了友好关系，积极参与国际性宗教组织活动，开展不同宗教信仰对话。中国基督教界于 2006 年和 2011 年先后两次赴美国、2007 年赴德国举办“中国教会圣经事工展”。中国佛教界于 2006 年、2009 年和 2012 年举办了三届世界佛教论坛。中国道教界于 2007 年、2011 年举办了两届国际道教论坛。中国伊斯兰教界于 2010 年、2012 年、2014 年分别赴印度尼西亚、土耳其、马来西亚举办伊斯兰文化展演活动。中美基督教会于 2011 年和 2013 年分别在华盛顿、上海举办“中美基督教领袖论坛”。2011 年，中国各全国性宗教团体积极响应联合国第 65 届大会通过的关于设立“世界不同信仰间和谐周”的决议，联合发表《倡导宗教和谐共同宣言》，倡导宗教和谐理念，把实现宗教和谐作为共同追求的价值目标。中国政府还支持宗教界积极参与北京奥运会、上海世博会、广州亚运会、深圳大运会和南京青奥会等重大活动的志愿服务工作，为各国宗教信徒提供良好的宗教服务。

2012 年，中国佛教界在香港举办第三届世界佛教论坛。

2011 年，中国各全国性宗教团体召开倡导宗教和谐座谈会。

宗教信仰自由作为一项重要的人权，应当得到尊重和保护，这是国际社会的共识。同时又应看到，各国国情不同，文化传统迥异，必然出现多元的实践方式和实现路径，由此形成的经验不仅独特，而且非常宝贵，应当得到重视和珍惜。中国政府将遵循“国家尊重和保障人权”的《宪法》规定，正确应对挑战，努力解决问题，继续推进符合本国国情、教情的宗教人权保障事业，并愿意通过对话方式，同其他国家进行对话，交流互鉴，寻求共识，共同致力于推进包括宗教信仰自由在内的人权事业的进步和发展。

New Progress in Religious Human Rights Protection in China

Wang Zuo'an, Director, State Administration for Religious Affairs

In 2004, "[t]he State respects and protects human rights" was articulated in the *Constitution of the People's Republic of China*. This addition fully affirms the significant progress that has been made in human rights protection since the founding of New China. It also provides a constitutional guarantee that more will be done to promote and improve human rights in China. That freedom of religious belief is a fundamental human right is a belief shared in the international community and the Chinese Government's basic attitude towards religion. With "human rights" written in the Constitution, the Chinese Government has, proceeding from respecting human rights and upholding the authority of the Constitution, protected citizens' right to freedom of religious belief. It has followed the principles "protection, administration, guidance and service" in the work concerning religious affairs, emphasized legislation regarding religion, taken action to protect the legitimate rights and interests of the religious community, promoted harmony between different religions and encouraged both renowned religious figures and ordinary believers to play a positive role in socio-economic development. These efforts have been remarkably successful and have become an important manifestation of progress in human rights protection in China.

I. Protecting the right to freedom of religious belief.

In the past decade, venues for religious activities increased from just over 100,000 to 140,000, religious workers increased from about 300,000 to 360,000, religious groups increased from over 3,000 to over 5,500 and religious schools increased from 74 to 81.

Ordination of Bishop, Chinese Catholic Church.

By organizing and supporting experts, scholars and people in religious circle, large classic religious texts such as the *Chinese Buddhist Canon,* the *Chinese Daoist Canon* and the *Complete Laozi* have been compiled and published. Various Chinese translations of the *Koran* as well as a re-translation of the *Koran* into the Uighur language have been published. More than 100 million copies of the Bible have been printed, placing China among countries that print the most copies of the Bible in the world. When traditional religious festivals are held by practitioners, the State Administration for Religious Affairs issue congratulatory letters and publish them on main Internet portals, local CPC and government leaders attend celebrations, and relevant government departments provide transportation and security facility for large-scale events. More than 17,000 religious figures are also deputies and committee members at various levels of People's Congresses and Chinese People's Political Consultative Congresses, engaging in discussion and consultation on national and social affairs and representing the aspirations and legitimate rights and interests of the religious circle.

II. Advancing legislative process.

In 2004, the State Council promulgated the *Regulations on Religious Affairs.* New China's first comprehensive administrative regulations pertaining to religion. The Regulations endows religious groups, venues for religious activities and religious citizens with the right to establish venues for religious activities, carry out religious activities, set up religious schools, publish religious books, accept religious donations, manage religious property, develop charities and conduct external exchanges. The Regulations also contain provisions on administrative actions by relevant government departments so as to ensure that power is exercised in strict accordance with their statutory mandates and legal procedures.

Since the implementation of the Regulations, the State Administration for Religious Affairs has developed and implemented a package of eleven departmental decrees, various provinces, autonomous regions and municipalities have enacted more than 60 local laws and government regulations, and various national religious organizations developed and improved 32 sets of rules and regulations. These formed a relatively complete system of laws, regulations, rules and institutions to provide legal guarantee for citizens' right to freedom of religious belief.

In order to enhance the positive role of religious organizations and improve the system of examination and approval with regard to religious affairs, the State Administration for Religious Affairs has revoked or adjusted 16 administrative approval items and sped up efforts to reduce bureaucracy and devolve power. The Administration promotes legal education among religious workers and believers to improve their legal and civil awareness and guide them to consciously carry out activities within the boundaries of law and use legal means to protect their legitimate rights and interests. Illegal and criminal activities under the guise of religion are dealt with strictly according to law.

III. Providing public services for the religious circle.

To the extent permitted by law, the Chinese Government assists to the best of its ability in resolving practical difficulties of various churches.

Over the past decade, the Central Government has invested over 800 million yuan in total to improve working conditions at national religious headquarters and reconstruct and repair six religious schools. In 2008, the State Council issued the *Notice on the Promotion of Conservation and Intensive Land Use,* which specified that land for religious use is special and may still be appropriated. In 2011, the Ministry of Housing and Urban-Rural Development set *Standards for Urban Land Classification and Land-Use Planning and Construction,* explicitly stating that land used for religious facilities is an important category of land for urban public service facilities. The Central Government has cumulatively invested over 200 million yuan to maintain and repair temples, mosques and churches and since 2011 has increased annual grant to 30 million.

Local governments have helped venues for religious activities with power, running water and access, reconstructed dilapidated buildings and improved the surrounding environment. In 2010, after the Yushu earthquake in Qinghai Province, the State Council put rebuilding of the destroyed Tibetan Buddhist temples and monasteries in the master plan for post-disaster recovery and reconstruction, and allocated a total investment of 1 billion yuan. Again, in 2013, after the Lushan earthquake in Sichuan Province, the State Council included 29 venues for religious activities in the master plan for reconstruction. In 2009, there was an influenza A (H1N1) outbreak before Haj. Free vaccinations were provided to pilgrims and experts in epidemic prevention and medicines and equipments were dispatched to Saudi Arabia to protect the safety of Chinese Muslim pilgrims. In 2010 and 2011, the State Administration for Religious Affairs, Ministry of Human Resources and Social Security, Ministry of Finance, Ministry of Civil Affairs and Ministry of Health jointly issued *Opinions on Properly Resolving Social Security Issues of Religious Personnel* and *Notice on Further Resolving Social Security Problems of Religious Personnel.* As a result, religious workers are also covered by the social security system. By the end of 2013, the social security system had basically covered all members of the clergy, with 96.5% of religious workers voluntarily participating in medical insurance and 89.6% in basic endowment insurance, and all those eligible receiving basic living allowances.

The newly completed Nanjing Union Theological Seminary.

IV. Protecting the legitimate rights and interests of people in religious circle.

Through unremitting effort, a number of Buddhist and Daoist temples, mosques and churches have been returned to the religious community and open for religious activity. Dozens of incidents offending religious people and harming the legitimate interests of the religious community were settled according to law. The religious affairs departments at all levels of government have helped people in religious circle to resolve conflicts of interests with other individuals or social entities. They have also participated in the handling of problems involving relocating religious organizations and their real estate holdings in urban development process so as to protect the interests of religious organizations from being undermined. In 2006, the State Council promulgated revised *Regulations for the Administration of Scenic Areas,* providing that venues for religious activities in scenic areas should be administered in accordance with the relevant regulations for the administration of religious venues. In 2008, the National Development and Reform Commission decided that tourist sites with religious venues should provide discounted tickets for members of the clergy and believers attending religious activities there. In 2011, the State Administration for Religious Affairs and the People's Bank of China jointly issued a document allowing venues for religious activities and religious schools to open entity settlement account with banking financial institutions in accordance with regulations governing settlement accounts. In 2012, the State Administration for Religious Affairs promulgated *Methods of Qualifications of Teachers at Religious Schools, and Their Assessment and Appointment to Professional Positions (for trial implementation)* and *Method for Granting Degrees in Religions Schools (for trial implementation),* which addressed issues of teacher qualifications, their professional titles, and degrees for religious schools. In 2012, the State Administration for Religious Affairs joined Central United Front Work Department of CPC Central Committee, National Development and Reform Commission, Ministry of Public Security, Ministry of Housing and Urban-Rural Development, Ministry of Culture, State Administration for Industry and Commerce, National Tourism Administration, China Securities Regulatory Commission and State Administration of Cultural Heritage to develop and issue *Opinions on the Handling of Issues Related to the Management of Buddhist and Daoist Temples.* Problems of Buddhist and Daoist temples "being put out to contract, operated for profit or listed" were rectified to protect the legitimate interests of the religious community. By a decree of the National Development and Reform Commission in 2013, venues for religious activities pay for electricity at the same tariff as residents and as a result the financial burden on such venues have been reduced.

V. Supporting charitable activities of the religious community.

The Chinese Government supports non-profit activities by people in the religious circle, such as providing disaster relief, assisting the disabled, the aging and the young, helping those in poverty and hardship, donating to education, providing healthcare services, protecting environment, and constructing public facilities. These all have a positive role in promoting social equity and justice. In 2010, the CPC Central Committee, the State Council and the Central Military Commission, in commending specific collectives and individuals for their contributions towards Yushu earthquake relief efforts, included institutions and individuals from the religious community in the commendation for the first time since the founding of New China. In 2012, the State Administration for Religious Affairs, in conjunction with the Central United Front Work Department, National Development and Reform Commission, Ministry of Finance, Ministry of Civil Affairs and State Administration of Taxation, published *Opinions on Encouraging and Regulating Involvement of the Religions Community in Charitable Activities,* providing a sound institutional environment and policy space for such involvement. In 2014, the State Administration for Religious Affairs and Ministry of Civil Affairs jointly issued *Notice on Regulating Adoption of Orphans and Abandoned Children by the Religious Community* to effectively protect such conduct. Since 2012, the religious community has celebrated an annual "religious charity week" with the theme of "Five faiths working together in kindness to humanity," which raised 560 million yuan in cash contributions alone and lifted the image of religious charity. With the Chinese Government supporting participation by the religious community in the construction of an ecological civilization, the Chinese Daoists proposed an "ecological Daoist temples" project and formulated *Opinions on Outline of Eight-Year Environmental Protection Plan (2010-2017) of Chinese Daoism.* The move has gained the attention of the United Nations Development Programme as well as support from relevant international environmental organizations.

Chinese Daoists donate to Yushu earthquake relief.

Ⅵ. Protecting freedom of religious belief for ethnic minorities.

The Chinese Government attaches special importance to protecting the religious practices of ethnic minorities. Today, Tibet has over 1,700 temples with over 460,000 resident monks and nuns and 358 living Buddhas. Tibetan Buddhism's traditional process of selecting reincarnated living Buddhas is fully honored. Traditional religious activities and temple-based learning of and progress in Buddhist classics have been carried out, including scriptural study and debate, ordination, initiation and Buddhist practices. During major religious festivals, a variety of activities are held according to tradition. Faith-based practices are respected, including maintaining prayer halls and Buddhist shrines at home, spinning prayer wheels, undertaking pilgrimages, or engaging monks and nuns to offer services. Each year, over a million Tibetans undertake the pilgrimage to Lhasa. The Central Government has allocated huge sums of money to the repair and maintenance of temples, the preservation of cultural artifacts such as murals, sculptures, statues, thangkas, rolls of scripture, ritual implements and shrines and the compilation and publication of Tibetan Buddhist classics. Since 2000, the Central Government has invested 2.04 billion yuan to implement a series of projects to protect cultural relics in Tibet. The traditional printing houses of various temples have been maintained and developed. There are nearly 60 traditional Tibetan printing houses such as the Meru Monastery Print House and the Potala Palace Print House, which put out an annual inventory of 63,000 scriptural compilations for distribution through some 20 popular outlets. The Chinese Government respects the faith and practices of the Muslim community and provides extensive facility for those making the pilgrimage to Mecca. Beginning in 2007, an average of over 10,000 people make the pilgrimage each year. In Xinjiang, there are over 24,000 mosques serviced by over 29,000 religious workers. Muslim customs in food, clothing, festivals, marriages and funerals are fully respected. In recent years, a series of violent terrorist incidents have occurred in succession in Xinjiang. While the Chinese Government takes steps to crack down on terrorism according to law, it also pays special attention to avoid linking violent terrorist incidents with any specific ethnic minority or religion. Special attention has been paid to respecting and protecting the religious belief of Muslims and to meeting their normal religious needs. The Chinese Government supports Islamic figures in interpreting the Islamic view of patriotism, peace, unity, moderation and kindness, and revealing the nature of extremist ideology as anti-humanity, anti-society, and anti-religion. It helps Muslims adopt right beliefs and right behaviors so that they will consciously oppose and resist violence or terrorist activities.

Tibetan Buddhists light butter lamps.

Chinese Muslims celebrate Eid al-Fitr.

VII. Encouraging the religious community to engage in friendly international exchanges.

The Chinese Government supports all religions to adhere to the principle of independence and self-administration and to develop exchanges and cooperation with their foreign counterparts on the basis of equality, friendship and mutual respect. In the past decade, the Chinese churches have become more active in international exchange activity. They have established friendly relations with religious organizations in over 80 countries, actively participated in international religious events, and engaged in dialogues among different faiths. The Chinese Christian community held Chinese Christian Bible Ministry Exhibition in the US in 2006 and 2011 and once in Germany in 2007. The Chinese Buddhist community hosted World Buddhist Forums in 2006, 2009 and 2012, and Chinese Daoists held International Forums on Daoism in 2007 and 2011. The Chinese Islamic community organized Islamic cultural exhibitions and performances in Indonesia, Turkey and Malaysia in 2010, 2012, and 2014. The Chinese Christian Church and its American counterpart held China-US Christian Leaders Forum in Washington and Shanghai in 2011 and 2013 respectively. In 2011, Chinese religious organizations responded positively to the 65th United Nation General Assembly's resolution on the establishment of World Interfaith Harmony Week and jointly issued *Common Declaration on Advocating Religious Harmony* to promote the concept of interfaith harmony as a common goal. The Chinese Government also actively supports religious organizations in providing volunteer religious service for followers of different faiths from around the world at the Beijing Olympics, Shanghai World Expo, Guangzhou Asian Games, Shenzhen Universiade, the Nanjing Youth Olympic Games and other major events.

In 2012, the Chinese Buddhist community held the Third World Buddhist Forum in Hong Kong.

In 2011, a number of Chinese national religious organizations held a forum to advocate religious harmony.

Freedom of religious belief is an important human right and should be respected and protected. This is the consensus of the international community. At the same time, countries obviously have different national conditions and their cultural traditions vary, so it is inevitable that there will be a diversity of practices of and paths to human rights protection. The experience gained in this process is not only unique to the relevant country but also extremely valuable and should be respected and cherished. The Chinese Government will follow the constitutional provision to respect and protect human rights. It will deal with challenges properly, work hard to resolve problems and continue advancing the protection of religious rights in light of national and religious conditions. China stands ready to have dialogue with other countries to exchange views and experiences and to seek consensus in a joint effort to promote progress in human rights protection including in protecting the right to freedom of religious belief.

(original translation by Cynthia Yume Ning)

完善信访制度　保障公民权利

国务院副秘书长、国家信访局局长　舒晓琴

信访制度作为中国特色民主政治制度的重要补充和权利救济制度，是中国人权事业的重要组成部分。“人权入宪”十年来，各级政府不断健全完善信访制度，大力畅通公民诉求表达渠道，广泛听取意见建议，积极推动解决合理诉求，有效维护群众合法权益，取得了积极成效。十年来，信访结构发生了重大变化，意见建议类在信访总量中占比逐年上升。这一积极变化，标志着中国公民权益保护取得的巨大进步，也从一个侧面彰显了中国人权事业取得的成就。

一、畅通和规范诉求表达渠道，有效保障公民的表达权

《宪法》第四十一条规定：“中华人民共和国公民对于任何国家机关和国家工作人员，有提出批评和建议的权利；对于任何国家机关和国家工作人员的违法失职行为，有向有关国家机关提出申诉、控告或者检举的权利。”为保障公民表达权落到实处，十年来，从中央到地方，各级人民政府进一步畅通信访渠道，规范信访工作行为，探索建立了具有中国特色的公民诉求表达方式和信访工作新方法。

（一）不断畅通和拓宽信访渠道

十年来，各级人民政府大力推广“绿色邮政”、网上信访、视频接访、

热线电话、信访代理、建议征集等做法，普遍建立起“信、访、网、电”四位一体的信访工作平台，方便群众通过多种方式反映情况、表达诉求。全国大部分市县实行了政府部门联合接访，实现了信访事项的“一站式接待、一条龙办理、一揽子解决”；建立横向到边、纵向到底的全国网上信访受理平台，引导群众多上网、少走访，让“数据多跑腿，群众少跑路”，逐步把网上信访打造成群众信访的主渠道。2013 年 7 月 1 日起，国家信访局全面放开网上投诉受理内容，方便了群众、降低了成本、提高了效率，取得初步成效，受到了社会和群众的广泛认同。

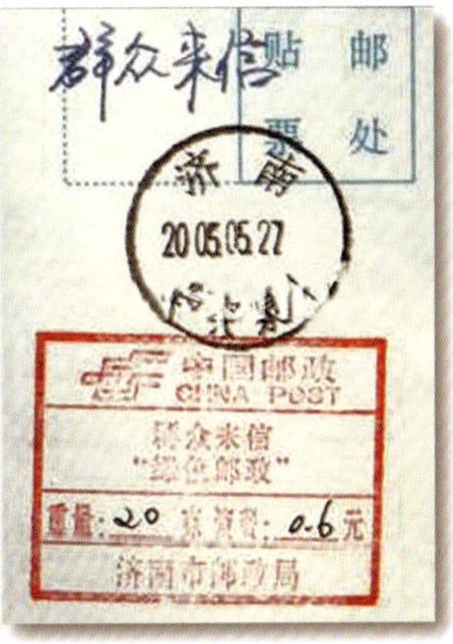

为方便群众信访，山东省在全省范围内开通群众来信“绿色邮政”。

（二）大力开展领导干部接访下访

十年来，各级人民政府把组织领导干部接待群众来访、机关干部深入群众下访作为密切联系群众的一项重要制度，通过重点约访、专题接访、带案下访、领导包案等方式方法，广泛听取群众反映的诉求和意见建议，深入了解群众疾苦，整合多方面资源解决信访问题。此举既方便了信访群众及时就地反映问题，也增强了各级干部服务基层一线的意识，促进了科学民主决策。

国务院副秘书长、国家信访局局长舒晓琴深入基层听取群众意见建议。

（三）积极引导公民依法有序表达诉求

十年来，从中央到地方开展了不同形式的宣传教育活动，将《信访条例》纳入普法培训、干部培训的内容，依法规范了各级各部门的信访工作行为。围绕依法规范信访秩序，积极引导群众以理性合法方式逐级表达诉求。2014 年 5 月 1 日全国开始全面推行依法逐级走访办法后，各级信访工作机构登记接待来访群众人次下降、结构渐趋合理，信访秩序环境进一步改善。

二、完善社会信息汇集机制，有效保障公民的参与权和监督权

《宪法》第二十七条第二款规定：“一切国家机关和国家工作人员必须依靠人民的支持，经常保持同人民的密切联系，倾听人民的意见和建议，接受人民的监督，努力为人民服务。”通过信访渠道汇集公民反映的情况和意见建议，是提升公民民主参与程度、接受公民批评与建议、监督各级人民政府工作的重要保障。十年来，中国社会信息汇集分析制度逐步完善，既健全了公民民主参与途径，又把公民意见和建议体现到国家决策中去，从程序和实体上切实保障了公民参与权和监督权。

（一）深入推进人民建议征集制度

各地普遍建立了人民建议征集制度，设立了专门的人民建议征集机构，为人民群众参与国家治理和社会事务开辟了一条绿色通道，引导人民群众对人民政府的工作献计献策，鼓励和支持公民积极参与国家和社会事务管理。许多地方和部门制定出台了优秀人民建议奖励办法，对国民经济和社会发展或者对改进国家机关工作以及保护社会公共利益有贡献的意见建议，给予奖励，极大地激励了公民民主参与的积极性和创造性。许多优秀有价值的建议转化为各级人民政府的工作决策，有的纳入有关部门工作规划，产生了良好的经济效益和社会效益。

北京市基本形成了以人民建议征集机构为龙头，网络单位为支撑，特邀建议人为基础的人民建议征集工作网络。

（二）建立健全信访信息汇集分析机制

各地各部门充分利用丰富的信访信息资源进行分析研判，及时发现问题，改进工作，完善政策，真正把公民的批评与建议落实到工作中去。十年来，根据群众的意见建议，中央制定出台了数十项政策措施，惠及数千万群众；着力完善收入分配制度、健全社会养老保险体系等重点领域的制度顶层设计，从政策源头层面防范化解信访突出问题。

（三）积极探索社会公众参与信访工作

普遍完善了党代表、人大代表、政协委员联系群众制度，组织老干部、老党员、老模范、老教师、老军人等共同参与解决和化解信访问题。充分发挥工会、共青团、妇联等人民团体优势，积极组织引导服务群众和维护群众权益工作。引导村（社区）制定符合国家法律的村规民约，运用道德、习俗、伦理的力量调节关系，化解矛盾纠纷。推广信访听证制度、重大决策社会稳定风险评估机制和决策纠错改正机制，增强了信访工作的透明度，提高了社会参与信访工作的广度和深度，有力促进了信访事项处理过程的民主、公开、公正。

三、着力推动信访问题解决，有效保障公民的合法权益

着力解决信访问题，是做好信访工作、维护公民合法权益的核心。十年来，各地各部门把维护群众合法权益作为工作的出发点和落脚点，认真落实信访事项办理责任，在及时就地解决群众合理诉求方面取得明显进展。

（一）大力推行“阳光信访”

全面推进信访信息化建设，将接访、办信、督查督办、网上投诉等全部信访事项网上流转，把受理、办理和结果等通过网络公开，实现了信访事项的可查询、可跟踪、可督办、可评价、可考核。建立“信访事项办理群众满意度评价体系”，2014年国家信访局对初次登记受理的非涉密署名求决类来信、来访和网上投诉事项，依托全国信访信息系统开展公民满意度评价，真正把办理群众利益诉求的工作置于群众的监督之下，受到群众的普遍欢迎。广东省各市、县及信访量较大的省直单位，全部建成开通了网上信访大厅，受理的信访量逐年上升。

淮安阳光信访网。

（二）大力推动信访问题及时就地解决

处理好信访问题，贵在“及时”、重在“就地”。做到了“及时”，群众就减少了等待的焦虑；做到了“就地”，信访问题就不会上行。各级信访工作机构高度重视初信初访工作，严格执行首接首办责任制，下大力气把好信访工作的“第一道关口”，协调相关职能部门及时解决问题，有效减少了信访问题在信访部门内部转来转去、信访群众在职能部门之间跑来跑去等现象。各职能部门切实承担起化解本领域职责范围内信访问题的责任，依法按政策处理信访事项，力戒推诿扯皮、敷衍塞责，切实提高了初信初访一次性办结率，防止了“初转重”、“信转访”，最大限度地减少了问题积累、矛盾上行。对于一些长期得不到化解的信访案件，通过调整办案人员或上提一级来办理，加大了推动解决的力度；对群众反应强烈、涉及面广、社会关注度高的重大疑难信访问题，提请人民政府督查机构督查督办，形成了解决问题的合力。2009年，中央设立了解决特殊疑难信访问题专项资金，带动地方配套相应资金，解决了大量特殊疑难信访问题。

（三）逐步完善信访工作责任追究机制

为确保各级政府高度重视、积极推动解决信访问题，切实维护群众合法权益，近年来，从中央到地方都建立起了比较完备的信访工作责任体系，形成了主要领导负总责、分管领导具体抓、其他领导“一岗双责”，一级抓一级、层层抓落实的良好局面；各地各部门紧密结合实际，采取多种方式，及时了解掌握群众反映的问题和建议，及时研究解决和吸收借鉴，及时督导检查和跟踪问效，有力地推动了工作责任的落实。特别是近年来，进一步加大了问责力度，对损害群众利益引发信访突出问题的，对群众反映的问题推诿扯皮、不认真解决造成不良影响的，严肃追究责任。

Optimizing Petition System to Protect Rights of Citizens

Shu Xiaoqin, Deputy Secretary General of the State Council,
Director of the State Bureau for Letters and Calls

The petition system, as a rights relief system and an important supplement to the democratic political system with Chinese characteristics, is an indispensable component of human rights cause in China. In the past ten years after the concept of human rights was enshrined in the *Constitution of the People's Republic of China*, governments at all levels have achieved fruitful results with great efforts in continuously optimizing the petition system, vigorously clearing channels for citizens to express views, extensively soliciting opinions and suggestions, actively helping solve legitimate appeals, and effectively upholding people's lawful rights and interests. The recent ten years witnessed a significant structural change of petition, with growing percentage of letters and calls containing people's opinions and suggestions. This positive change marks a tremendous progress in protecting the rights and interests of Chinese citizens and it partly demonstrates the achievements in human rights protection in China.

I. Keeping open and standardized channels of expression of appeals to effectively protect citizens' freedom of expression.

Article 41 of the Constitution stipulates that "citizens of the People's Republic of China have the right to criticize and make suggestions to any state organ or functionary. Citizens have the right to make complaints and charges against, or exposures of, violation of the law or dereliction of duty by any state organ or functionary to relevant state organs". In the past ten years, in order to materialize freedom of expression, the people's governments at all levels have explored and established ways with Chinese characteristics for people to express their views and new methods to deal with letters and calls by further clearing channels of petition and standardizing the handling of petitions.

1. Keeping open and expanding channels of petition

In the past ten years, people's governments at all levels have built petition platforms to handle "letters, visits, emails and calls" through such measures as postage-free mails, online petition, reception of petitioners via video chat, telephone hotlines, agents of petition and opinion collection, making it convenient for whistleblowing and expression of views. Government departments in most cities and counties have joint hands in receiving petitions so that petitions can enjoy "one-stop reception, coordinated management, and complete resolution". We have established an all-round online platform to receive petitions, encouraging people to make more use of this online platform instead of paying personal visits to the relevant authorities. By so doing, data, instead of people, travel (on the Internet) to government departments and gradually the online platform will become the main channel of petitions. On 1 July 2013, the State Bureau of Letters and Calls started to receive all types of petition online, which has brought convenience to people, lowered cost, improved efficiency and achieved preliminary results. This has been widely praised.

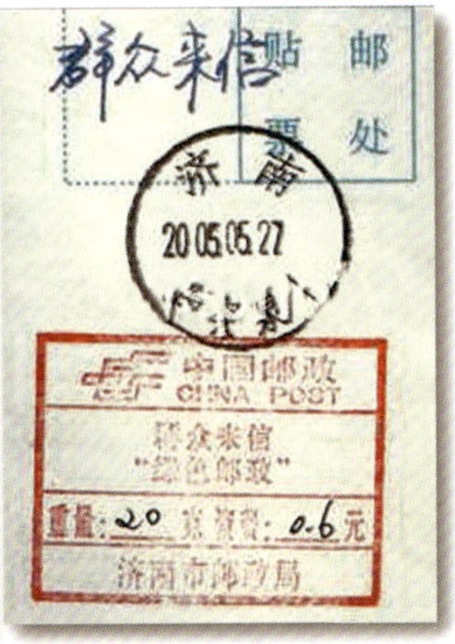

In order to facilitate petitions from the masses, Shandong Province launched the postage-free mails of petition all across the province.

2. Encouraging leading officials to directly receive and visit petitioners

In the past ten years, governments at all levels has taken it as an important institution for maintaining close ties with the masses to organize leading officials to directly receive petitioners and government functionaries to go deep among the masses to visit petitioners. People's appeals, views and suggestions are extensively collected and their sufferings better understood so that different resources are mobilized to address the problems by means of appointments on key petitions, reception of petition on specific themes, visiting petitioners with cases and leader responsibility system. This not only brings convenience to the masses to report problems on the spot in a timely manner but also raises the awareness of cadres at different levels to serve the grass-roots, thus promoting scientific and democratic decision-making.

Shu Xiaoqin, Deputy Secretary General of the State Council and Director of the State Bureau for Letters and Calls went deep among the masses to solicit opinions and suggestions.

3. Actively guiding citizens to express their appeals in an orderly manner and according to law

In the past ten years, various forms of publicity and education have been carried out by governments at the central and local levels. *The Regulations on Letters and Calls* have become part of cadre training and programs to popularize legal knowledge. The handling of petitions by different departments at various levels has been standardized. We encourage the masses to express their appeals step by step up the administrative hierarchy in a rational and lawful manner to ensure the order of petition according to law. Since the introduction of the practice of government officials visiting ordinary households to hear their appeals all across the country on 1 May 2014, the registered number of petitioners received in petition-handling institutions has dropped and the order of petition is further improved with a more reasonable composition of petitioners.

II. Improving social information collection mechanism to effectively ensure citizens' rights to participation and supervision.

Item 2 of Article 27 of the Constitution stipulates that "all state organs and functionaries must rely on the support of the people, keep in close touch with them, heed their opinions and suggestions, accept their supervision and do their best to serve them." Collecting information and suggestions through the petition channel is an important way to improve people's participation in democracy, to accept citizens' criticisms and suggestions, and to supervise over the work of people's governments at all levels. In the past ten years, we have gradually improved the social information collection and analysis system, improving the ways for people to participate in democracy and informing the decision-making process of people's opinions and advices, thus procedurally and substantively ensuring citizens' rights to participation and supervision.

1. Thorough implementation of the system to solicit public opinions

The system to solicit public opinions has been generally established all across China. Specific organizations for soliciting public opinions have been set up to serve as a green channel for the masses to participate in the management of state and social affairs, guide the masses to contribute ideas and exert efforts for the work of people's governments and encourage and support their active involvement in the management of the state and social affairs. Many local governments and relevant departments offer incentives for valuable suggestions from the people. Those opinions and suggestions that are useful in promoting economic and social development, improving the work of state organs or protecting public interests are rewarded, which greatly stimulates the initiative and creativity of people's participation in democracy. Many valuable suggestions have informed decision-making by people's governments at different levels and some of them have been integrated into relevant work plans and produced good economic and social benefits.

Beijing Municipality has basically formed a network to solicit public opinions and suggestions led by the office to collect people's suggestions supported by member organizations in the network operators and with specially invited individuals.

2. Instituting and improving the petition information collection and analysis mechanism

All localities and departments at all levels make full use of the abundant resources of petition information to find out problems in time, improve work and policies, thus truly reflecting citizens' criticisms and suggestions on government work. In the past ten years, in the light of people's opinions and suggestions, the CPC Central Committee has issued dozens of policies and measures that have brought benefits to millions of people. Focused efforts have been made to improve the income distribution system and the top-level design in key areas such as social endowment insurance so that prominent problems triggering petition can be addressed and prevented at the source of their policy origins.

3. Actively exploring public participation in the handling of petitions

Party representatives, NPC deputies and CPPCC members are encouraged to maintain close ties with the masses. Veteran cadres, Party members, model workers, teachers and soldiers are invited to participate in the handling and addressing of petition problems. The strength of people's organizations such as trade unions, Youth Leagues and Women's Federations is fully tapped to actively organize, guide and serve the masses and protect their rights and interests. Villages (communities) are guided to formulate rules that are consistent with laws and to mediate relationships and tackle conflicts and contradictions by the force of morality, customs and ethics. Systems and institutions of hearing on petitions, social stability risk evaluation on important decisions and policy mistake correction. All of these have increased the transparency of petition handling, stimulated a wider and deeper social participation in petition handling and promoted democracy, openness and justice of petition handling process.

Ⅲ. More effort to address petition demands to effectively protect citizens' legitimate rights and interests.

Striving to address petition demands is at the core of performing our duty and maintaining citizens' legitimate rights and interests. In the past ten years, different departments at various levels across the country have taken citizens' legitimate rights and interests as the starting point and foothold of their work, conscientiously handled different petition matters and made remarkable progress in addressing the legitimate appeals of the public in a timely fashion.

1. Vigorously putting "petition-related work in sunshine"

We have comprehensively advanced the building of online petition system through which all the procedures including reception of letters and calls, supervision over the handling process and online complaints are conducted online and the public can access information on the reception, handling and results online. As such, petition cases can be searched, traced, supervised, evaluated and assessed. A "Satisfaction Evaluation System on Petition Handling" has been created. In 2014, with the help of this system, the State Bureau of Letters and Calls conducted a survey on whether the masses had been satisfied or not on the handling of the non-confidential mails with name of sender and containing specific demands, physical visits and online complaints that had been registered for handling for the first time. The handling of people's appeals is thus truly placed under the supervision of the masses, which is widely welcomed by the public. Cities and counties in Guangdong Province and departments directly administered by the province with large numbers of petitions all offer the option to petition online, with the number of petitions presented and registered increasing year by year.

Home page of the website "Petition in the Sunshine" of Huai'an.

2. Vigorously promoting timely and on-the-spot resolution of petition problems

A better handling of petition demands requires settlement in a timely fashion and on the spot. If a problem is addressed in a timely manner, people will wait for results with less anxiety. If a problem is addressed on the spot, it will not be escalated. Bureaus of letters and calls pay close attention to first-time petitions and stick to the rule of responsibility on first recipient. We devote great efforts to coordinating related departments to solve petition problems when they arise for the first time, which effectively reduces the buck passing of problems and petitioners' back and forth among different government departments. Functional departments undertake the responsibility to resolve petition problems within their mandate, handle petitions according to law and relevant policies and restrain themselves from buck passing or perfunctory performance of duty. As a result, more petition demands are now addressed at the first time when they are raised. Then first-time petitioners do not return for the same matter and people do not come to visit the authorities after receiving a response to their mails. In the end, petition problems no longer accumulate and the conflicts are not escalated to higher authority. Petition cases that have not been solved for a long time are processed by new personnel in charge by referral to authority one step higher. Major tough petition problems that influence many people, cause strong complaint and attract wide attention are submitted to the supervisory organs of the people's governments for their oversight, thus creating synergy for their resolution. In 2009, the CPC Central Committee set up a special fund to solve special and difficult petition problems, which, together with matching funds from local governments, have helped address a large number of special and difficult petition demands.

3. Gradually improving accountability in petition handling

In order for governments at various levels to pay close attention to and actively help resolve petition problems to earnestly maintain the legitimate rights and interests of the masses, a relatively complete responsibility system of petition work has been established at both the Central Government and local government levels in recent years, with chief leaders taking overall responsibility, leaders in charge taking specific care and all other functionaries helping. Government departments at various levels across the country have adopted many ways pursuant to their individual conditions to grasp problems and suggestions provided by the masses, to carry out investigation, solve problems, draw lessons, supervise over and review the handling process and results in a timely fashion, thus fulfilling the relevant responsibilities. Especially in recent years, with further strengthening of accountability, officials have been held accountable for prominent problems harming people's interests and triggering petitions and for buck passing or perfunctory handling of petition demands leading to adverse effect.

(original translation by Jiang Yu)

积极探索　多策并举

公安机关全力做好尊重和保障人权工作

公安部常务副部长　杨焕宁

2004 年，“国家尊重和保障人权”被正式写入《宪法》，这是中国人权事业发展的一个重要里程碑。十年来，在宪法精神引领下，中国人权事业得到了长足的发展，相关立法渐趋完善，人权保障机制日益健全，尊重和保障人权理念更加深入人心。公安机关肩负打击犯罪和保护人民的重大职责，是中国人权事业的重要参与者、保护者、捍卫者。近些年来，公安机关积极顺应国家民主法治发展大势，切实贯彻依法治国方略，全面部署开展执法规范化建设，创新社会治理方式方法，充分发挥职能作用，切实保障公民合法权益，真正把“国家尊重和保障人权”这一宪法原则落到实处。

一、依法打击违法犯罪活动

违法犯罪活动严重侵害人民群众的人身财产权益，破坏社会正常秩序，是对人权特别是生命权、健康权、财产权的严重侵害。

近年来，在做好日常侦查办案工作的同时，全国公安机关针对侵害人民群众切身利益的严重违法犯罪活动部署开展了一系列专项行动，严厉打击黑恶势力、涉枪涉爆、严重暴力、两抢一盗、[①] 拐卖妇女儿童、跨国电信诈骗、危害食品安全、毒品、假币等严重侵犯人权的犯罪活动，一大批犯罪分子受到依法惩处，社会公平正义得到伸张，人民群众的安全感和满意度大幅提高，为人权的实现提供了安全稳定的环境。此外，中国公安机关积极同外国警方开展执法合作，建立“中老缅泰湄公河流域执法安全合作机制”，与马来西亚、新加坡、越南、柬埔寨等东南亚国家合作打击跨国电信犯罪和拐卖妇女儿童犯罪，开创了中国与周边国家执法安全合作新模式，坚决惩治各种形式跨国犯罪和国际犯罪，侦破了很多大案要案，有力打击了犯罪分子的嚣张气焰，有效保护了广大人民群众的合法权益，进一步树立了中国公安机关严格执法、保障人权的良好形象。

积极同周边国家开展打击拐卖儿童犯罪警务合作。

二、不断提升公安机关执法规范化水平

规范文明执法不仅提高工作效率，而且能有效保障人民群众的合法权

① 即“抢劫、抢夺、盗窃”。

益。2008 年 9 月以来，公安部在全国公安机关部署开展了执法规范化建设，采取一系列措施，不断推进公安机关公正文明规范执法。

首先，大力加强执法主体建设。通过集中培训、网上培训、实战演练、案例点评、旁听庭审等多种培训形式，使民警树立既要严格、公正、规范执法，又要理性、平和、文明执法的理念。同时，在全国公安机关推行执法资格等级考试，将保障人权列为考试的重要内容，并明确要求未取得基本级执法资格的民警不得办案，派出所所长、刑警队长等执法勤务类机构负责人必须取得中级执法资格，有效提升了人民警察的法律素养和执法能力。

其次，不断严密执法制度。公安部出台一系列规定，从接处警到案件终结的全过程形成了较为系统、严密的制度规范，有效解决了民警“干什么、怎么干、干到什么程度”的问题。根据修改后的《刑事诉讼法》，公安部全面修订了《公安机关办理刑事案件程序规定》，明确要求“尊重和保障人权”、“不得强迫任何人证实自己有罪”、“严禁刑讯逼供”，建立完善了依法保障律师会见、非法证据排除、讯问犯罪嫌疑人全程录音录像等一系列制度，使保障人权的规定更加具体化、制度化、严格化。

第三，积极构建执法管理体系。近年来，公安机关借鉴现代企业管理经验，探索建立系统、规范的执法管理体系。强化源头管理，在一线执法单位配备或派驻专兼职法制员，加强对执法办案初始环节的质量把关；持续开展执法质量考评，强化对有无刑讯逼供等侵犯人权情形的监督，严格追究执法过错责任；加强问题管理，针对执法中的突出问题在全国公安机关大力开展专项治理活动，及时发现和纠正执法不规范和安全隐患等问题。

第四，规范执法办案场所设置和使用管理。公安部要求各地公安机关对执法办案场所进行规范化改造，严格按要求加强使用管理：办案区与其他功能区实行物理隔离，并按照执法办案的流程和要求安排功能室的顺序和布局；讯问室全部安装同步录音录像设备；民警将违法犯罪嫌疑人带至公安机关后一律直接进入办案区讯问询问；进入办案区，要先对违法犯罪嫌疑人进行人身检查和信息采集，并由专人负责看管；对于在办案区内开展执法活动，要有视频监控并记录。规范的场所设置和专业化的环境，既有助于防止刑讯逼供等侵犯人权问题的发生，又促进了民警规范执法的习惯养成。

讯问时实现办案民警与犯罪嫌疑人隔离。

第五，加快执法办案信息化建设。为强化执法监督的即时性、全面性，各地公安机关普遍建立运行了全省统一的执法办案和监督信息系统，推行“执法信息网上录入、执法流程网上管理、执法活动网上监督、执法质量网上考核”的执法办案和监督管理新模式，实现了对执法活动的全程、实时监控。同时，加强对现场执法活动的监督，不断加大科技投入，为一线民警配备执法现场记录仪等装备，对接处警等重要执法环节实行同步录音录像，有效固定了现场证据，防止了执法不规范等问题的发生。

利用网络平台监督执法办案。

第六，加大执法公开力度。为强化人民群众对公安机关执法活动的监督，促进执法公正，公安部出台了《公安机关执法公开规定》，要求各级公安机关依照规定向社会公众和特定对象公开执法的依据、流程、进展、结果等信息，并积极推行刑事案件立破案告知、案件回访、110短信评警、案件回访、窗口单位满意度评价、互联网评议、聘请特邀监督员等制度，有效保障群众的知情权、监督权、参与权，真正把执法活动置于阳光之下。

三、改革创新公安管理机制

在打击违法犯罪、维护社会治安工作中加强对人权保障的同时，公安机关在日常行政管理工作中更加重视服务和保障民生，不断加强和改进各项管理服务工作，进一步提升人民群众的满意度。

首先，加强公共安全管理。公安机关与时俱进，积极拓宽管理服务领域，改进管理服务方式，提高管理服务水平。强化对公路客运道路交通安全管理，推行“文明交通行动计划”，增强人民群众文明交通意识，着力纠正各类违反交通法规现象；强化校车安全管理，消除安全隐患，保障校车通行安全；开展“护卫天使行动”，采取多种形式向广大师生宣传道路交通安全法律法规和交通常识，提高学生、儿童的交通安全意识和安全防护技能，一些地方还专门抽调女民警在校园周边值守，加强交通疏导维护，保障中小学生上下学交通安全。强化消防安全管理，设置“96119”火灾隐患举报投诉中心，及时发现并消除火灾隐患；开展形式多样的消防宣传活动，向人民群众传授消防知识、防火常识和安全逃生技能，提高全民消防安全意识；强化校园安全管理，大力整治校园及周边治安环境，开展“护校安园”专项行动，严厉打击涉校违法犯罪活动，在校园周边设立“护学岗”，增强校园安防力量。

积极在群众中开展普法宣传教育。

其次，推出便民利民措施。近年来，公安机关紧紧围绕人民群众的需求，先后推出多批便民利民措施，涉及户政、交管、消防、出入境管理、报警求助等方方面面，有效地提高了服务群众、管理社会的能力和水平。对于群众在办理证件和行政许可过程中提出的问题，要求及时答疑解惑；对需要补充的事项要一次性告知，能够让群众跑一趟办妥的事情决不让群众跑第二趟，能够在网上办理的事情尽量在网上办理，真正把方便让给群众。为提高边检通关和出入境办理服务的效率和质量，推出了非户籍地居民就近办理出入境证件、提供全国互联网查询本人出入境记录服务、简化边检查验手续等一系列措施；为方便群众快捷办理机动车驾驶证业务，推行远程自助预约驾驶人考试服务，方便群众根据自身需要，合理选择时间参加考试；对行动不便的孤寡老人、残疾人等特殊群体，提供上门办理户口、居民身份证服务。近期，公安部又推行提高户口办理时效、推行网上预约办理出入境证件服务、实行机动车省内跨地市检验等 16 项便民利民措施，及时下放取消了一批行政审批事项，并在法律政策规定的范围内最大限度地减少审批环节、简化办事程序、缩短办理时间，努力让人民群众感到管理更人性、服务更贴心、办事更便利。

第三，改进工作作风和方式。2011 年以来，公安部在全国公安机关深入开展“大走访”开门评警活动，敞开大门访民意、敞开心扉听民声，主动征求群众意见、自觉接受群众评议，按照人民满意的标准不断加强和改进公安工作。针对群众反映强烈的“门难进、脸难看、话难听、事难办”等突出问题，严格要求执法服务窗口单位民警语言文明、动作规范、改进服务态度、转变工作作风。各地公安机关适应网络时代工作的新特点，积极依托网络管理服务新平台，设立“网上公安局”、“网上服务大厅”、“公安微博”，拓展警民互动的新渠道，全面推广网上受理、网上审批、网上办公等管理服务新模式，努力为社会和公众提供方便快捷的服务。同时，开通网上监督窗口，畅通群众对违法违规问题的举报投诉渠道，自觉接受社会监督。

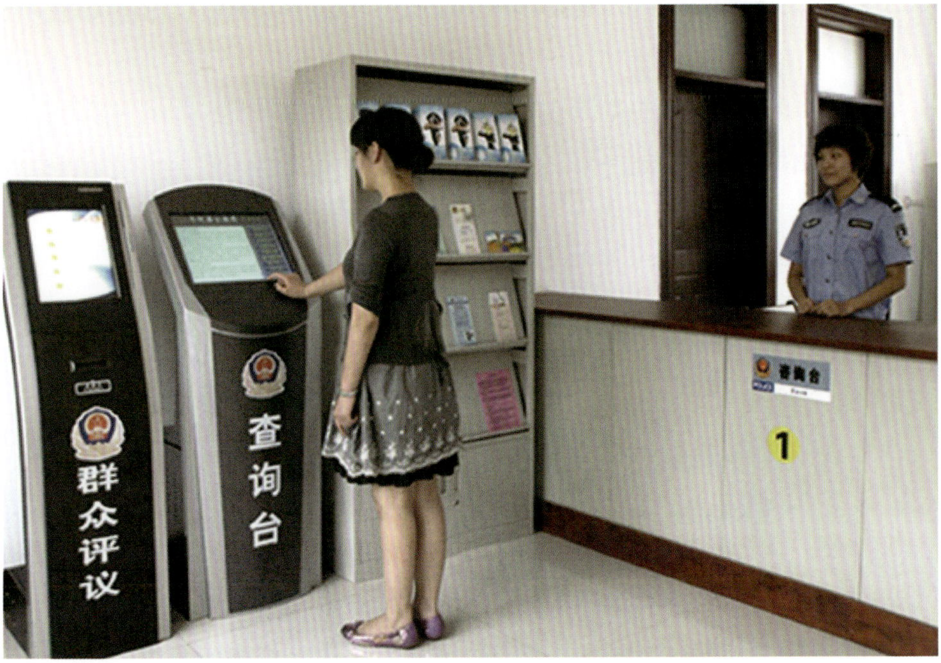

群众在派出所查询信息。

四、积极保障在押人员的合法权益

公安机关高度重视保障在押人员合法权益，创新建立了系统全面的在押人员人身权利保障制度和诉讼权利保障制度，并取得了良好的实践效果。

首先，保障在押人员的诉讼权利。修改后的《刑事诉讼法》施行后，各地看守所普遍推出了律师会见预约、建立法律援助中心驻看守所工作站等保障辩护权的措施，及时安排律师会见，保障在押人员的诉讼权利。严格落实在押人员出入所身体检查制度，犯罪嫌疑人被送看守所后，首先进行入所健康检查，对发现有外伤或者不宜羁押的疾病的，及时告知办案部门；因侦查工作需要提解在押人员出所的，办案机关应当严格履行相关手续，送返时，看守所应对其进行体表检查；规范在押人员随身携带的物品的保管和发还，确保其财产权不受侵犯；规范提讯活动，对在押人员的提讯必须在看守所讯问室进行，并对讯问室实行物理分隔，确保讯问人不直接接触在押人员，对讯问过程全程录音录像，杜绝刑讯逼供现象。

其次，保障在押人员的投诉权。看守所普遍实行在押人员权利义务告知制度和投诉机制，每个监室都设有报警装置和检察信箱，及时受理并转达在押人员有关上诉、申诉、控告、检举等材料，对在押人员反映侵害其合法权益的行为，相关部门将及时予以查处。

第三，主动接受社会监督。将看守所视频监控与驻所检察室联网，接受检察机关实时动态监督。建立特邀监督员制度，受聘的特邀监督员可凭有效身份证件随时进入看守所进行巡查，了解在押人员在看守所的待遇。截至目前，全国看守所共聘请特邀监督员 13000 余名，2500 余个看守所实现了对社会开放。2011 年以来，美国、英国等 47 个国家的 69 名驻华使领馆警务联络官、红十字国际委员会东亚代表处、国外媒体等参观了北京市第一、第二看守所，对中国看守所羁押条件、管理水平、医疗卫生、人权保障等工作给予高度评价。

外国驻华警务联络官参观看守所。

第四，给予在押人员更多人性化关怀。不断推进看守所基础设施和装备建设，改善在押人员生活、放风场所条件。注意科学合理安排在押人员的生活，提高伙食标准并保证必要的休息、自由活动时间。积极推行医疗卫生社会化，由医院在看守所设立门诊或医院，医生定期在监室巡诊，对患病在押人员及时医治，病情严重的及时送医院治疗，充分保障在押人员的生命健康权益。民警定期对在押人员进行谈话、教育等心理疏导，及时发现、解决其心理存在的问题。通过开展家属亲情会见等活动，让在押人员感受到亲情的温暖，促使其真正悔过，早日回归社会。

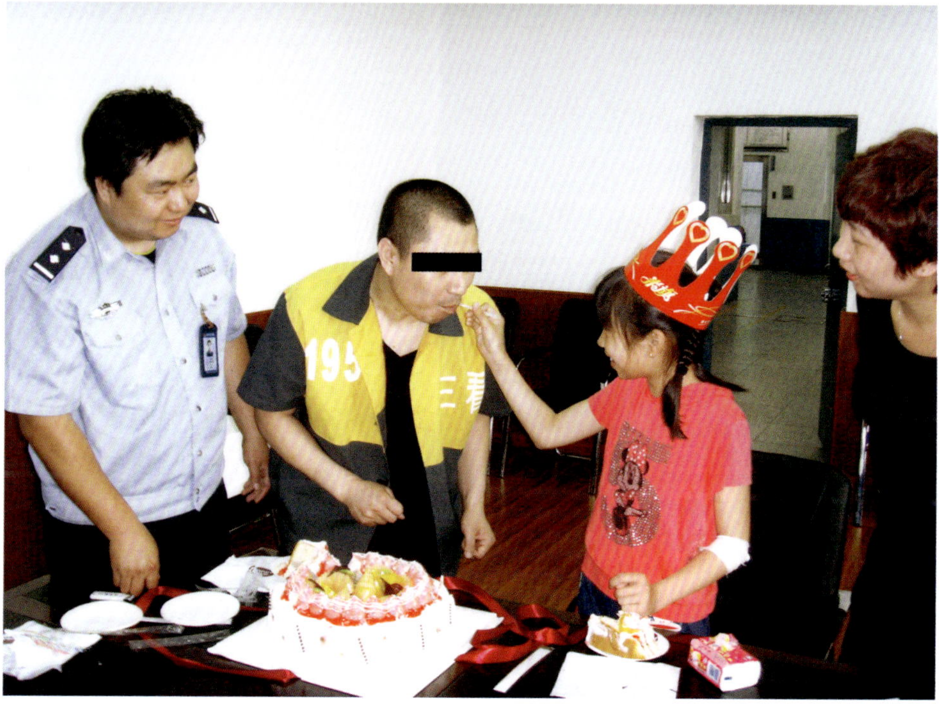

看守所开展与家属亲情会见。

五、积极开展对一些特殊群体的救助

公安机关一贯重视保障刑事案件被害人以及刑满释放人员、吸毒人员等群体的权益，采取多种方式予以特殊的关爱和救助。在打击拐卖人口犯罪中，对于被解救的被拐卖妇女，公安机关积极帮助其返家并会同民政、妇联等部门通过提供法律援助、心理咨询等措施，及时对其提供救助、安置和康复服务。对于被解救的被拐卖儿童，公安机关通过不断健全完善儿童失踪快速查找、来历不明儿童摸排比对、DNA 比对等方式，帮助其寻找家人。对刑满释放人员，公安机关始终坚持"教育、感化、挽救"方针，及时对其进行教育疏导，并积极协调民政、司法、工商等部门，帮助其解决生活、就业困难，预防其重新犯罪。对于吸毒人员，公安机关依法运用自愿戒毒、社区戒毒、强制隔离戒毒、社区康复等戒毒措施，促使其戒断毒瘾，回归社会。

积极帮助戒毒康复人员就业。

总之，尊重和保障人权是一项系统工程，需要全社会共同努力，公安机关将一如既往地做好相关工作，不断完善相关规章制度，全面提升依法保障人权的能力和水平，并进一步加强与世界各国在人权领域的交流与合作，共同将人权事业推向前进。

Actively Exploring and Applying Various Policy Measures

Public Security Organs Spare No Effort to Respect and Protect Human Rights

Yang Huanning, Executive Vice Minister of Public Security

In 2004, that "[t]he State respects and protects human rights" was officially articulated in the *Constitution of the People's Republic of China*. It was an important milestone in China's human rights protection cause. During the ten years since then, under the guidance of the spirit of the Constitution, human rights protection cause has gained great improvement, with the relevant legislation becoming more full-fledged and institutions more robust. The respect for and protection of human rights have taken root in people's minds. The public security organs shoulder the duty of punishing crimes and protecting people and are important participants, protectors and guardians of human rights protection in China. During these years, public security organs have actively followed the trend of democracy and rule of law, earnestly implemented the strategy of "governing the country according to law", made comprehensive efforts to harmonize law enforcement, innovated in ways of social management, fully played its role in protecting people's lawful rights and interests and fulfilled the constitutional principle of respecting and protecting human rights.

I. Cracking down on illegal and criminal activities according to law.

Illegal activities and crimes severely violate people's personal and property rights, and undermine social order, thus seriously violating human rights especially the rights to life, health and property.

In recent years, while carrying out regular investigation and case handling, the public security organs all over the country have conducted a series of campaigns against serious illegal activities and crimes that harm people's immediate interests. With severe crackdown on crimes that seriously violate human rights such as mafia-like gangs, crimes involving the use of guns or explosives, serious violence, robbery, looting and theft, trafficking in women and children, transnational telecommunications fraud, crimes endangering food safety, drugs trafficking, and counterfeit money, a multitude of criminals have been punished, social fairness and justice have been upheld, people's sense of security and satisfaction have been improved, and a safe and stable environment for the realization of human rights has been created. Besides, Chinese public security organs have cooperated with their foreign counterparts in law enforcement. The Mechanism of Law Enforcement and Security Cooperation in the Mekong River Basin was established with Laos, Myanmar and Thailand. Cooperation has also been conducted with Malaysia, Singapore, Vietnam, Cambodia and other Southeast Asian countries to crack down on transnational telecommunications fraud and trafficking in women and children, creating a new model of cooperation with neighboring countries to resolutely punish all forms of transnational and international crimes. A lot of major cases have been cracked down, powerfully crashing the criminals' arrogance, effectively protected the legitimate rights and interests of the people and further establishing the Chinese public security organs' good image in strict law enforcement and protection of human rights.

China has actively cooperated with neighboring countries to crack down on the crime of children trafficking.

Ⅱ. Constantly improving the level of law enforcement standardization of public security organs.

Standardized and civilized law enforcement not only improves work efficiency but also help protect effectively people's legitimate rights and interests. Since September 2008, the Ministry of Public Security has directed public security organs in China to standardize law enforcement and taken a series of measures to roll out just, civilized and standardized law enforcement.

First, efforts have been taken to build up the capacity of law enforcement officers. Through group training, online training, drills, case review, attending trials and other forms of training, the policemen set up the idea of combining strict, fair and standard law enforcement with rational, calm and civilized manners. In the meantime, law enforcement qualification examinations are conducted in public security organs all over the country, with human rights protection as an important content of the exam. It is clearly required that the policemen failing to obtain a basic qualification will not be allowed to handle cases, station chiefs and heads of criminal police team must have intermediate qualification. The measure has effectively improved the legal accomplishment and law enforcement capability of the police.

Second, the law enforcement system is constantly improved to minimize loopholes. The Ministry of Public Security has published a series of regulations to create a comprehensive and rigorous system covering the whole process from alarm and response to closure of case, thus effectively answering questions of what, how and to what extent for policemen. According to the amended *Criminal Procedure Law*, the Ministry of Public Security revised the *Provisions on the Procedures for Handling Criminal Cases by Public Security Organs,* explicitly requiring that the police respect and protect human rights, refrain from forcing anyone to prove his own guilt, and be forbidden to extort confession by torture. Rules have been developed with regard to lawyers' meetings, illegal evidence exclusion and tape or video recording of interrogation. Human rights protection provisions have thus become more specific, systematic and strict.

Third, a law enforcement management system is actively developed. In recent years, the public security organs have drawn upon the management experience of modern companies and explored a systematic and standard law enforcement management system. They have enhanced source management by deploying full-time or part-time legal inspector to frontline law enforcement agencies to guarantee the quality of the primary steps of law enforcement. Law enforcement quality assessment is carried out to strengthen supervision over potential violations of human rights, such as extorting confession by torture, and strictly investigate into and hold accountable law enforcement faults. Problem management has been enhanced with special campaigns carried out throughout the country's public security organs to detect and rectify in time irregular law enforcement and security loopholes.

Fourth, the law enforcement and case handling site setup and usage management have been standardized. The Ministry of Public Security required public security organs at all levels to standardize the law enforcement and case handling site setup and enhance usage management according to requirements: the case handling area should be physically separated from other functional areas and the layout of the functional rooms should be arranged according to the procedure and requirements of case handling; interrogation rooms should be equipped with synchronized video and audio recording equipments; when the illegal or criminal suspects are taken to the public security organs, they should be directly taken into case handling area to be consulted or interrogated; when entering the case handling area, the police should first verify the person and collect information collection of the suspects and the suspects should be watched over by designated staff members; law enforcement activities in the case handling area should be video monitored and recorded. Standardized site setup and professional environment help prevent human rights violations like extorting confession by torture and foster habits of standardized law enforcement among the police.

In interrogation, police and suspect are physically separated.

Fifth, application of information technology in law enforcement and case handling has been sped up. In order to enhance the instantaneity and comprehensiveness of law enforcement supervision, the public security organs at all levels have unified law enforcement and supervision systems at the provincial level, carried out the new mode of law enforcement and supervision management that includes online information input, process management, activity supervision and quality inspection of law enforcement, achieving real-time monitoring of the whole process of law enforcement activities. Meanwhile, the public security organs have enhanced inspection of on-site law enforcement, with increased technology input to equip frontline policemen with scene recording machine and to have synchronized recording of important law enforcement procedures like alarm receipt and response, thus effectively securing on-site evidence and preventing irregular law enforcement.

Online platforms are used to inspect law enforcement and case handling.

Sixth, law enforcement has been made more transparent. In order to enhance people's supervision over public security organs' law enforcement activities and promote impartial law enforcement, the Ministry of Public Security published *Provisions on the Transparency of Law Enforcement by Public Security Organs,* requiring public security organs at all levels to disclose to the general public and specific groups of population the basis, procedures, progress and results of law enforcement according to the provisions. The public security organs have also actively practised notification on filing and closing of criminal cases, case follow-up visit, evaluation of the 110 police hotline by text messages, satisfaction survey on service units, online comments solicitation and recruitment of guest supervisors to secure people's rights to information, supervision and participation and to truly put law enforcement in the sunshine.

III. Reforming and innovating public security management system.

While improving human rights protection by punishing crimes and safeguarding public security, the public security organs have attached more importance to serve and protect people's livelihood in daily administrative work and constantly improved various administration and services to increase people's satisfaction.

First, public security management is enhanced. In keeping pace with the times, the public security organs have expanded areas of management and service, improved the way of management and service and enhanced the level of management and service. They have strengthened highway passenger transportation safety management, carried out the action plan for civilized transportation to increase people's awareness and rectify traffic violations. They have strengthened school bus safety management and eliminated hidden dangers to ensure safe passage of school buses. They have conducted the "guardian angel" campaign to advocate road safety laws and regulations as well as traffic knowledge in schools so that students and children are mindful of road safety and relevant protection skills. In some localities, policewomen were deployed to guard areas around schools and enhance traffic dispersion to protect the safety of primary and middle school students. Fire safety management has been enhanced and 96119 fire hazard report and complaint center has been set up so as to discover and eliminate fire hazard. Various fire safety campaigns have been conducted to spread fire safety and prevention knowledge and train people on fire survival skills so that they are more fire aware. School safety management has been enhanced by improving the surrounding and campus security environment, conducting special campaigns to crack down on illegal and criminal activities involving school, instituting security posts near school to increase school security.

Popularizing legal knowledge among the people.

Second, measures of convenience and benefit to people have been adopted. In recent years, public security organs, bearing in mind people's needs, have introduced various measures that bring convenience and benefits to the people, including in household registration, traffic management, fire safety, entry and exit control, calling the police for help and so on, with the ability and level of serving people and social management effectively enhanced. Questions raised during application for credentials and administrative licensing are answered in time. Full and complete information must be provided to the visiting applicant so that he or she will settle the matter during one visit and won't need additional visits and issues that can be dealt with online are so processed, thus bringing true convenience to people. Public security organs have taken a series of measures to increase the efficiency and quality of border control and exit and entry service. For example, applicants not at the seat of their registered residence may apply for entry and exit document at the nearby public security organ and people may search online their own exit and entry records. Border examination procedures have also been simplified. In order to make sure people receive driving license quickly, the public security organs introduced remote self-service appointment system for driving license test so that people may choose a proper test time according to their needs. For special populations like the elderly of no family and the disabled, household registration and resident identification card may be done at home by visiting policemen. Recently, the Ministry of Public Security has again introduced 16 measures to bring convenience and benefits to people, including higher efficiency in household registration, online reservation for exit and entry documents and motor vehicle examination across cities within the province. It has also canceled or transferred to lower levels some items of administrative approval and reduced approval procedures and handling time to the extent permitted by law so that the people enjoy more humanized management, more considerate service and more convenient procedures .

Third, the style and mode of work has been improved. Since 2011, the Ministry of Public Security have conducted extensive interviews and surveys among the people to seek their opinions and comments on public security organs so as to improve the public security work according to people's satisfaction standard. Aiming at solving problems of "difficult access, unfriendly look, unpleasant words and tough process" that people feel very strongly about, the Ministry urged policemen at service counters to speak and act politely, improve attitude and change work style. In this new Internet era, public security organs at all levels should have made use of new online platforms such as "online public security bureau", "online service hall" and "public security Weibo" to increase interaction with the people and promote new management and service mode of online acceptance, approval and conduct of office work, thus providing convenient and quick service for the public. Online supervision is also made possible with unblocked channels of reporting of and complaint about illegal behaviors and irregularities.

Searching information in the police station.

Ⅳ. Actively protecting the legitimate rights and interests of detainees.

The public security organs pay much attention to protecting the detainees' legitimate rights and interests and created innovative mechanisms to protect their personal rights and litigation rights, which have achieved great results.

First, the litigation rights of detainees are protected. After the implementation of the amended *Criminal Procedure Law,* detention houses at all localities have introduced measures to protect the right to defense including lawyer's meeting with detainees and setting up work station of legal aid center in the detention houses so as to arrange lawyers' meetings in time and guarantee detainees' litigation rights. They have implemented strictly the physical examination system upon detainees' exit and entry. When a suspect is sent to the detention house, he or she first receives a health examination and any injury or illness that makes it inappropriate to detain the person is notified to the case handling department immediately. When a detainee needs to be taken out of the detention house for investigation, the case dealing organs must go through the relevant procedures strictly and when the detainee is sent back, the detention houses carries out body surface examination. The storage and returning of detainees' personal belongings have been standardized to make sure that their property rights are not violated. Rules for arraignment have been formulated and strictly followed. For example, arraignment of detainees must be conducted in the interrogation room of the detention house, the interrogation room must be physically arranged in a way that the interrogator cannot have direct body contact with the detainee, and the whole interrogation process must be audio and video recorded to avoid extorting confession by torture.

Second, the detainees' right to complaint is protected. The detention houses have implemented the system of informing the detainees of their rights and duties and the complaint system. Every cell is equipped with an alarm and procurator's mailbox so as to accept and convey in time the detainees' materials about appeal, complaint, accusation and impeachment. Acts of infringement reported by detainees are investigated into and handled promptly by the relevant departments.

Third, proactive measures have been taken to increase supervision by the public. The surveillance cameras in the detention houses are connected to the procurator's office for continuous real-time monitoring by the procuratorate. Guest supervisors are invited to check on the detention house at anytime upon presentation of valid ID to ask for information about treatment of the detainees. There are now 13,000 such supervisors and 2,500 detention houses are open to the society. Since 2011, 69 police liaison officers from embassies and consulates of 47 countries such as the US and UK as well as officers from East Asian representative office of the International Committee of the Red Cross and foreign media have visited Beijing No.1 and No.2 detention houses and spoken highly of the detention environment, management level, medical treatment and hygiene as well as human rights protection in Chinese detention houses.

Police liaison officers from foreign embassies in China visited a detention house.

Fourth, more humane care is given to the detainees. The infrastructure and facilities of the detention houses have been improved together with the detainees' living and recreational spaces. Attention is paid to arrange the detainees' life scientifically and properly, increase the food standard and make sure they get necessary rest and exercise time. Medical treatment and healthcare are socialized with clinics opened in detention houses by hospitals. Doctors visit the cells regularly, give timely treatment to sick detainees and refer the severely ill to hospital in time, thus protecting the detainees' right to life and health. Prison police offer regular psychological counselings through conversation and education so as to detect and solve detainees' psychological problems in time. Family reunions are arranged for detainees to feel the warmth of family affection and genuinely repent so as to return to the society at an early date.

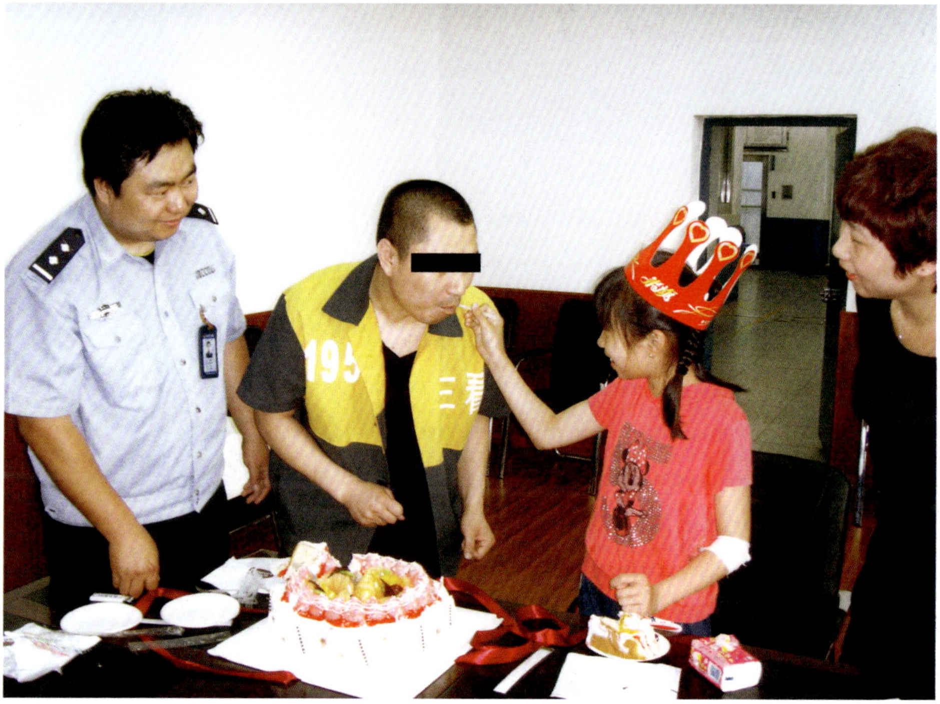

A family reunion in detention house.

Fifth, assistance is provided for special groups of detainees. The public security organs always pay much attention to the rights and interests of the crime victims, persons released upon completion of sentence and drug addicts and take various measures to offer special care and assistance. During the crackdown on human abducting and trafficking, public security organs actively help the rescued women to go back home and cooperate with the civil affairs departments and women's federations to provide aid, make arrangement for settlement and offer rehabilitation service through legal aid and psychological counseling. They also help the rescued children to find their families through improving the missing children quick search mechanism, investigation into and comparison of children of unknown background and DNA comparison. The public security organs insist on the policy of "education, reformation and rescue" towards persons released upon completion of sentences to educate them in time and cooperate with the civil affairs, judicial, and industry and commerce departments to help them resolve difficulties in life and employment, thus prevent relapse. Public security organs implement according to law such measures as voluntary detoxification, community-based detoxification, compulsory isolation detoxification, community rehabilitation to help drug addicts stop using drugs and return to society.

Former drug addicts are assisted in getting employed after rehabilitation.

In conclusion, respecting and protecting human rights is a systematic project that takes the concerted efforts of the whole society. The public security organs will, as always, perform well its functions, constantly improve relevant rules and institutions, comprehensively build up the capacity to protect human rights according to law and enhance exchanges and cooperation with other countries in human rights protection to jointly advance human rights protection.

(original translation by Niu Ya'nan)

中国国际人权交流合作成果丰硕

外交部副部长　李保东

2004年3月，第十届全国人大第二次会议通过《宪法》修正案，将“国家尊重和保障人权”载入《宪法》，开启了用《宪法》保障人权的新时代。2014年10月，中国共产党第十八届中央委员会第四次全体会议就全面推进依法治国做出战略部署，为推动人权保障法治化绘制了新蓝图。

十年来，中国人权成就举世瞩目，走出了一条符合自身国情的人权发展道路。同时，中国秉持平等互信、包容互鉴、合作共赢精神，全面深入参与全球人权治理，认真履行国际人权义务，积极推进对外人权交流与合作，取得丰硕成果。

一

中国全面深入参与全球人权治理，秉持公道，坚持正义，推动建立公正国际人权体系。中国三度高票当选联合国人权理事会成员，成为履职时间最长的人权理事会成员之一，反映了各国对中国人权成就与作用的肯定。

（一）推动人权理事会建立公平公正运作机制

人权理事会是全球人权治理主要平台。2005年，时任联合国秘书长安南提交改革报告，首次将人权与安全、发展并列为联合国三大支柱，主张提升人权在联合国系统地位，将人权委员会升格为人权理事会。联合国人权机构改革大幕自此拉开。2005 年至 2011 年，各方围绕人权理事会设立、建章立制和重审展开激烈较量。中国与观点相近国家密切协作，经过艰苦努力，维护了发展中国家利益。

2006 年 5 月 9 日，中国当选联合国人权理事会首届成员。

在设立人权理事会的谈判中，中国联合其他发展中国家据理力争，实现了理事会成员国在各地区组均衡分配，增加了亚洲国家席位，明确人权理事会应遵循公正、客观、非选择性原则，为人权理事会工作奠定了良好基础。

在人权理事会建章立制工作中，中国与观点相近国家旗帜鲜明地反对人权问题政治化，反对借此干涉他国内政，成功为国别人权提案设立“门槛”；坚持国别人权审查机制由各国政府主导，国别人权审查机制应秉持公正、客观原则；明确人权特别机制专家须由人权理事会核准，推动制定人权特别机制专家《行为准则》，防止西方操纵妄为。

在人权理事会重审谈判中，中国与广大发展中国家共同努力，实现了人权理事会地位不变、组成选举方式不变、审查机制和运行模式基本不变等目标，挫败了西方借此重开人权理事会谈判的图谋，维护了发展中国家在人权理事会设立和建章立制谈判中取得的成果。

（二）积极影响联合国人权条约机构改革

联合国于上世纪80年代启动人权条约机构改革工作。发展中国家批评有关机构职能交叉、政治化、选择性严重，主张规范条约机构工作。西方则认为条约机构对各国履约监督不够，希望扩大条约机构权限，将其打造成“人权准司法机构”。

2009年，联合国人权高专办在缺乏充分授权情况下自行启动“加强人权条约机构体系进程”。为集思广益、凝聚共识、发挥主导作用，中国与俄罗斯等观点相近国家倡议联大设立条约机构改革政府间进程。有关谈判于2012年启动，2014年4月达成改革方案。改革方案要求加强缔约国地位和作用，促进履约能力建设，条约机构应该严格遵守职责授权等。方案平衡反映了发展中国家关切。中国作为主要发起者和推动者，为条约机构改革进程取得有利于发展中国家的成果发挥了重要作用。

（三）捍卫国家利益，积极宣传中国特色人权理念和实践

中国建设性参与每年联大三委、人权理事会及其下属社会论坛、发展权工作组等多边人权会议，结合和谐世界、科学发展观、“两个一百年”目标、中国梦以及党的十八大、十八届三中全会、十八届四中全会的精神，宣传中国促进和保护人权政策、举措和成就，介绍中国对各类专题性人权问题的主张，坚决驳斥西方国家和反华敌对势力无理指责和污蔑，用法律、数据和事实争取到越来越多国家对中国人权工作的理解和支持。

2004年，中国在友好国家和发展中国家支持下，连续第11次挫败西方国家在人权委员会提出的反华提案，鲜明表达了反对借人权搞政治施压的严正立场。2014年初中国在接受第二轮国别人权审查时，西方国家怂恿和支持反华敌对势力滋事。中国沉着应对，干净利落挫败西方和反华敌对势力有关图谋，取得重大胜利。

在白俄罗斯、斯里兰卡等发展中国家受西方整治时，中国挺身而出，仗义执言，明确反对将人权问题作为地缘政策工具、干涉别国内政。中国和人权问题“观点相近国家小组”其他成员一道，不断加强小组机制化建设，集体发声，共同行动，抵制西方人权攻势。

中国积极倡导国际社会同等重视经社文权利和发展权，推动各方讨论反对种族歧视、非洲人后裔权利、移民权利、和平权等发展中国家关心的问题，支持人权理事会设立安全饮用水、文化权、残疾人权利、人权与国际团结、促进民主公平国际秩序等专题性特别机制。中国还倡导召开关于粮食安全、国际金融危机的特别会议，将国际人权合作聚焦发展中国家最关切的生存权和发展权。

二

十年来，中国认真履行国际人权义务，不断加强人权保障体系、制度和能力建设。

中国根据承担的国际人权条约义务，制订修订与保障人权相关的国内法律法规，包括社会法、行政法、刑法、诉讼法等多个法律类别。截至 2014 年 9 月，中国现行有效法律共 242 部、行政法规 738 部、地方性法规 9000 部左右，形成了以《宪法》为统帅的中国特色社会主义法律体系。

中国切实履行《经济、社会和文化权利国际公约》、《消除对妇女一切形式歧视公约》、《儿童权利公约》、《残疾人权利公约》、《消除一切形式种族歧视公约》、《禁止酷刑公约》等 6 项核心人权公约和《防止及惩治灭绝种族罪公约》、《关于难民地位的公约》、《男女同工同酬公约》、《消除就业和职业歧视公约》等其他 20 项与人权有关的国际条约。过去十年，中国 15 次接受上述 6 项核心人权公约履约审议，得到有关条约机构充分肯定。2014 年 5 月，中国接受《经济、社会和文化权利国际公约》第二次履约报告审议。中国优秀的履约成绩、中国代表团开放自信的态度、出色的现场答问得到委员会专家高度评价，被誉为“履约审议典范”。中国专家担任联合国经社文权利委员会、消除对妇女歧视委员会、消除种族歧视委员会、禁止酷刑委员会、残疾人权利委员会委员，建设性参与上述条约机构工作，推动其公正履职，发挥了积极作用。

2013 年 10 月 22 日，中国代表团团长、外交部特使吴海龙率团出席中国接受联合国人权理事会第二轮国别人权审查会议。

2009 年和 2013 年，中国两次接受人权理事会国别人权审查。中国专门成立近 30 家立法、行政和司法部门组成的跨部门工作组，撰写高质量的《国家人权报告》，并广泛征询非政府组织和学术机构以及公众意见。中国用事实和数据向各国全面介绍中国人权事业进展、面临的挑战和努力目标，充分展示中国政府促进和保护人权的坚定决心和取得的成绩。2009 年，中国接受了各国提出的 42 条建议，这些建议在随后四年中得到全面落实。2013 年，中国接受了 204 条建议，占各国所提建议总数的 81%，涵盖减贫、司法、民族、宗教、社会保障等 20 多个领域，展现了中国政府积极负责、开放包容的良好姿态。

三

十年来，中国与联合国人权高专办积极开展务实合作，不断拓宽双方合作广度和深度。

2005 年，中国第 8 次接待联合国人权高专访华，与人权高专办签署第二份《合作谅解备忘录》，内容涵盖司法改革、人权教育、履行人权条约等多个领域，合作效果良好，增进了双方相互了解，促进了中国人权能力建设。在与人权高专办合作中，中国不回避敏感问题，与高专办就死刑等问题深入交流，并邀请国际知名专家和中国相关学者举行研讨会。2014 年，中国向新任人权高专扎伊德·侯赛因发出访华邀请，旨在进一步加强与人权高专和人权高专办的合作。中国每年均向人权高专办捐款，已承诺于 2014 年至 2017 年大幅增加捐款额度。今后，中国将与人权高专办开展更多、更丰富的合作。

过去十年，中国先后接待联合国人权理事会任意拘留问题工作组、酷刑问题特别报告员、粮食权问题特别报告员和消除对妇女歧视问题工作组等 4 个特别机制访华，其中任意拘留问题工作组已是第 3 次访华。中国政府结合人权特别机制专家访问要求，安排其走访立法、司法、执法、行政等政府部门，与学术机构、民间组织等进行充分交流，分别赴山东、上海、四川、云南、西藏、新疆等地考察。中国政府官员、学者、民间组织代表等与访华的人权特别机制专家进行了良好互动，增进了他们对中国人权政策和人权状况的了解。2014 年，中国邀请人权理事会外债问题独立专家、健康权问题特别报告员和安全饮用水问题特别报告员访华。

2013 年 12 月 15 日，联合国消除对妇女歧视问题工作组在访华期间走访云南少数民族村寨，听取当地少数民族妇女介绍妇女平等参与基层民主工作。

四

十年来，中国本着开放自信态度，与数十个国家开展了双边人权对话与交流，取得积极成果。

中国重视在平等和相互尊重基础上与西方国家开展人权对话。过去十年，中国与美国开展 5 次人权对话和 5 次法律专家交流，与欧盟举行 16 次人权对话，与英国、德国、瑞士、荷兰等国举行近 30 次人权对话和磋商，与澳大利亚举行 8 次人权对话，中澳还就扶贫、司法、妇女、少数民族权利保护等问题开展了内容丰富的人权技术合作。上述对话与合作在一定程度上增进了中国与西方国家在人权领域的相互了解，有效管控双方分歧，促进了两国政府部门、司法机构、学术团体的深入交流，为双边关系发挥了积极作用。

2014 年 2 月 20 日，外交部副部长李保东和澳大利亚外交贸易部副秘书长伯德共同主持中澳第 15 次人权对话。

中国与发展中国家也保持经常性的人权交流，相互学习借鉴，深化合作。中国与俄罗斯、巴基斯坦、古巴等建立了多边人权事务磋商机制，定期交流各自参与国际人权工作的做法和经验，协调立场和行动，共同维护发展中国家利益。中国多次与老挝、斯里兰卡进行人权交流，介绍中国参加联合国人权理事会、筹备国别人权审查和人权条约履约审议、与联合国人权机制合作等方面做法。中国还与埃及、南非、巴西、墨西哥等就人权领域重要问题保持沟通，交换看法。在交流中，越来越多的发展中国家认同中国人权发展道路，希望学习和借鉴中国做法和经验。

2014 年 2 月 11 日，外交部长王毅在北京与来访的斯里兰卡总统特使、外长佩里斯举行会谈。

中国在南南合作框架下向发展中国家提供力所能及的援助，支持和帮助发展中国家特别是最不发达国家减少贫困，改善民生，保障人民生存权和发展权。目前，中国共向 120 多个发展中国家提供过援助，援建项目超过 2000 个，涉及农业、粮食援助、医疗卫生、教育培训、能源开发、免债等领域。2010 年至 2012 年，中国对外援助金额就达 893.4 亿元人民币。2014 年 3 月西非国家爆发埃博拉疫情以来，中国已向疫区国家提供了 4 批紧急援助，总额达 7.5 亿元人民币，全力保障疫区国家人民的生命权和健康权。

五

“人人得享人权”，是各国人民共同追求的崇高理想，也是中国人民孜孜以求的奋斗目标。然而，世界上不存在放之四海而皆准的人权发展道路，也不存在统一的人权保障模式。在人权问题上，没有最好，只有更好。在国际人权合作中，各国唯有平等相待、相互尊重，才能交融互鉴，共同进步。展望未来，中国在国际人权合作道路上将继续秉持以下原则和目标：

恪守《联合国宪章》宗旨和原则。人权交流与合作必须遵循《联合国宪章》宗旨和原则以及国际关系基本准则，尊重各国独立、主权和领土完整；必须摒弃政治化和双重标准，使人权国际合作回归本真，真正发挥促进和保护人权的作用。

尊重各国自主选择的人权发展道路。“各美其美，和而不同。”各国价值观、历史文化传统、政治制度没有高下优劣之分，人权事业发展必须注重历史和现实、理论和实践的有机结合，必须坚持从实际出发、从人民意愿出发。

通过对话与合作妥善处理人权分歧。东西方人权观念各有千秋，人权实践也千差万别。各国只有开展平等和建设性的对话与合作，才能增进了解，减少分歧，共同寻求促进和保护人权的有效途径。事实证明，在人权问题上，“点名羞辱”解决不了问题，对抗冲突只会破坏互信和国际人权合作基础。

平衡推进人权概念的健康发展。民主和民生是人权的两面，一切人权都是普遍的、不可分割的。经社文权利、公民政治权利和发展权相互依存、同等重要。各国应将人权的普遍性和特殊性结合起来，统筹个人权利和集体权利，兼顾权利和义务。

2014 年是中国“人权入宪”十年。这是中国人权事业发展进程中里程碑式的重要历史事件。值此庄严时刻，我们纪念“人权入宪”，总结人权成就与经验，旨在坚持走中国特色人权发展道路，推动中国人权、民主与法治建设迈上新台阶，为国际人权事业作出更大贡献。

China Has Scored Remarkable Achievements in International Human Rights Cooperation

Li Baodong, Vice Minister of Foreign Affairs

In March 2014, the Second Session of the Tenth National People's Congress of China passed an amendment to the Constitution, articulating the sentence "[t]he State respects and protects human rights". This ushered in a new era in China for protection of human rights by the Constitution. In October 2014, the Fourth Plenary Session of the 18th Central Committee of the Communist Party of China (CPC) set out the strategy for advancing the rule of law on all fronts in China and drew a new blueprint for protecting human rights under the rule of law.

Over the past ten years, China has scored remarkable achievements in the protection of human rights and found a path of development suited to its national conditions. In the meantime, on the basis of equality and mutual trust, tolerance and mutual learning, and win-win cooperation, China has actively participated in international human rights governance, performed in good faith its international human rights duties, and engaged in human rights exchanges and cooperation. Fruitful results have been achieved in these areas.

I

China has actively participated in global human rights governance. China upholds fairness and justice and champions an equitable international human rights system. For three times in a row, China was elected to the UN Human Rights Council with a huge majority of votes, and is now one of the members who have served the Council for the longest time. This reflects the world's recognition of China's achievements and its role in human rights protection.

1. Working for the establishment of a fair and equitable operation mechanism at the UN Human Rights Council

On 9 May 2006, China was elected as one of the first members of the UN Human Rights Council.

The UN Human Rights Council is a major platform for global human rights governance. In 2005, the then UN Secretary-General Kofi Annan submitted a report on UN reform, in which the promotion of human rights, for the first time, was listed as one of the three UN pillars along with security and development. The report maintained that greater emphasis should be placed on human rights in the UN system and the Commission on Human Rights should be upgraded into the Human Rights Council. The reform of UN human rights institutions has since set off. From 2005 to 2011, parties wrestled over the establishment of the Council, its institution building as well as its review mechanism. Thanks to their hard work and close collaboration, China and like-minded countries managed to safeguard the interests of developing countries.

Together with other developing countries, China argued strongly and convincingly during the negotiations on the establishment of the Human Rights Council, achieved the goal of equal representation among regional groups and increasing the number of Asian members, and established the principles of fairness, objectiveness and non-selectivity, thus laying down a good foundation for the work of the Human Rights Council.

In the process of building institutions for the Council, China and like-minded countries unequivocally condemned politicization of human rights issues and interference in other countries' internal affairs under the pretext of human rights. Thus thresholds were introduced for country-specific human rights resolutions. China insisted that the Universal Periodic Review (UPR) of the Human Rights Council must be led by the government concerned, and carried out under the principle of fairness and objectiveness. We made it clear that experts of the Human Rights Special Procedures must be approved by the Human Rights Council and pushed for formulation of a code of conduct for these experts to prevent manipulation and willful acts by Western countries.

During the negotiations on the review of the Human Rights Council, working in concert with other developing countries, China achieved the goal of retaining the status and the voting mechanism of the Human Rights Council and keeping its review mechanism and operational modality generally unchanged, thus defeating the attempt of some Western countries to reopen negotiations on the Council and successfully upholding the outcomes achieved by developing countries during the negotiations on the establishment of the Council and on building its institution.

2. Exerting positive influence on the reform of the UN human rights treaty body system

In the 1980s, the UN started to reform its human rights treaty body system. Many developing countries complained about the overlapping functions of some treaty bodies as well as the problems of politicization and selectivity and urged that the treaty bodies be regulated. Western countries, on the other hand, accused that the treaty bodies were not doing enough to supervise treaty implementation and hoped to expand their mandates and turn them into quasi-judicial organs for human rights.

In 2009, the Office of the UN High Commissioner for Human Rights started to "strengthen the effective functioning of the human rights treaty body system" on its own in absence of full authorization. To pool wisdom, build consensus and play an active role, China worked with Russia and other like-minded countries to urge the UN General Assembly to set up inter-governmental process to reform human rights treaty bodies. Related negotiations were launched in 2012, with reform plan reached in April 2014. The plan demanded enhanced status and role for the states parties, and strengthened capacity building for implementation. It also required the treaty bodies to strictly honor their responsibilities and mandates. The plan accommodated the concerns of developing countries in a balanced way. As a major initiator and driving force, China played an important role in securing favorable outcomes for developing countries in the reform process of the treaty body system.

3. Safeguarding China's interests and advocating China's human rights concepts and practices

China has constructively participated in multilateral human rights meetings such as the meetings of the Third Committee of the UN General Assembly, the UN Human Rights Council and its subsidiary Social Forum and Working Group on the Right to Development. In line with the vision on a harmonious world, the scientific outlook on development, China's "two centenary goals", the Chinese Dream as well as the spirit of the meetings of the 18th CPC Central Committee and the Third and the Fourth Plenary Sessions of the 18th CPC Central Committee, China communicates to the world its policies, measures and achievements related to human rights promotion and protection as well as its positions and views on various human rights issues. In the meantime, China uses data, facts and legal tools to refute the groundless accusations and vilification by some Western countries and anti-China forces, and has won the understanding and support of an increasing number of countries on the issue of China's human rights protection.

In 2004, with the support of developing countries and other friendly countries, China defeated an anti-China resolution sponsored by a few Western countries at the UN Commission on Human Rights, the 11th time in a row. And on the occasion China gave clear expression to its firm stance against using human rights as an excuse to impose political pressure. At the beginning of 2014 when China received the second round of UPR by the Human Rights Council, some Western countries instigated and supported the attempts of anti-China forces to stir up trouble. China composedly responded to the situation and neatly defeated their attempts, thus achieving a great success in the process.

When Western countries ganged up to criticize Belarus, Sri Lanka and other developing countries, China stood by the sides of these developing countries, spoke out for them and clearly expressed its opposition to hijacking human rights issues as a geopolitical tool to interfere in other countries' internal affairs. Working with the Like-Minded Group on Human Rights, China has helped to strengthen the institution building of the Group and contributed to the Group's efforts to air its views and take actions together to fight against the human rights attacks by the West.

China urges the international community to attach equal importance to the economic, social and cultural rights as well as the rights to development, and has pushed forward the discussions about combating racial discrimination, protecting the rights of people of African descent, the rights of migrants and the right to peace, and other issues of concern to developing countries. China supports the Human Rights Council's decision to set up special procedures for safe drinking water, cultural rights, the rights of disabled people, human rights and international solidarity, as well as the promotion of a democratic and equitable international order. China also proposed the convening of special sessions on food security and international financial crisis, which focused international human rights cooperation efforts on the rights to subsistence and development, an issue of gravest concern to developing countries.

II

Over the past ten years, China has fulfilled its international human rights obligations in real earnest and made consistent efforts to strengthen its human rights protection system, mechanism and capacity building.

In light of its obligations as defined by international human rights conventions, China formulates and amends the laws and regulations related to human rights protection, including social laws, administrative laws, criminal laws, and procedural laws. As of September 2014, 242 laws, 738 administrative regulations and about 9,000 local laws and regulations were in force in China, forming a socialist legal system with Chinese characteristics centering around the Constitution.

China has implemented in good faith six core human rights conventions, namely, *International Covenant on Economic, Social and Cultural Rights, Convention on the Elimination of All Forms of Discrimination Against Women, Convention on the Rights of the Child, Convention on the Rights of Persons with Disabilities, Convention on the Elimination of All Forms of Racial Discrimination,* and *Convention Against Torture,* as well as 20 other international conventions related to human rights, such as *Convention on the Prevention and Punishment of the Crime of Genocide, Convention on the Status of Refugees, Convention Concerning Equal Remuneration for Men and Women Workers,* and *Convention Concerning Discrimination in Respect of Employment and Occupation.* In the past ten years, China has received 15 reviews on its implementation of the above six core conventions and its work has gained full recognition from the relevant treaty bodies. In May 2014, China received the second round review on its implementation of *International Covenant on Economic, Social and Cultural Rights.* China's good implementation results, the open-mindedness and confidence of the Chinese delegation, and its outstanding performance in the Question and Answer session were highly acclaimed by the experts of the implementation committee and China was hailed as a good example in the implementation review process. As members of the UN Committee on Economic, Social and Cultural Rights, the Committee on the Elimination of Discrimination Against Women, the Committee on the Elimination of Racial Discrimination, the Committee Against Torture, and the Committee on the Rights of Persons with Disabilities, Chinese experts have constructively participated and played an active role in their work, pushing for these committees to perform their duties impartially.

On 22 October 2013, Mr. Wu Hailong, Special Envoy of the Ministry of Foreign Affairs of China, led a Chinese delegation to attend the second round of UPR by the UN Human Rights Council.

In 2009 and 2013, China received two rounds of UPR. China set up an interagency working group composed of nearly 30 government departments responsible for legislative, administrative and judicial affairs to prepare a high quality *National Report on Human Rights* and widely solicited opinions from NGOs, academic institutions and the general public. Citing facts and data, China communicated to the world its progress, the challenges and its goals, which fully reflected the strong resolve of the Chinese Government and its remarkable achievements in the promotion and protection of human rights. China accepted 42 recommendations from various countries in 2009 and comprehensively followed through on these recommendations in the following four years. In 2013, China accepted 204 recommendations, or 81% of the total, which covered over 20 fields, such as poverty reduction, justice, ethnic groups, religion, and social welfare. This demonstrated the Chinese Government's high sense of responsibility and its open and inclusive attitude.

III

Over the past ten years, China has carried out and expanded in width and depth its practical cooperation with the Office of the High Commissioner for Human Rights.

In 2005, China hosted the 8th visit by the UN High Commissioner for Human Rights, during which the two sides signed their second *Memorandum of Understanding* covering judicial reform, human rights education, implementation of human rights conventions and a variety of other areas. The cooperation achieved fruitful results, deepened mutual understanding and promoted China's human rights capacity building. In the cooperation with the Office of the High Commissioner for Human Rights, China has not evaded sensitive issues. Rather, it has engaged in in-depth exchanges with the Office on death penalty and other issues and invited internationally reputable experts to join in seminars on the relevant topics with Chinese scholars. In 2014, China invited Mr. Zeid Ra'ad Al Hussein, the newly appointed High Commissioner for Human Rights, to visit China with a view to further deepening the cooperation with the High Commissioner and his Office. China makes donations to the Office every year, and has pledged to substantially increase its contributions from 2014 to 2017. China will engage in more activities and various forms of cooperation with the Office in the years to come.

Over the past ten years, China has also received visits by four Special Procedures of the Human Rights Council, including the UN Working Group on Arbitrary Detention, the UN Special Rapporteur on torture, the UN Special Rapporteur on the right to food, and the UN Working Group on the issue of discrimination against women in law and in practice. The UN Working Group on Arbitrary Detention has visited China three times. At the request of the Special Procedures experts, we arranged for them visits to China's legislative, judicial, law enforcement, and administrative departments, exchanges with academic institutions and social organizations, and field trips to Shandong, Shanghai, Sichuan, Yunnan, Tibet and Xinjiang. The sound interactions they had with Chinese officials, scholars, and representatives from social organizations enhanced their understanding of China's human rights policies and situation. In 2014, China also sent invitations to the Independent Expert on the effects of foreign debt, the Special Rapporteur on the right to health, and the Special Rapporteur on the human right to safe drinking water and sanitation for a visit to China.

On 15 December 2013, the UN Working Group on the issue of discrimination against women in law and in practice visited ethnic minority villages in Yunnan and was briefed by an ethnic minority woman on equal participation of women in grass-roots democracy.

IV

Over the past ten years, China has carried out bilateral human rights dialogues and exchanges in an open and confident manner with dozens of countries and achieved positive results.

China attaches great importance to its human rights dialogues with Western countries on the basis of equality and mutual respect. In the past ten years, China has had five human rights dialogues and five legal experts dialogues with the US. There have been 16 dialogues with the EU and a total of nearly 30 dialogues and consultations with the UK, Germany, Switzerland, the Netherlands and other countries. Apart from 8 human rights dialogues, China has also engaged in comprehensive human rights technical cooperation with Australia on poverty relief, justice, women, and protection of the rights of ethnic minorities. The above-mentioned dialogues and cooperation have deepened mutual understanding between China and Western countries in the field of human rights, helped to effectively manage our differences and intensified exchanges between the governments, judiciaries, and academic organizations of the two sides, thus contributing significantly to the growth of bilateral relations.

On 20 February 2014, Mr. Li Baodong, Vice Minister of Foreign Affairs of China, co-chaired the 15th China-Australia human rights dialogue with Ms. Gillian Bird, Deputy Secretary of the Department of Foreign Affairs and Trade of Australia.

China has also maintained regular human rights exchanges with other developing countries to promote mutual learning and deepen cooperation. China has established consultation mechanisms on multilateral human rights affairs with Russia, Pakistan and Cuba to exchange on a regular basis the practices and experience of participating in the international human rights activities, coordinate their stance and actions and jointly uphold the interests of developing countries. China has had a number of human rights exchanges with Laos and Sri Lanka, during which we shared China's experience in participating in the work of the UN Human Rights Council, preparing for UPR and review of human rights conventions implementation and strengthening cooperation with UN human rights institutions. China has also maintained communication and exchange of views with Egypt, South Africa, Brazil, Mexico and other countries on important human rights issues. Through these exchanges, more and more developing countries have come to recognize China's model of human rights development and want to learn from China's practices and experience.

On 11 February 2014, Chinese Foreign Minister Wang Yi held a meeting with Professor Gamini Lakshman Peiris, Presidential Envoy and Cabinet Minister of External Affairs of Sri Lanka.

China has provided within its capacity assistance to developing countries under the framework of the South-South cooperation to support and help these countries, the Least Developed Countries in particular, in their efforts to alleviate poverty, improve people's lives and protect their rights to subsistence and development. Up to now, China has offered assistance to over 120 developing countries and undertaken more than 2,000 projects in areas such as agriculture, food assistance, medical service, education and training, energy development, and debt relief. From 2010 to 2012, China devoted 89.34 billion yuan to foreign assistance. Since the outbreak of Ebola epidemic in West Africa in March 2014, China has made every effort to protect the rights to life and health of the people in the affected countries and provided the affected countries with four tranches of emergency aid worth 750 million yuan in total.

V

"Human rights for all" is a lofty ideal of people across the world and a long-standing aspiration pursued by the Chinese people. There is no one-size-fits-all model for human rights development in the world. Nor is there a single paradigm for human rights protection. When it comes to human rights, there is always room for improvement. In international human rights cooperation, countries must treat each other as equals and respect each other in order to promote mutual learning and achieve common development. Looking ahead, China will stick to the following principles and purposes in international human rights cooperation:

Abide by the purposes and principles of the UN Charter. Human rights exchanges and cooperation must follow the purposes and principles of the UN Charter and the basic norms of international relations. It is essential to respect the independence, sovereignty and territorial integrity of all countries and discard politicization of human rights issues and application of double standards. We must make sure that international human rights cooperation plays its due role and makes a real difference in promoting and protecting human rights.

Respect each country's approach to human rights development. The choice of individual countries should be respected and there can be harmony without uniformity. "Each should enjoy its own beauty and strive for harmony but not sameness with others." The difference between the values, historic and cultural traditions and political systems of countries is not about which is superior. Human rights development must be a process that takes into account both history and reality and stresses both theory and practice. And it must be based on reality and the will of the people.

Resolve human rights-related disputes through dialogue and cooperation. People in the East and the West see and approach the issue of human rights differently.

Only through equal and constructive dialogue and cooperation can countries enhance mutual understanding, bridge their gaps and find an effective way to jointly promote and protect human rights. Experience shows that human rights issues cannot be solved by using "name-and-shame" tactics and confrontation and conflict will only erode mutual trust between countries and undermine the foundation of international human rights cooperation.

Promote the healthy development of human rights in a balanced manner. Democracy and people's livelihood are two sides of human rights. All aspects of human rights are universal and inseparable. The economic, social and cultural rights, civil and political rights, and development rights are interdependent and equally important. Countries need to emphasize both the universality and particularity of human rights and strike a balance between individual rights and collective rights and between rights and obligations.

The year 2014 marks the tenth anniversary of the articulation of the human rights clause in the *Constitution of the People's Republic of China*, a historical event of milestone significance in terms of human rights development in China. At this historic moment, we commemorate the articulation of human rights in the Constitution, and take stock of our achievements and experience. Our mission is to pursue a path of human rights development with Chinese characteristics, bring the development of China's human rights, democracy and rule of law to a new level, and thus make greater contribution to international human rights endeavors.

(original translation by Yang Ji)

中国基本民生保障和基层民主政治建设的重大成就

民政部副部长　顾朝曦

2004年，中国《宪法》第三十三条增加了“国家尊重和保障人权”一款，党和政府作出了一系列保障和改善民生、创新社会治理体制、发展基层民主的重大决策部署，有效维护了人民群众的基本生存权、基本发展权和民主政治权利。

一、完善民生保障托底网络，更好地维护了人民群众的基本生存权

保障和改善人民群众尤其是困难群众的基本生活，是维护人的生存权的首要任务，是反映国家人权状况的重要标志。十年来，通过不断健全完善社会救助体系、提高优待抚恤水平，有效地改善了广大低收入群众、受灾群众、优抚对象等群众的基本生活。

一是健全社会救助制度。在2006年农村五保供养制度实现由农民互助共济向以财政保障为主的历史转型、2007年全面建立农村低保制度、相关专项救助制度不断健全完善的基础上，2014年国务院颁布《社会救助暂行办法》，建立了以最低生活保障、特困人员供养、受灾人员救助、医疗救助、

教育救助、住房救助、就业救助、临时救助等制度为主要内容，与社会力量参与相结合、与其他社会保障制度相衔接，统筹城乡的社会救助体系，将全体公民的基本生活纳入了制度保障。

新疆维吾尔自治区博尔塔拉蒙古自治州博乐市顾力木图街道北郊社区发放低保金。

二是扩大群众受益范围。纳入经常性保障的救助对象从2004年的2693万人增加到2013年年底的7989.4万人，增长了1.97倍。享受医疗救助的人次从673.7万人增加到8485.2万人，增长了11.6倍。26个省份建立了临时救助制度。全国范围内开展了重特大疾病医疗救助试点。享受国家抚恤补助的优抚对象从462万人增加到950.5万人。

三是大幅增加资金投入。城市低保资金从2004年的172.7亿元增加到2013年的756.7亿元，增长了3.4倍。农村低保资金从2006年建制时的47.7亿元增加到866.9亿元，增长了17.17倍。医疗救助资金从3.2亿元增加到257.4亿元，增长了79.44倍。重点优抚对象抚恤补助资金从104.1亿元增加到618.4亿元，增长了4.94倍。

四是着力提高保障水平。建立社会救助标准与物价上涨挂钩的联动机制、重点优抚对象抚恤补助标准自然增长机制。城市低保标准从152元/

人・月增加到373元／人・月，农村低保标准从建制时的850.8元／人・年增加到2434元／人・年。农村五保集中供养标准从1608元／人・年增加到4685元／人・年，分散供养标准从1224.5元／人・年增加到3499元／人・年。连年大幅提高重点优抚对象抚恤补助标准，显著改善了优抚对象生活、医疗、住房等条件。

五是强化自然灾害救助。制订《自然灾害救助条例》，修订《国家自然灾害救助应急预案》，实施《国家综合减灾“十一五”规划》和《国家综合防灾减灾“十二五”规划》，建立救灾准备、应急救助、灾后救助和恢复重建相衔接的灾害救助制度，完善灾害预警和应急响应机制，高效有序应对了汶川特大地震、甘肃舟曲特大山洪泥石流、青海玉树地震、四川芦山地震、南方低温雨雪冰冻等各类重特大自然灾害，确保了灾区社会稳定和人心安定。提高自然灾害救助标准，增加过渡性生活救助项目，统一不同灾害农产和倒损住房恢复重建补助标准。建立了从中央到地方、覆盖多灾易灾地区的救灾物资储备网络，将卫星遥感等科技应用于灾害监测评估，形成了常态减灾和非常态救灾有效结合的机制。

六是做好生活无着流浪乞讨人员救助。对生活无着的流浪乞讨人员，按照“自愿受助、无偿救助”，由政府提供基本的食物、住宿和突发疾病医疗等服务。出台了流浪未成年人救助保护政策，开展了“接送流浪孩子回家”、“流浪孩子回校园”等专项活动，开展了未成年人社会保护试点工作，强化了对未成年人流浪现象的源头治理，实现了城市街面基本无流浪未成年人的目标。

二、推进社会福利服务，不断增进了特殊群体的基本发展权

向老年人、残疾人、孤残儿童等特殊群体提供社会福利服务，是落实人的发展权的必然要求。十年来，国家不断扩大社会福利惠及范围，提高社会福利服务水平，有力推动了社会福利服务事业的发展。

在老年人福利服务方面，推进建立了以法规政策为保障，以居家为基础、社区为依托、机构为补充，资金保障与服务保障相匹配、公办与民营相

结合的社会养老服务体系。对于无劳动能力、无生活来源、无法定赡养人的老年人，由政府负责保障基本生活，提供无偿的养老服务。对于 80 周岁以上的老年人，全国已有 19 个省份建立了高龄补贴制度。对于生活困难的老年人，全国已有 22 个省份建立了养老服务补贴制度。一些省份还探索建立了专项护理补贴制度。采取政策扶持、民办公助、公建民营、购买服务等方式，积极鼓励和引导民间资本参与社会养老服务发展，逐步使社会力量成为发展养老服务业的主体。2013 年起，中央财政还安排专项彩票公益金支持"农村幸福院"建设，提升了农村互助式养老服务水平。养老服务设施建设取得重大成绩，养老机构数由 2004 年年底的 3.79 万个增加到 2013 年年底的 4.25 万个，增长了 12.4%；床位数由 139.5 万张增加到 493.7 万张，增长了 2.54 倍；每千名老年人拥有养老床位数达到 25 张，增长了 2.5 倍；老年人日间照料服务覆盖近 50% 的城市社区和 30% 以上的农村社区。

广州市老人院的工作人员与在院老人谈心。

在孤儿保障方面，建立了孤儿国家保障制度，将孤儿抚养、教育、医疗、康复、成年后就业、住房等纳入国家保障范围。定期向艾滋病病毒感染儿童发放基本生活费。制定实施了规范宗教界收留孤儿、弃婴的政策。着眼于逐步把事实上无家庭抚养儿童分类纳入保障范围，在部分地区开展了适度普惠型儿童福利制度试点。实施了孤残儿童手术康复"明天计划"等一系列儿童福利项目，先后为 8 万多名孤残儿童开展了手术矫治和康复训练。

西安市儿童福利院小小运动会。

在残疾人福利服务方面，国家制定了加快推进残疾人社会保障体系和服务体系建设的指导意见，全国有 17 个省份建立了困难残疾人生活补贴制度，11 个省份建立了重度残疾人护理补贴制度。全国民政系统共创办精神卫生福利机构 261 所，床位 7.4 万张，长期在院人员 6 万余人。出台了支持福利企业发展的税收优惠政策，全国 1.8 万个福利企业吸纳残疾职工 53.9 万人。

三、广泛动员城乡居民参与社会治理，依法扩大了人民群众的民主政治权利

保证人民群众依法行使民主选举、民主决策、民主管理和民主监督权，建立和完善中国共产党领导下的多元主体共同治理机制，是实现人民当家做主、维护人民民主政治权利的重要内容。十年来，通过不断完善党组织领导的充满活力的基层群众自治机制，创新城乡社区治理机制，支持社会组织健康发展、发挥积极作用，人民群众的选举权、知情权、参与权、表达权、监

督权等得到依法保障。

在基层群众自治方面，修订了《村民委员会组织法》，规范了民主选举程序，完善了选民登记、民主议事、民主管理和民主监督制度。依法保障群众的选举权，制定了《村民委员会选举规程》，全国有98%以上的村委会和30%以上的居委会依法推行了直接选举，村民平均参选率达到95%，一些城市社区居委会的直选比例达到了100%。无记名投票、公开计票、秘密写票普遍实行，竞职演讲、治村演说广泛推行。落实村（居）民会议、村（居）民代表会议、村（居）民议事会等制度，对涉及基层群众利益的重要问题进行讨论决议，实现了人民群众有序参与公共事务管理和决策。进一步扩大村务公开，全国90%以上的县（市、区）编制了统一的村务公开目录，实现了村务公开由事后公开向事前、事中延伸；全国91%的村建立了村务公开机制，采取公开栏、明白纸、听证会、广播等各种形式公开村务政务；完善村民评议村干部和财务监督制度，更好地落实了群众的民主监督权。截至2013年年底，全国共有村委会58.9万个、成员232.3万名；居委会9.46万个、成员48.4万名。

江苏省苏州市开展“小巷里的实话实说”。

在创新社区治理体制机制方面，以满足居民群众需求、扩大居民参与为导向，不断健全社区服务体系，构建社区多元主体参与机制。全国城市社区综合服务设施覆盖率从2004年年底的10.3%提高到2013年年底的75.4%。日间照料、康复照料、四点半课堂、慈善超市等特色服务不断普及，社区信息化建设普遍开展。加快推进社会工作专业人才队伍建设，建立了社会工作人才职业水平评价制度，以社区为依托，逐步开展专业社会工作服务。大力发展社区公益性、服务性、互助性组织，推行社区社会组织社区备案制，促进了社区建设主体多元化，形成了以社区党组织为核心、社区自治组织为主导、社区居民为主体、社区社会组织和驻区单位共同参与的社区治理体制。

在社会组织发展方面，着眼于建立政社分开、权责明确、依法自治的现代社会组织体制，优化了社会组织发展环境，出台了政府向社会力量购买服务的指导政策，2012年起中央财政每年列支2亿元资金购买社会组织服务。改善行业协会商会类、科技类、公益慈善类、城乡社区服务类社会组织登记体制，取消业务主管部门审批，实行登记部门直接登记，全国26个省份开展了直接登记工作，截至2013年年底已直接登记社会组织2万个。简化社会组织登记程序，取消了全国性社会团体分支机构和代表机构的登记、变更、注销，取消了在华外国商会设立的前置许可，将异地商会和非公募基金会的登记权限下放到县级登记部门。推进行业协会与行政机关脱钩，完善公益性捐赠税前扣除等优惠政策，政社关系进一步理顺，社会组织发展空间进一步拓展。指导社会组织加强信用建设、提升公信力，支持社会组织提高开展活动、提供服务的能力，开展了行业协会行业自律与诚信创建活动、民办非企业单位塑造品牌与服务社会活动，解决了社会组织人才队伍建设的相关问题。社会组织数量从2004年年底的28.9万个增加到2013年年底的54.7万个，人民群众和社会各方有更多渠道和机会依托社会组织理性表达利益诉求，有序参与民主协商、社会治理和公共服务。

回首过去的十年，党和政府始终坚持人民在改革和发展中的主体地位，坚持把保障和改善民生作为发展的根本目的，坚持完善和落实相关法律法规制度，为保障人民的基本生存权、发展权和民主政治权利提供了有力保证。

我们相信，随着中国特色社会主义制度的优越性不断发挥，随着中国经济社会持续快速发展，人民群众的基本权益将得到更好保障，中国的人权事业将取得更大的进步，不断为全面建成小康社会、实现中华民族伟大复兴的中国梦汇聚正能量。

Major Achievements in Basic Livelihood Security and Grass-Roots Democracy in China

Gu Zhaoxi, Vice Minister of Civil Affairs

Since "[t]he State respects and protects human rights" was added to Article 33 of the *Constitution of the People's Republic of China* in 2004, the Communist Party of China and the Chinese government have made a series of major policy arrangements for protecting and improving people's livelihood, innovating the system of social governance and promoting democracy at the grass-roots level, effectively protecting people's fundamental rights to subsistence, development and democracy.

I. The social safety net has been further improved for better protection of people's basic right to subsistence.

Protecting and improving people's basic livelihood, particularly that of poor people, is the primary task in protecting the right to subsistence and an important indicator of human right protection. In the past decade, continuous improvement of the social assistance system and higher state pension and preferential treatment subsidies have effectively improved the basic living of low-income people, disaster victims and beneficiaries of the state pension or preferential treatment subsidies.

First, the social assistance system has been improved. In 2006, the five-guarantee system (guarantee of food, clothing, housing, medical care and burial services/ education for the elderly, disabled and minors in the countryside who have lost the ability to work, have no source of income and have no people to support them) went through a historic transformation from mutual aid among peasants to mainly relying on fiscal support. In 2007, an extensive subsistence security system for people in the rural areas was established. On the basis of these and the improvement of other special relief mechanisms, the State Council promulgated the *Interim Measures for Social Assistance* in 2014. A social assistance system was thus set up, consisting of minimum living security, support for extremely poor people, assistance for people affected by disaster, medical assistance, assistance in education, housing and employment, and temporary assistance. Participation of social forces in such assistance is encouraged. The system ties in nicely with other social security systems and covers people in both urban and rural areas, thus providing institutional guarantee for all citizens' basic livings.

Subsistence allowance was handed out at Beijiao Community, Gulimutu Subdistrict, Bole, Bortala Mongol Autonomous Prefecture, Xinjiang Uygur Autonomous Region.

Second, the range of beneficiaries has been expanded. People supported by regular assistance increased from 26.93 million in 2004 to 79.894 million by the end of 2013, an increase of 1.97 times. People who enjoyed medical assistance increased from 6.737 million to 84.852 million, a 11.6-fold increase. Temporary assistance mechanism has been set up in 26 provinces. Medical assistance for major and critical diseases has been provided on pilot basis throughout the country. Beneficiaries of state pension or preferential treatment subsidies increased from 4.62 million to 9.505 million.

Third, investment has been increased by a large margin. Funds for urban minimum living security increased from 17.27 billion yuan in 2004 to 75.67 billion in 2013, an increase of 3.4 times. Investment in rural minimum living security increased from 4.77 billion in 2006 when the system was created to 86.69 billion, an increase of 17.17 times. The medical assistance increased from 0.32 billion to 25.74 billion, an increase of 79.44 times. State pension and preferential treatment subsidies for key entitled groups increased from 10.41 billion to 61.84 billion, an increase of 4.94 times.

Fourth, the amount provided in social assistance has been increased with concentrated effort. Amounts provided in social assistance is linked to inflation and a mechanism is in place to increase automatically of state pensions and preferential treatment subsidies for key entitled groups. Minimum living allowance in urban areas has increased from 152 yuan per month to 373 yuan and that in rural areas from 850.8 yuan per year to 2,434 yuan per year. Allowance provided under the system of five guarantees for those living in government facilities has increased from 1,608 yuan to 4,685 yuan per year while that for those living in separate households has increased from 1,224.5 yuan to 3,499 yuan per year. State pension and preferential treatment subsidies for key entitled groups have also increased significantly for consecutive years, thus obviously improving the beneficiaries' living, health care and housing conditions, among other things.

Fifth, assistance for people affected by disaster has been consolidated. *Regulations for Natural Disaster Relief* has been formulated, *National Natural Disasters Relief Emergency Plan* has been revised and *National 11th Five-Year Plan on Comprehensive Disaster Reduction* and *National 12th Five-Year Plan on Comprehensive Disaster Reduction* have been implemented. A disaster relief system that connects disaster preparedness, emergency assistance, post-disaster relief and recovery and reconstruction has been put in place, with rather full-fledged early warning and emergency response mechanisms. The system operated efficiently in response to major natural disasters, such the Wenchuan earthquakes, the mudslide at Zhouqu, Gansu Province, the earthquakes at Yushu, Qinghai Province and Lushan, Sichuan Province, and extreme freezing rain and snow in South China, which helps to stabilize situation and reassure the public in disaster-stricken areas. Amounts paid in this form of assistance have also been increased, with additional interim items for living assistance and criteria of assistance for affected agricultural produces and rebuilding of collapsed or damaged houses have been unified. A network of reserved disaster relief supplies involving both central and local governments and covering all disaster-prone regions is in place. Technologies, such as satellite remote sensing, are used to monitor and evaluate disasters. Disaster reduction at normal times and relief after disasters are thus effectively combined.

Sixthly, best efforts are made to help vagrants and beggars without any assured source of living. The government provides services such as basic food, sheltering, and emergency medical treatment for free for these people, who may choose to accept the assistance or not. A policy to assist and protect vagrant minors has been adopted. Special campaigns have been conducted to "take vagrant children home" and "bring vagrant children back to school". Social protection of minors has been piloted and action has been taken to address the root cause of vagrancy of minors, achieving the objective of no vagrant minors in urban streets.

II. Social welfare service has been promoted to advance special groups' right to basic development.

Providing social welfare services for special groups such as the elderly, people with disabilities, orphans and children with disabilities is a necessary requirement out of the right to development. In the last decade, the coverage of social welfare service has expanded and the level of service has increased, leading to great progress in the development of social welfare services.

With regard to senior citizens, a social old-age service system with family caring as its basis to be complemented by community caring and supported by institution caring is promoted. The system enjoys legal and policy support, matches financial input with services and involves both public and private providers. The basic living of senior citizens who have lost the ability to work, with no source of income or legal support person is secured by the government, which also provides gratuitous old-age services. Nineteen provinces have instituted subsidies for people at the age of 80 and above. Twenty-two provinces have special allowances for the elderly with financial difficulties to enjoy old-age care. Some provinces have explored the provision of special allowances for nursing service. Various ways of policy support, public-private partnership and purchase of service are used to guide private capital in providing social care for the elderly so that private entities will gradually become the main providers of old-age services. Since 2013, arrangements have been made to use special lottery fund from the budget of the central government to support the construction of rural nursing homes, elevating the level of mutual care services for the old in rural areas. Great achievements have been made in the construction of facilities for caring of the old, as nursing homes increased by 12.4% from 37,900 by the end of 2004 to 42,500 by the end of 2013 and available beds increased by 254% from 1.395 million to 4.937 million. There are 25 nursing-home beds per 1,000 old people, an increase of 2.5 times. Nearly 50% urban communities and over 30% rural ones are covered by day care service for senior citizens.

Employees of a nursing home in Guangzhou had a chat with residents of the home.

A security system for orphans has been set up, covering upbringing, education, medical services, rehabilitation, employment in adulthood and housing. The government provides regular basic living allowance for children living with HIV. A policy to regulate the adoption of orphans and abandoned babies by religious organizations has been developed and implemented. In some areas a universal child welfare system is being piloted with a view to gradually expand security coverage to children who effectively have no family support. A series of welfare programs have been carried out. For example, the "Project Tomorrow" has benefited over 80,000 orphans with disabilities with corrective surgery and rehabilitation.

Mini games are held in Xi'an Children's Welfare Center, Shaanxi Province.

With regard to persons with disabilities, guiding opinions have been issued to advance the construction of a social security system and service system for them. Seventeen provinces provide living allowances for people with disabilities who are in financial hardship and 11 provinces provide nursing allowances for people with severe disabilities. The civil affairs system in the whole country oversees 261 social welfare institutes for people with mental health problems, with 74,000 beds and over 60,000 long-term inpatients. The government has adopted preferential tax policies to support the development of welfare enterprises. There are 18,000 welfare enterprises in China, providing 539,000 jobs for people with disabilities.

Ⅲ. Residents of both urban and rural areas are mobilized to take part in social governance and people's democratic and political rights have been expanded according to law.

For the people to manage their own affairs and safeguard their democratic and political rights, it is important to make sure that the people exercise their rights to democratic elections, democratic decision-making, democratic management and democratic supervision according to law and to set up and improve the pluralistic co-governance mechanism under the leadership of the Communist Party of China. In the last decade, the people's rights to election, information, participation, expression and supervision have been protected according to law by improving the vigorous self-governance led by CPC at the grass-roots level, innovating community governance mechanisms in urban and rural areas and supporting the healthy development and positive role of social organizations.

With regard to grass-roots self-governance, the *Organic Law of the Villagers' Committees* has been revised to standardize the democratic elections procedures and improve the systems of registration of the voters, democratic consultation, democratic management and democratic supervision. *Rules for Villagers' Committee Elections* has been formulated to protect people's right to elections. Over 98% villagers' committees and over 30% residents' committees in the country hold direct elections in accordance with the law. Over 95% villagers, on average, participate in elections and the percentage of direct elections for residents' committees reached 100% in some cities. Anonymous voting, public counting of ballots and privacy in ballot writing are a general practice and campaigning speeches are widely introduced. Institutions such as villagers'/residents' assembly, villagers/residents representatives meeting and villagers/residents consultative councils have been put in place to deliberate and decide on important matters concerning the interests of people at the grass-roots level, thus realizing an orderly participation by the people in public affairs management and decision-making. The level of openness of village affairs has increased. Over 90% counties (cities, or districts) in the country have compiled village affairs directories, making the handling of village affairs more open with disclosure of information before, during and after events. 91% villages have mechanisms in place to make village affairs known to villagers by way of bulletin board, hearing and broadcasting. Mechanisms for the assessment and financial supervision of village officials by the villagers have been improved, further facilitating the exercise of people's right to democratic supervision. By the end of 2013, there were 589,000 villagers' committees with 2,323,000 committee members and 94,600 resident's committees with 484,000 members in the country.

The "Tell it like it is in the alleys" event in Suzhou, Jiangsu Province.

To innovate community governance, a pluralistic participation mechanism has been created to meet the needs of residents and increase participation from the residents with continuously improved community services. The coverage of comprehensive service facilities in urban communities areas increased from 10.3% at the end of 2004 to 75.4% at the end of 2013. Featured services such as day care, rehabilitation care, 4:30 pm classes, charity stores have been rolled out. Information technology has been widely applied at the community level. Efforts have been made to increase human resources for social work by, inter alia, establishing a system to evaluate the vocational proficiency of social workers and providing specialized social services based on the communities. Public welfare organizations, service organizations and mutual help clubs have been vigorously developed. Community social organizations are registered in the community. With more parties involved, a community governance system has come into being with the CPC as the core, community self-governance organizations playing a leading role, community residents as the main players and social organizations and work units in the relevant community also taking part.

With regard to the development of social organizations, the focus is to build modern social organizations that are independent of the government, have clear rights and responsibilities and are autonomous in accordance with the laws. The environment has been optimized for the development of social organizations. The policy to guide government purchase of services from social organizations has been adopted and since 2012 the central finance budgets 200 million yuan annually for such service. Registration of such social organizations as industry associations, chambers of commerce, and those in the fields of technology, public welfare and charity as well as urban and rural community services has been streamlined. Direct registration with the registration authority now suffices and approval by the departments in charge of the relevant industries is no longer required. Twenty-six provinces accept direct registration and by the end of 2013, 20,000 social organizations had been registered in this way. The registration procedure has been simplified and branches and representative offices of national social organizations are no longer required to register, change or cancel their organizations. Pre-approval is no longer required for the setting up of foreign chamber of commerce in China. Registration of foreign chambers of commerce and non-public fund has been delegated to county-level registration department. Industry associations have been pushed to dissociate themselves from government departments. Preferential policies such as pre-tax deduction for public welfare donations have been improved. The relationship between government and social organizations has been further sorted out and social organizations now have greater room for development. Social organizations are guided to increase their credibility and are given support to strengthen their ability to carry out activities and provide services. Industry associations endeavor to strengthen self-discipline and enhance credibility and private non-enterprise organizations to establish brand image by providing social services. Problems related to human resources development have been solved. The number of social organizations rose from 289,000 at the end of 2004 to 547,000 at the end of 2013. People now have more channels and opportunities to express their interests and appeals through social organizations and to participate in democratic consultation, social governance and public services in an orderly manner.

Over the last decade, the Party and the government have always insisted that the people should play a main role in reform and development and that protecting and improving people's livelihood is the ultimate purpose of development. Consistent efforts have been made to improve and implement related laws and regulations thus providing a powerful guarantee for the exercise of people's fundamental rights to subsistence, development and democracy and other political rights. We believe that with the superiority of socialism with Chinese characteristics being given full play and with the sustained rapid socio-economic development in China, the fundamental interests and rights of the people will be better protected and even greater progress will be made in human rights protection, thus contributing to the building of a moderately well-off society in an all-round way and the realization of the Chinese Dream of great national rejuvenation.

(original translation by Yang Shouxun)

促进就业，加强保障，维护劳动者合法权益

人力资源和社会保障部副部长　王晓初

2004年，"国家尊重和保障人权"写入中国《宪法》。在党中央、国务院的坚强领导下，原劳动和社会保障部、人力资源和社会保障部制定完善法律法规，及时出台政策措施，千方百计保民生、促就业，保护劳动者权益，扩大社会保障覆盖面，努力实现尊重和保障人权，取得丰硕成果。

一、实施就业促进法，促进劳动者充分就业

中国有超过13亿人口，是一个人口和劳动力大国，就业工作任务艰巨。中国政府始终高度重视就业问题，提出就业是民生之本、安国之策，把促进充分就业作为经济社会发展的优先目标，实施就业优先战略和更加积极的就业政策。主要采取了以下措施：

一是2008年实施了《就业促进法》。从法律上确立了促进就业的政策体系、制度保障和长效机制，明确了就业援助和公共就业服务制度，还对实现公平就业、消除就业歧视、保障各类群体的平等就业权利作出了具体规定。

二是坚持通过促进经济增长扩大就业，实现经济增长与扩大就业的良性互动。把稳增长、保就业作为经济运行合理区间的下限。既通过产业转型升

级创造更多高质量的就业岗位，也鼓励大力发展劳动密集型的第三产业，鼓励发展个体、私营、外商投资等多种所有制经济，注重发展中小企业和微型企业，千方百计扩大就业岗位，促进劳动者多渠道、多形式就业。

“春风行动”招聘会现场。

三是实施积极的就业政策，支持劳动者就业创业。 2002年以来，中国制定实施了积极的就业政策，主要内容包括：通过税费减免、场地安排、小额担保贷款及财政贴息等措施，积极扶持劳动者自谋职业、自主创业；通过给予定额税收减免、发放社会保险补贴、小额担保贷款贴息等措施，鼓励企业更多吸纳就业；通过开发公益性岗位，给予社会保险补贴、岗位补贴等措施，健全就业援助制度，帮扶就业困难人员和零就业家庭人员实现就业再就业。

积极开展零就业家庭就业援助活动。

四是加强人力资源市场建设，提供公共就业和人才服务。中国已逐步建立起完善的公共就业和人才服务体系，初步形成了市、区县、街道（乡镇）、社区四级公共就业服务网络，对城乡劳动者实行免费就业服务。

五是加强职业培训，提高劳动者就业创业能力。围绕构建劳动者终身职业培训体系，依托技工学校、就业训练中心、企业培训机构以及民办职业培训机构，大规模开展就业技能培训、岗位技能提升培训和创业培训。不断完善职业培训和技能鉴定补贴政策，创新技能人才培养模式，提高职业培训的针对性、有效性，畅通技能人才职业发展的通道。

职业培训指导实训基地进行技能培训。

十年来，我们妥善安置了3000多万国有企业下岗职工，成功应对了国际金融危机对就业的严重冲击，有效缓解了新一轮青年就业高峰的压力，对此国际社会给予了比较高的评价。国际劳工组织认为，中国积极的就业政策是现代就业理念、世界各国经验与中国实际的良好结合。到2013年年末，中国就业人员达76977万人，其中城镇就业人员38240万人。三产业就业人员的比重由2002年的50：21.4：28.6调整到2013年31.4：30.1：38.5，城镇登记失业率为4.05%。每年开展政府补贴性培训2000多万人次。

二、切实维护劳动者合法权益，保持劳动关系总体和谐稳定

中国政府非常重视劳动者工作中的权益保护，通过完善立法、加强执法和建立新型的劳动关系调整机制，维护广大劳动者的合法权益。

一是完善法制。继《劳动法》之后，出台了《劳动合同法》、《就业促进法》、《劳动争议调解仲裁法》、《社会保险法》以及《劳动保障监察条例》、《劳动合同法实施条例》、《职工带薪年休假条例》、《女职工劳动保护特别规定》、《劳务派遣暂行规定》等配套法律法规和规章。中国已初步形成了以《劳动法》为核心，内容涉及工时、休息休假、工资支付、禁止使用童工、女职工和未成年工特殊劳动保护、劳动保障监察、劳动争议调解仲裁等领域的劳动保障法律体系，较好地保护了劳动者的合法权益。

二是建立适应社会主义市场经济体制的劳动关系调整机制，努力实现劳动关系的和谐稳定。劳动合同制度全面实施，集体协商和集体合同制度稳步推进。协调劳动关系三方机制建设不断加强。截至2013年年底，全国各类企业劳动合同签订率达到88.2%。劳动人事争议调解仲裁制度建设取得新进展，机构队伍和基础保障建设加快。基层调解组织组建率达60%，地市级和县级仲裁院建院率分别达到81%和71%，仲裁结案率保持在90%以上。

三是加强劳动保障监察执法。劳动保障监察网格化、网络化管理覆盖率稳步提高。劳动保障监察工作体系不断完善，制定了重大违法案件查处、跨地区案件协查、劳动保障监察执法与刑事司法衔接等制度。劳动保障监察执法能力不断加强，机构组建率达97.8%，投诉、举报案件结案率达到99%以上。

三、推进城乡社会保障体系建设，扩大社会保障覆盖面

《宪法》明确规定，国家建立健全同经济发展水平相适应的社会保障制度，将社会保障作为人人应当享有的基本权利。改革开放以来，特别是近十年来，中国政府不断深化社会保障制度改革，确定适应社会主义市场经济体制的制度模式，建立了以社会保险、社会救助、社会福利和住房保障为基础，以基本养老、基本医疗、最低生活保障制度为重点，以慈善事业、商业保险

为补充的社会保障体系。其中，社会保险包括养老保险、医疗保险、失业保险、工伤保险、生育保险五项。中国政府作出不懈努力，坚持“广覆盖、保基本、多层次、可持续”的方针，社会保险事业取得了突破性进展。集中体现在以下方面：

一是制度建设取得突破性进展，体系框架基本形成。2003 年建立农村医疗救助制度；2004 年试点建立新型农村合作医疗制度；2005 年建立城镇居民医疗救助制度；2007 年建立城镇居民基本医疗保险制度，同年建立农村最低生活保障制度；2009 年试点建立新型农村社会养老保险制度；2010 年颁布《社会保险法》；2011 年启动城镇居民社会养老保险制度试点；2012 年《社会保障“十二五”规划纲要》颁布，提出“十二五”末基本实现新农保和城居保全覆盖。

农村居民积极参加新型农村社会养老保险。

二是覆盖面迅速扩大，越来越多的人享受到社会保障。社会保障的覆盖范围，从城镇扩大到农村，从国有企业扩大到各类用人单位及灵活就业人员，从各单位职工扩大到城乡居民。截至 2013 年年底，基本养老、基本医疗（含城乡统筹）、失业、工伤、生育五项保险参保人数分别达到 81968 万人、

57322 万人、16417 万人、19917 万人和 16392 万人。基本医疗保险（含新型农村合作医疗）参保总人数超过 13 亿。同时，集中解决了一批历史遗留问题：先后将 800 多万关闭破产企业退休人员、500 多万集体所有制企业等职工、300 多万国有企业“老工伤”人员（指 2004 年《工伤保险条例》实施前认定工伤、由企业自行保障的职工）分别纳入了医疗、养老、工伤保险制度。实行社会保险补贴政策，帮助下岗失业人员实现再就业。对于农村进城务工人员，先后实施两期“平安计划”，近 7200 万名农民工被纳入工伤保险，职业伤害风险得以化解。

三是不断加大政府投入，逐步提高社会保险待遇水平。2005 ～ 2013 年，中国政府连续九年调整企业退休人员基本养老金，2013 年月人均水平达到 1856 元；城乡居民基本养老金月人均额有大幅度提高，2013 年达到 82 元。逐步提高基本医疗保险报销比例和最高支付限额，逐年提高城乡居民医保的财政补助标准，2013 年达到每人每年 280 元，全面开展城乡居民医保门诊统筹工作。失业、工伤、生育保险待遇均有明显提高。

参保职工领取社会保障卡。

四是社会保障公共服务体系初步形成，服务网络逐步延伸。在完善制度、增加投入的同时，大力加强社会保障管理服务体系建设，确保各项社保惠民政策能够及时准确得到落实。

在过去十年中，中国的人力资源和社会保障事业取得了长足发展，但今后一段时期内，城镇化进程加速、人口老龄化加剧都将给中国的就业、劳动关系和社会保障带来巨大挑战，我们的工作任重而道远。中国政府将继续牢牢抓住民生这一关键点，加大工作力度，创新工作方法，推动中国的人力资源和社会保障事业取得新发展，为实现中华民族伟大复兴的中国梦作出积极贡献。

Promoting Employment, Enhancing Security and Protecting Laborers' Lawful Rights and Interests

Wang Xiaochu, Vice Minister of Human Resources and Social Security

In 2004, that "[t]he State respects and protects human rights" was articulated in the *Constitution of the People's Republic of China*. Under the strong leadership of the Central Committee of the Communist Party of China and the State Council, the then Ministry of Labor and Social Security and its successor Ministry of Human Resources and Social Security have worked to formulate and improve laws and regulations and adopted policies in a timely manner to protect people's livelihood, facilitate employment and safeguard the rights and interests of laborers. The coverage of social security programs have been expanded and human rights are respected and protected. Great results have been achieved in the relevant areas.

I. Implementing the *Employment Promotion Law* and facilitating full employment.

With 1.3 billion people, China is a big country in terms of population and labor force. Employment is a big task. The Chinese Government always attaches great importance to the employment issue and regards it as the basis for people's well being and the guarantee for the country's stability. The promotion of full employment is thus a priority in socio-economic development. The government implements a strategy to prioritize employment and more proactive employment polices. The major measures are as follows.

First, the *Employment Promotion Law* was promulgated in 2008. Policies, institutional guarantees and long-term mechanism to promote employment were thus established in law. The law institutes employment assistance mechanism and public employment service and contains detailed provisions on equal employment opportunities, elimination of employment discrimination and protection of equal employment rights of all groups of people.

Second, employment opportunities are increased through the promotion of economic growth, achieving a sound interaction between economic growth and employment. Steady economic growth and employment security are regarded as the bottom line of the reasonable range for economic dynamics. Good employment opportunities are created via industry transformation and upgrading. The labor-intensive tertiary industry is encouraged, so are enterprises with different types of ownership such as self-employment, private businesses and foreign invested companies. Development of SMEs and mini enterprises is emphasized. All these measures are aimed at increasing jobs and facilitating employment through different channels and in different forms.

Campaign Spring Breeze: a job fair for migrant workers.

Third, proactive employment policies are adopted to support people in finding a job or starting their own business. Since 2002, China has implemented proactive employment policies as follows: supporting independent search for a job and self-employment with tax and fee deductions and exemptions, venue facility, guaranteed micro loans and fiscal discounts; encouraging enterprises to create more job opportunities with quota tax relief, social insurance subsidies and interest discount for guaranteed micro loans; improving employment assistance system and helping people with difficulties in finding an employment and zero-employment families by offering public welfare positions and providing social insurance subsides and post allowances.

Activities are carried out to provide employment assistance for zero-employment families.

Fourth, human resource markets are further developed and public employment and human resources service are provided. China has gradually established a public employment and human resources service system. A four-tiered employment service network covering cities, counties, subdistricts/towns and communities has been initially created to offer free employment service for urban and rural laborers.

Fifth, vocational training is strengthened to enhance the employability and

entrepreneurial skills of the unemployed. With the objective of creating a life-long vocational training system, vocational schools, employment training centers, corporate training institutions and private vocational training institutions are mobilized to provide training on employability enhancement, improvement of job skills as well as business startup. The subsidies polices on vocational training and skills evaluation continue to be improved. New modes of training talented workers are created. The vocational training is becoming more targeted and effective. The channels for skilled workers to develop their career are unblocked.

Skills training is provided at vocational training centers.

In the past ten years, we have provided jobs for over 30 million laid-off workers of state-owned enterprises, successfully dealt with the huge impact of the international financial crisis and effectively mitigated the pressure of a new youth employment peak. The international society gives high praise to China's efforts. The International Labor Organization regards China's employment policies as a nice combination of modern employment concepts, best practices of various countries and China's own situation. At the end of 2013, China had a workforce of 769.77 million. Among them, 382.40 million were from cities and towns. The ratio of workers in the three industries changed from 50:21.4:28.6 in 2002 to 31.4:30.1:38.5 in 2013. Urban registered unemployment rate was 4.05%. Government-funded training programs were offered to more than 20 million people each year.

Ⅱ. Safeguarding laborers' lawful rights and interests and maintaining harmony and stability of labor relations.

The Chinese Government attaches great importance to and protect laborers' rights and interests at work via improved legislation, strengthened law enforcement and establishing new adjustment mechanisms of labor relations.

First, the legal system has been improved. Following the *Labor Law*, the Chinese Government has promulgated *Labor Contract Law, Law on Promotion of Employment, Law on Labor-Disputes Mediation and Arbitration*, and *Social Insurance Law,* as well as *Regulation of Labor Insurance and Supervision, Implementation Regulation for Labor Contract, Implementation Measures for Paid Annual Leave for Employees, Special Provisions for the Work Protection of Female Employees,* and *Interim Provisions on Labor Dispatch.* Based on *Labor Law,* a legal system centering on the *Labor Law* and consisting of rules on working hours, rest and vacation, salary payment, ban on child labor, special protection for female workers and underage workers, labor security inspection and mediation and arbitration of labor disputes has basically taken shape. Laborers' lawful rights and interests are thus well protected.

Second, a labor relations adjustment mechanism suited to the socialistic market economy has been established and efforts have been made to achieve harmony and stability in labor relations. The labor contract system has been universally implemented and institutions of collective consultation and collective contract have steadily developed. The tripartite coordination mechanism has been strengthened. By the end of 2013, the labor contract signing rate of all types of enterprises was 88.2%. New progress has been made in developing the system of mediation and arbitration of labor disputes, with more people and basic institutions in place and increasing. 60% townships have set up mediation organizations and 81% prefectures and 71% counties have court of arbitration. The arbitration settlement rate has been kept at

90% and above.

Third, inspection and law enforcement of labor security is strengthened. The grid and network management of labor security have expanded steadily. The working system of labor security inspection has been improved. Rules concerning investigation into serious cases of illegality, cross-regional assistance in case investigation, connection between labor security inspection and enforcement and criminal justice have been set. The law enforcement capacity is constantly improving. 97.8% labor security inspection teams have been established, and over 99% complaints and accusations have been addressed and concluded.

III. Further developing urban and rural social security systems and expanding social security coverage.

The Constitution explicitly states that "[t]he State establishes and improves the social security system fitting in with the level of economic development" and regards social security as a basic right for everyone. Since Reform and Opening up, especially in the past ten years, the Chinese Government has continued to deepen reform of the social security system and set up a system suited to the socialistic market economy. The system thus established is based on social insurance, social assistance, social welfare and housing security, focuses on basic endowment insurance, basic medical insurance and minimum living allowances supplemented with charities and commercial insurance. The social insurance system includes endowment insurance, medical insurance, unemployment insurance, employment injury insurance and maternity insurance. In line with the guideline of "wide and multi-leveled coverage, affordable and sustainable service", the Chinese Government makes great efforts to achieve breakthroughs in developing social insurance in the following aspects:

First, breakthroughs have been made in institutional setup with a basic system framework taking shape. In 2003, the rural medical assistance scheme was set up and a new type of rural cooperative medical service was tried out in 2004. Urban medical assistance scheme was established in 2005. Basic medical insurance was provided for urban residents in 2007 and the minimum living security system was set up for rural residents in the same year. In 2009, a new type of social endowment insurance for rural residents was tried out. In 2010, the *Social Insurance Law* was promulgated. In 2011, the pilot program of social endowment insurance for urban residents was launched. In 2012, *Outline of 12th Five-Year Plan on Social Security* was issued, proposing that the new social endowment insurance for rural residents and basic medical insurance for urban residents will achieve universal coverage by the end of the 12th Five-Year Plan period.

Rural residents actively get enrolled in the new rural social endowment insurance.

Second, with the coverage of social security programs expanding rapidly, more and more people benefit from social security. The coverage of social security programs has expanded from urban areas to rural areas, from state-owned enterprises to all types of enterprises and people in flexible employment, from employees to urban and rural residents. By the end of 2013, the number of people covered by the basic social endowment insurance, basic medical insurance (including urban-rural balance), unemployment insurance, employment injury insurance and maternity insurance amounted to 819.68 million, 573.22 million, 164.17 million, 199.17 million and 163.92 million respectively. Over 1.3 billion people are insured under basic medical insurance (including the new cooperative medical insurance for rural residents). Problems left over by history have been resolved: over 8 million retirees from closed or bankrupt enterprises, over 5 million employees of collectively owned enterprises and over 3 million SOE employees with "old" work-related injury (referring to people recognized as having work-related injury before *Regulation on Work-Related Injury Insurances* was issued in 2004 and secured by their own enterprises) are included in medical insurance, endowment insurance and work-related injury insurance respectively. Subsidies on social insurance are offered to help laid-off workers to find a new job. Two "safety programs" were offered to migrant workers and nearly 72 million of them have been covered by work-related injury insurance with the risk of occupational injury lessened.

Third, the government makes increasing investment to raise social insurance benefits. From 2005 to 2013, the Chinese Government increased pension for corporate retirees for nine consecutive years, reaching on average 1,856 yuan per person per month in 2013. Basic monthly pension for urban and rural residents increased substantially and reached 82 yuan in 2013. The reimbursement ratio of basic medical insurance and the medical payment cap are steadily increased. Fiscal subsidies for urban and rural medical insurances have increased with each passing year and reached 280 yuan per person per year in 2013. The out-patient pool of urban and rural residents' medical insurance is widely carried out. The benefits of unemployment insurance, work-related injury insurance and maternity insurance are also substantially increased.

Insured workers receive social security cards.

Fourth, the social security public service system has basically taken shape with extending service network. While the system is improved with more investment, efforts are made to further develop social security management service system so as to make sure that all policies bringing social security benefits to the people be accurately implemented without delay.

In the past ten years, human resource and social security programs in China have achieved substantial development. For some time to come, the urbanization process and accelerated population aging will present big challenges to employment, labor relations and social security in China. We are faced with a big task in the long run. The Chinese Government will continue to focus on people's livelihood, devote more efforts and invent new ways to promote human resource development and social security and thus contribute to the realization of the Chinese Dream of great national rejuvenation.

(original translation by Yang Ji)

中国住房和城乡建设领域人权保障的主要做法和成就

住房和城乡建设部副部长　齐　骥

第一部分　实施城镇保障性安居工程　推进各类棚户区改造

中国政府高度重视解决城镇中低收入家庭住房困难问题。中央政府提出，要努力实现全体人民住有所居。《国民经济和社会发展第十二个五年规划纲要》明确指出，"十二五"时期，开工建设城镇保障性住房和棚户区改造住房3600万套，到"十二五"末，中国城镇保障性住房覆盖面达到20%左右。各级政府大力推进廉租住房、公共租赁住房、经济适用住房和限价商品住房等保障性住房建设，推进城市棚户区、国有工矿棚户区、国有林区（场）棚户区（危旧房）、农垦危房和中央下放地方煤矿棚户区等五大类棚户区改造，加快解决城镇中低收入家庭的住房困难，取得了明显成效。2011~2013年，中国开工建设城镇保障性住房和棚户区改造住房2490万套，基本建成1577万套。截至2013年年底，中国累计解决了3600多万户城镇家庭的住房困难。

各级政府高度重视，积极推行目标责任制管理。中央政府多次召开专题会议研究支持政策，地方各级政府精心组织实施。各部门密切协作，形成了省级负总责、市县抓落实、中央给支持的住房保障工作机制，建立了相应的目标责任管理机制，并将保障性安居工程建设纳入对各地的督查和问责范围。人大、政协、纪检及相关部门，通过开展专题调研、专项督查等方式，加强督促和指导。

探索建立多层次的城镇住房保障体系。经过探索实践，初步形成了多层次的城镇住房保障体系，面向各类住房困难群体分别供应廉租住房、公共租赁住房等租赁型保障房和经济适用住房、限价商品住房等购置型保障房以及棚户区改造安置住房。

完善住房保障支持政策。国家实施土地优先供应、财政补助、税费减免和信贷扶持等支持政策，将保障性住房尽可能安排在重点发展、交通便利、设施完备的区域，方便居民就业、就医、就学、出行。据估算，2011～2013年，中国各级财政城镇保障性安居工程建设支出10000多亿元。同时，各级政府还鼓励民间资本参与保障性安居工程建设与运营，享受与国有企业同等的贴息、投资补助等支持政策。

建立完善保障性住房管理制度。从2012年起，中央政府正式启动了住房保障立法工作，《城镇住房保障条例》即将报送中央政府批准实施。同时，各地按照廉租住房、公共租赁住房和经济适用住房的管理规定，结合本地区实际，制定和完善了地方性管理办法，进一步规范了保障性住房建设、分配、上市交易、退出、后续管理等行为，确保了保障性住房资源的公平善用。

保障房建设前。

保障房建设后。

第二部分　改造农村危房　改善农民居住条件

一、基本情况

2008 年中央政府支持贵州省率先开展了农村危房改造试点。从 2009 年起，住房城乡建设部、国家发展改革委、财政部启动了扩大农村危房改造试点。随后，中央政府支持的地区范围逐步扩大，2012 年实现了全国农村地区全覆盖。农村危房改造以优先帮助住房最危险、经济最贫困农户解决最基本安全住房为目标，补助对象重点是居住在危房中的农村分散供养五保户、低保户、贫困残疾人家庭和其他贫困户。

2008 ～ 2013 年，各级政府累计安排 1384 亿元补助资金，支持 1559 万贫困农户改造危房，其中五保户 47.8 万户、低保户 262.3 万户、贫困残疾人家庭 102.6 万户。

二、主要成效

困难群众住房条件明显改善。 7 年来，1500 多万农户改造了危房，这些贫困群众告别了原来存在严重安全隐患的破旧泥草房、土坯房、杈杈房、树皮房等危房，住上了结构牢靠的安全房。据对中西部地区 20 个省份 2008 ～ 2011 年实施农村危房改造农户的随机调查，92.2%的受访农户认为改造危房是家中的头等大事，93.4%的受访农户认为改造后住房条件改善很大，87.6%的受访农户对危房改造表示很满意。

农房质量安全水平明显提升。据对 2013 年年底 1559 万危房改造户的统计，改造前农房砖混及以上结构的比例仅占 4.7%，改造后提高到了 60.1%，土坯、简易砌体等结构的比例大幅下降。农房抗震标准大幅提高。例如 2012 年 6 月下旬，云南省宁蒗县与四川省盐源县交界处、新疆维吾尔自治区新源县与和静县交界处先后发生 5.7 级和 6.6 级地震，极震区烈度均达到 8 度。经灾损评估，未经改造的农房受损较重，受损率分别达 58%和 36%，而经危房改造后的农房受损极小，云南仅 2%轻微或中度受损，新疆无一受损。

推动了农村住房建筑节能发展。中央政府对寒冷地区结合危房改造开展建筑节能示范户予以额外补助，引导农户在墙体、门窗、屋面、地面等围护结构中采用节能措施。2009 ～ 2013 年，已有 68.6 万农户结合农村危房改造开展了建筑节能示范。通过实施建筑节能示范，有效提高了农房居住舒适度，降低了冬季采暖支出，推动了农房降低能耗、节约资源和减少环境污染。

中国东北地区某贫困农户危房改造前。

中国东北地区某贫困农户危房改造后。

第三部分　尊重和保障房屋征收拆迁当事人的合法权益

城镇房屋征收拆迁关系到地方经济社会发展，关系到人民群众居住条件和生活环境的改善。城镇房屋征收拆迁过程中一度产生的矛盾纠纷，是社会关注的热点问题之一。

一、加强房屋征收拆迁法制建设

中国政府高度重视在房屋征收拆迁中保障被征收拆迁人的合法权益。1991 年，国务院公布了《城市房屋拆迁管理条例（国务院令第 78 号）》，对规范房屋拆迁行为、维护拆迁当事人的合法权益发挥了积极作用。随着市场经济的发展和城市化建设的推进，2001 年国务院对该条例进行了修改，出台了修订后的《城市房屋拆迁管理条例（国务院令第 305 号）》。2011 年 1 月，按照《物权法》规定，国务院公布了《国有土地上房屋征收与补偿条例（国务院令第 590 号）》（以下简称"条例"）。《条例》界定了公共利益的范围，规定了政府是房屋征收与补偿主体，确立了公众参与、公开透明的征收程序，明确了补偿标准、补助和奖励措施，取消了行政机关自行强制拆迁。这些规定有利于从根本上避免和减少房屋征收中的矛盾纠纷，更好地维护被征收人的合法权益。

二、房屋征收法规制度的主要内容

一是界定了公共利益的范围。根据《物权法》规定，《条例》第八条对公共利益的范围做出了界定，明确为了保障国家安全、促进国民经济和社会发展等公共利益的需要，有下列情形之一，确需征收房屋的，由市、县级人民政府作出房屋征收决定：（一）国防和外交的需要；（二）由政府组织实施的能源、交通、水利等基础设施建设的需要；（三）由政府组织实施的科技、教育、文化、卫生、体育、环境和资源保护、防灾减灾、文物保护、社会福利、市政公用等公共事业的需要；（四）由政府组织实施的保障性安居工程建设的需要；（五）由政府依照城乡规划法有关规定组织实施的对危房集中、基础设施落后等地段进行旧城区改建的需要；（六）法律、行政法规规定的其他公共利益的需要。

二是完善了房屋征收补偿制度。房屋征收补偿是被征收人最为关心的问题，也是产生矛盾纠纷的焦点，《条例》对此做出了一系列的规定。首先，规定了市场化补偿和独立评估的原则。《条例》第十九条规定："对被征收房屋价值的补偿，不得低于房屋征收决定公告之日被征收房屋类似房地产的市场价格。被征收房屋的价值，由具有相应资质的房地产价格评估机构按照房屋征收评估办法评估确定。"第二十条规定："房地产价格评估机构应当独立、客观、公正地开展房屋征收评估工作，任何单位和个人不得干预。"其次，强化了对房屋征收中特殊人群的保障。《条例》第十七条规定："市、县级人民政府应当制定补助和奖励办法，对被征收人给予补助和奖励。"解决房屋征收过程中需要生活困难救助、重大疾病救助以及住房困难家庭的被征收人的困难。第十八条规定："征收个人住宅，被征收人符合住房保障条件的，作出房屋征收决定的市、县级人民政府应当优先给予住房保障。"再次，强调了对旧城区改建中原住居民的保护。《条例》第二十一条规定："因旧城区改建征收个人住宅，被征收人选择在改建地段进行房屋产权调换的，作出房屋征收决定的市、县级人民政府应当提供改建地段或者就近地段的房屋。”

三是确立了公众参与、公开透明的征收程序。《条例》赋予被征收人在征收补偿方案的制定与修改、房屋征收评估办法的制定、房地产价格评估机构的选择、补偿方式的选择等方面的知情权、参与权，让群众真正参与到整个征收工作中，表达诉求、发表意见。《条例》第十条、第十一条对征收补偿方案公示及征求公众意见等进行了规定；第二十条确立了房屋征收评估机构由被征收人选定的制度；第十五条、第二十九条确立了被征收房屋调查结果、初步分户评估结果、补偿结果等在征收范围内向被征收人公布的制度；第二十九条规定审计机关应当加强对征收补偿费用管理和使用情况的监督。

四是规范了房屋征收强制执行活动。房屋征收强制执行事关房屋征收工作的顺利开展，涉及被征收人的切身利益。《条例》第二十六条规定，对达不成补偿协议或被征收房屋产权不明的，市、县级人民政府可以依法作出房屋征收补偿决定。第二十八条规定：“被征收人在法定期限内不申请行政复议或者不提起行政诉讼，在补偿决定规定的期限内又不搬迁的，由作出房屋征收决定的市、县级人民政府依法申请人民法院强制执行。”2012 年 4 月，最高人民法院出台了《关于办理申请人民法院强制执行国有土地上房屋征收补偿决定案件若干问题的规定》，规范房屋征收补偿决定案件的审查、受理和执行。按照该司法解释，法院审理房屋征收补偿决定案件实行“裁执分离”，即只有在法院做出准予执行的裁定后才能实施强制执行，这从法律制度上保障了被征收人的合法权益。

三、工作成效

住房和城乡建设部会同有关部门认真宣传、贯彻《条例》，大力推进房屋征收规范化、法制化建设。对地方房屋征收部门、政府法制工作机构负责人和业务骨干进行了重点培训，增强有关人员的法制意识；制定了国有土地上房屋征收评估和征收补偿信息公开办法，规范房屋征收评估活动，促进房屋征收与补偿活动公开、公平、公正；配合国务院有关部门开展征地拆迁专项检查，严肃查处违法征地拆迁行为。目前，房屋征收工作依法有序开展，新发生的矛盾纠纷明显减少。

重庆市北碚区石岩村拆迁前。

重庆市北碚区石岩村拆迁后。

Major Measures and Achievements of Human Rights Protection in China's Housing and Urban-Rural Development

Qi Ji, Vice Minister of Housing and Urban-Rural Development

Part 1: Implementation of urban indemnificatory housing project and promotion of shantytowns renovations

The government of China attaches great importance to resolving the housing difficulties of low- and medium-income families in urban areas. The Central Government has set the goal of solving housing problems for all citizens in China. The *Outline of the 12th Five-Year Plan for Economic and Social Development* clearly stated that urban indemnificatory housing would be built and shantytowns would be renovated during the 12th Five-Year Plan period, providing a total of 36 million new units. The coverage of urban indemnificatory housing will reach 20% by the end of the 12th Five-Year Plan period. Governments at all levels make great efforts to advance the construction of indemnificatory housing including low-rent housing, public-rental housing, economically affordable housing and price-restricted commercial housing. In the meantime, the renovation of five major types of shantytowns will be facilitated – those in cities, in state-owned mining areas, in state-owned forest areas, and in coal mines transferred from central to local governments as well as dilapidated buildings in agricultural reclamation farms. The government has sped up moves to solve the housing difficulties of low- and middle-income families in cities and towns and achieves positive results. From 2011 to 2013, construction for 24.9 million units of indemnificatory housing and shantytowns transformation were started, and 15.77 million were completed. By the end of 2013, China had solved the housing difficulties of 36 million urban families.

Governments at all levels place great stress on the housing issues and target-oriented responsibility system is actively carried out. The Central Government holds special meetings to discuss about supportive policies and local governments make efforts to implement these policies. All government departments work closely with each other. In the work mechanism on indemnificatory housing, the provincial governments shoulder overall responsibility, city and county governments are responsible for the implementation, and the Central Government provides support. Corresponding target-oriented responsibility system is established and the implementation of indemnificatory housing project is included in the scope of supervision and accountability of local governments. The People's Congresses, Chinese People's Political Consultative Conference committees, disciplinary inspection departments and other relevant departments provide stronger supervision and guidance via themed researches and special supervisory campaigns.

A multi-level urban indemnificatory housing system is being explored. A multi-level urban indemnificatory housing system has been initially established on the basis of such exploration and practices. A variety of indemnificatory housing is available for various populations with housing difficulty including both housing for rent such as low-rent housing and public-rental housing and housing for purchase such as economically affordable housing and price-restricted commercial housing as well as resettlement for shantytowns.

Supportive policies of indemnificatory housing have been improved. Supportive polices such as the prioritized land supply, financial subsidy, tax and fee deduction and exemption and credit support are implemented. Arrangements are made for indemnificatory apartments to be built in key development areas with convenient access and rich service facilities to facilitate the employment, medical care, education and travel. According to a rough calculation, the fiscal expenditure on indemnificatory housing amounted to 1 trillion yuan by governments at all levels from 2011 to 2013. In the meantime, governments at all levels encourage the investment of private capital in the construction and operation of such projects with the same interest discount, investment subsidies and other supportive polices as state-owned enterprises.

The indemnificatory housing management system has been established and improved. Since 2012, the Central Government has started to legislate for housing security. The *Regulations on Urban Housing Security* will soon be submitted to the Central Government for approval and implementation. Furthermore, in light of the relevant regulations on low-rent housing, public-rental housing and economically affordable housing, local governments have made and improved local administrative measures to further regulate the construction, allocation, transaction, withdrawal, and follow-up management to ensure fair and good use of the indemnificatory housing resources.

Before the construction of indemnificatory housing.

After the construction of indemnificatory housing.

Part 2: Renovation of dilapidated houses in rural areas and improvement of farmers' living conditions

I. Background.

In 2008, the Central Government supported Guizhou province to take the lead to pilot renovation of dilapidated houses in rural areas. In 2009, Ministry of Housing and Urban-Rural Development, National Development and Reform Commission and Ministry of Finance launched expanded pilot programs, followed by gradual geographical expansion of Central Government support to universal rural coverage in 2012. The renovation program aims to provide basic safe housing to the poorest rural families living in the most dilapidated houses. The key beneficiaries are the families enjoying "five guarantees" in their own households or minimum living allowance, poor families of people with disabilities and other poor families living in the dilapidated houses.

From 2008 to 2013, governments at all levels provided 138.4 billion yuan to help 15.59 million poor rural families renovate the dilapidated houses, including 478,000 "five guarantees" families, 2.623 million families receiving minimum living allowance, and 1.026 million poor families of people with disabilities.

II. Major achievements.

The living conditions of poor families are substantially improved. In the past 7 years, 15 million dilapidated houses have been renovated. The relevant poor rural families bade farewell to their dangerous houses of straw, mud, bamboo or bark and moved into solid and safe houses. According to random surveys conducted in 20 provinces in central and western China from 2008 to 2011, 92.2% respondents regarded the renovation as their families' most important event, 93.4% said that their living conditions had been greatly improved after the renovation and 87.6% were satisfied with the renovation.

The safety level of rural houses is substantially improved. According to statistics at the end of 2013 about 15.59 million households whose dilapidated houses had been renovated, brick-concrete structure houses only took up 4.7% before the renovation project and the proportion raised to 60.1% after the renovation. In the meantime, the proportion of mud brick houses and simple masonry houses substantially declined. As a result, the seismic capacity of rural houses was improved by a large margin. For example, at the end of June 2012, earthquakes took place at the juncture of Ninglang, Yunnan Province and Yanyuan, Sichuan Province and at the juncture of Xinyuan and Jingxian Counties, Xinjiang Uygur Autonomous Region, with magnitudes of 5.7 and 6.6 on the Richter scale respectively and the seismic intensity of 8 at most intense points in both areas. According to disaster loss assessment, the unrenovated farm houses suffered a great loss, with 58% and 36% damaged respectively. In contrast, the renovated houses suffered very little loss. Only 2% renovated houses suffered slight or moderate loss in Yunnan and the rate was zero in Xinjiang.

The houses in rural areas are more energy-friendly. The Central Government offers additional subsidy to energy-efficient building demonstration households in cold areas. Rural families were encouraged to use energy-saving measures in the walls, doors, windows, roofs, floors and other exterior-protected structures. From 2009 to 2013, 686,000 rural households participated in the energy-efficient housing demonstration in the dilapidated housing renovation process. With these energy-efficient measures, the houses are more comfortable to live in, the heating expense in winter is lower, with energy and resources saved and environmental pollution reduced.

A rural household in Northeast China before renovation.

The same household after renovation.

Part 3: Respect for and protection of lawful rights and interests of parties concerned in house expropriation and demolition

House expropriation and demolition is closely related to local economic and social development as well as improvement of living conditions and environment of ordinary people. Disputes occurring in house expropriation and demolition are hotspots of major social concerns.

I. Strengthening legislation.

The Chinese Government places great stress on the lawful rights and interests of the persons whose housing units are expropriated and demolished. In 1991, the State Council issued *Regulations on Urban Housing Demolition Management (No.78 Decree of the State Council),* which played an positive role in regulating housing demolition activities and protecting the legal rights of the parties concerned. With the development of the market economy and the urbanization process, the State Council amended the Regulations and issued the revised *Regulations on Urban Housing Demolition Management (No. 305 Decree of the State Council)* in 2001. In January 2011, the State Council issued *Regulation on the Expropriation of Buildings on State-Owned Land and Compensation (No. 590 Decree of the State Council)* (hereinafter referred to as "the Regulation") in accordance with the *Property Law.* The Regulation defined the scope of public interests and made it clear that the government is the one that expropriates such buildings and makes compensation. The Regulation also established the housing expropriation procedures that involve public participation and are open and transparent. Compensation standards, assistance and incentive measures are introduced and the administrative organs are no longer allowed to practise forced demolition by themselves. These provisions are very helpful to reduce and avoid disputes during housing expropriation, and thus better protect the legal rights of the house owners.

II. Main content of the regulations and rules on housing expropriation.

First, the scope of public interests is defined. According to the *Property Law,* Article 8 of the Regulation defines the scope of public interests and reads the following: In order to protect national security, promote economic and social development and for other public interests, if houses are absolutely required to be expropriated in any of the following circumstances, decisions on house expropriation shall be made by municipal and county governments: (1) The needs of national defense and foreign affairs; (2) The needs of energy, transportation, water conservation and other infrastructure construction projects carried out under the organization of the governments; (3) The needs of science and technology, education, culture, health, sports, environmental and resource protection, disaster prevention and mitigation, heritage conservation, social welfare, municipal utilities and other public utility projects carried out under the organization of the governments; (4) The needs of construction projects for affordable residential houses carried out under the organization of the governments; (5) The needs of old city reconstruction projects for districts where dilapidated buildings are concentrated and poor infrastructure facilities are located that are carried out by the governments pursuant to relevant provisions of the urban and rural planning law; or (6) The needs of other public interests as set forth in laws and administrative regulations.

Second, the compensation system is improved. The compensation is not only a major concern of house owners but also the focus of disputes. The Regulation has a series of provisions in this respect. First, it sets out the principles of market-based compensation and independent evaluation. According to Article 19, the compensation for the value of houses to be expropriated shall not be less than the market price of the real estate comparable to the houses to be expropriated on the date of the public notice of the house expropriation decisions. The value of the houses to be expropriated shall be assessed and determined by real estate appraisal agencies with appropriate qualifications in accordance with the procedures for evaluating houses to be expropriated. According to Article 20, real estate appraisal agencies shall carry out the assessment of the houses to be expropriated in an independent, objective and fair manner, free from interference from any unit or individual. Secondly, the Regulation provides better protection to special populations. According to Article 17, city and county people's governments shall formulate the procedures for subsidies and incentives, and grant subsidies and incentives to the persons whose houses are to be expropriated so as to resolve the difficulties of such persons who need hardship allowance, assistance for major disease and have housing difficulties. In Article 18, if the residential houses of any individuals are to be expropriated and the persons whose houses are to be expropriated meet the conditions for affordable houses, the city and county people's governments that have made the decisions on house expropriation shall give priority to providing affordable houses to such persons. Furthermore, the Regulation places emphasis on the protection of the indigenous residents in old urban areas. According to Article 21, if personal houses are required to be expropriated due to reconstruction of old city districts, and the persons whose houses are to be expropriated choose property rights exchange with houses located at the site of reconstruction, the city and county people's governments that have made the decisions on house expropriation shall provide the houses located at or near the sites of reconstruction.

Third, open and transparent procedures with public participation are established. The Regulation confers on the persons whose houses are to be expropriated the rights to information and participation in making and revising compensation schemes, formulating method of housing evaluation, selecting real estate appraisal agencies and the way of compensation so that the people may truly participate in the expropriation process and express their appeals and views. Articles 10 and 11 contain provisions on disclosure of compensation programs and soliciting public opinions. Article 20 establishes that real estate appraisal agencies shall be selected by the persons whose houses are to be expropriated. Articles 15 and 29 establish the system to disclose to persons whose houses are to be expropriated within the scope of house expropriation the survey results of houses to be expropriated, initial appraisal results and compensation paid to individual households. Article 29 also provides that auditing organs shall strengthen their supervision over the management and use of the expenses for expropriation compensation.

Fourth, the enforcement of housing expropriation is regulated. The enforcement bears on the smooth conduct of house expropriation and the important interests of the persons whose houses are to be expropriated. According to Article 26, in case of failure to enter into compensation agreements or if the owners of the houses to be expropriated are uncertain, the city and county people's governments that have made the decisions on house expropriation may make decisions on compensation in accordance with the Regulations. Article 28 provides that "[i]f the persons whose houses are expropriated fail to apply for administrative reconsideration or institute administrative proceedings within the statutory time limit, and fail to relocate within the period set forth in the compensation decision, the city and county people's governments that have made the decisions on house expropriation shall petition the people's court for enforcement. In April 2012, the Supreme People's Court issued *Provisions on Several Issues Concerning Petitioning the People's Courts for Enforcement of Decision on Expropriation of Building on State-Owned Land and Compensation* to regulate the review, acceptance and enforcement of the relevant cases. According to this judicial interpretation, the courts exercise separation of judgment and enforcement when dealing with these cases. The enforcement may only be carried out after the court has ruled in agreement of enforcement, thus legally protecting the lawful rights and interests of the persons whose houses are to be expropriated.

III. Achievements.

The Ministry of Housing and Urban-Rural Development works together with other related government departments to publicize and implement the Regulation. In the meantime, we actively push for the standardization and legislation of house expropriation. Focused training has been provided for leaders and key staff members of local house expropriation departments and government legal work institutions to raise their legal awareness. Methods of disclosure of information on appraisal and compensation in the expropriation of buildings on state-owned land have been formulated to regulate housing appraisal and promote open, fair and just housing expropriation and compensation. The Ministry is working with other relevant departments of the State Council in special inspections on land expropriation and housing demolition and in serious investigation and punishment of illegal conducts in this area. Now, housing expropriation is conducted in an orderly manner according to law and there have been substantially fewer new disputes.

Shiyan Village in Beibei, Chongqing before demolition and relocation.

Shiyan Village in Beibei, Chongqing after demolition and relocation.

(original translation by Yang Ji)

卫生领域人权事业进展显著

国家卫生和计划生育委员会副主任　马晓伟

自2004年“国家尊重和保障人权”写入中国《宪法》以来，中国的人权事业发展取得巨大成就。其中，健康权是公民的一项核心权利，是公民参与一切社会活动、享有其他一切权利的基础。特别是在中国这个有着13亿多人口的发展中大国，医疗卫生关系亿万人民健康，是民生问题的重头戏。中国政府高度重视国民健康改善和医药卫生事业发展。《宪法》规定：“国家发展医疗卫生事业……保护人民健康。”多年来，中国坚持“以农村为重点，预防为主，中西医并重，依靠科技与教育，动员全社会参与，为人民健康服务”的卫生工作方针，努力发展具有中国特色的医疗卫生事业，无论在卫生法律体系还是居民健康状况上都取得了显著进展。

一、卫生法律体系基本形成

“国家尊重和保障人权”写入《宪法》以来，中国医药卫生领域迎来了立法的新时期，卫生领域人权事业和卫生法制建设取得了长足进展。截至目前，中国医药卫生领域已有11部法律、39部行政法规、近140部部门规章，内容涵盖了食品药品安全、医疗服务与监督管理、妇幼保健与社区卫生、疾病预防控制与生物安全、传染病防治、精神卫生和医疗纠纷预防与处理等，充分体现了中国充分尊重和保障人权，切实保障人民生命健康、保护患者隐私、尊重患者人格尊严的宪法精神。具体情况如下：

（一）法律

2009 年 2 月 28 日，第十一届全国人大常委会第七次会议通过了《中华人民共和国食品安全法》（以下简称“食品安全法”）。该法顺应时代要求，为解决现实生活中出现的食品安全问题确立了食品安全生产管理、食品安全风险监测和评估为基础的科学管理制度，从食品原料与添加剂的使用、食品生产者与服务者的责任、政府部门监督与管理、食品安全事故预防与应急处理等方面进行了全方位、体系化的制度设计，力争在食源方面把好关，为人民的生命安全和身体健康保驾护航。2013 年 6 月 17 日，《食品安全法》修订工作启动，列入国务院 2013 年立法工作，充分体现了中国立法工作高度重视食品安全卫生，心系百姓，立法为民。

2009 年 12 月 26 日，第十一届全国人大常委会第十二次会议通过了《中华人民共和国侵权责任法》（以下简称“侵权责任法”）。《侵权责任法》第一次把医疗损害责任设立专章进行规范，不仅规范了医患双方的行为，而且明确了医疗损害赔偿制度，更加注重维护医患关系和谐、尊重患者权利、保护弱势群体。医疗损害责任的有关规定内容涵盖了医疗机构或医护人员的侵权情形、责任认定和法律责任、病历资料的书写与提供、诊疗规范的介绍说明、诊疗风险的预先告知、就医患者的隐私保护和资料保密等方面，为维护患者合法权益提供了有力的法律支持。

2012年10月26日，第十一届全国人大常委会第二十九次会议通过了《中华人民共和国精神卫生法》（以下简称“精神卫生法”）。《精神卫生法》是一部承载着全民厚重权利期待的法律，不仅填补了中国精神卫生领域的法律空白，而且勾勒出了中国精神障碍患者人权保障的美好蓝图。《精神卫生法》规定：“精神障碍患者的人格尊严、人身和财产安全不受侵犯。精神障碍患者的教育、劳动、医疗以及从国家和社会获得物质帮助等方面的合法权益受法律保护。有关单位和个人应当对精神障碍患者的姓名、肖像、住址、工作单位、病历资料以及其他可能推断出其身份的信息予以保密”，并设专章规定了政府及有关部门、用人单位、学校、医务人员、监狱等场所，社区、家庭、媒体、心理咨询等人员在心理健康促进和精神障碍预防方面的法律责任。

《精神卫生法》首次明确："精神障碍的住院治疗实行自愿原则"，不得非法限制精神障碍患者人身自由。这部规范精神障碍患者医疗、保障精神障碍患者权益、促进精神障碍患者康复的法律经过了27年的酝酿与磨砺，从立项到公布都广泛征求社会不同群体的意见和建议，注重保护社会弱势群体，以人为本，努力实现权利平等与机会平等，充分体现了中国尊重和保障人权的法治理念。

（二）行政法规

目前，医药卫生领域的行政法规涵盖生物安全、预防接种和疫苗流通、麻醉品与精神药品管理、艾滋病防治、血吸虫病防治、传染病防治、食品安全、计划生育、女职工劳动保护等多个方面，如已制定出台《病原微生物实验室生物安全管理条例》、《疫苗流通和预防接种管理条例》、《麻醉药品和精神药品管理条例》、《艾滋病防治条例》、《血吸虫病防治条例》、《国务院关于加强食品等产品安全监督管理的特别规定》、《护士条例》、《乳品质量安全监督管理条例》、《流动人口计划生育工作条例》、《中华人民共和国食品安全法实施条例》、《女职工劳动保护特别规定》等多个行政法规，均集中体现了以人为本，注重保障人民生命健康权。

（三）部门规章

为保证医药卫生法律法规得到有效贯彻，切实保障人民生命健康，2004年以来中国卫生领域出台多个部门规章，内容涵盖放射诊疗、医疗质量安全、新生儿疾病筛查、托儿所幼儿园卫生保健、计划生育药具、传染病防治、性病防治、职业病诊断与治疗、结核病防治、食品安全、餐饮服务安全、食品添加剂、铁路运营食品安全、药品安全、医疗器械临床使用等，分别从不同领域和角度为保障人民生命健康确立了具体制度。

二、以人为本，着力促进医改

在卫生法律体系的保障下，中国长期致力于推动医药卫生体制改革，始终把维护人民健康权益放在第一位。2009年，中国确定了到2020年基本建立覆盖城乡居民的基本医疗卫生制度的目标，通过卫生改革与发展，努力保障每个居民不论性别、民族，不论城市、农村，都能享有安全、有效、方便、价廉的基本医疗卫生服务。

（一）城乡医疗卫生体系基本建立

中国已建立起覆盖城乡的医疗卫生体系，包括公共卫生服务体系、医疗服务体系、医疗保障体系和药品供应保障体系。截至2012年年底，全国基层医疗卫生机构达91.2万个，包括社区卫生服务中心8176个，社区卫生服务站2.5万个，乡镇卫生院3.7万所，村卫生室65.3万个，共有123.4万张床位。国家实施万名医师支援农村卫生工程，2009～2011年，1100余家城市三级医院支援了955个县级医院，中西部地区城市二级以上医疗卫生机构每年支援3600多所乡镇卫生院。截至2012年年底，基本药物制度实现基层全覆盖，所有政府办基层医疗卫生机构全部配备使用基本药物，实行零差率销售，并向村卫生室和非政府办基层医疗卫生机构延伸。

（二）基本公共卫生服务均等化水平显著提高

中国人均基本公共卫生服务经费标准从2009年的15元提高到2012年的25元。国家免费向全体居民提供10类41项国家基本公共卫生服务。2011年，国家免疫规划疫苗接种率总体达到90%以上，全国住院分娩率达到98.7%。艾滋病、结核病、血吸虫病、包虫病、麻风病、疟疾等重大及重点传染病患者获得免费药物治疗，并率先在全球83个丝虫病流行国家和地区中消除了丝虫病。

（三）积极开展社会医疗救助服务

在医疗救助方面，国家制定了《关于开展重特大疾病医疗救助试点工作的意见》，并在全国273个试点地区开展试点工作。2012年，全国医疗救助人次9134万，支出资金221亿元。在流浪乞讨人员救助方面，国家发布了《关于加强和改进流浪未成年人救助保护工作的意见》，开展了“接送流浪孩子回家”专项行动。截至2012年，全国共有救助机构（救助管理站、流浪未成年人救助保护中心）1788个。2010～2011年，全国共救助流浪乞讨人员4128709人次。在公共卫生突发应急方面，国家有关部门齐心协力充分做好了“非典”、“H1N9”、汶川大地震、芦山地震等重大事件的医疗救援和保障工作，充分体现了党和国家以人为本，充分保障民生。

三、居民健康水平提高

经过多年的不懈努力，覆盖城乡的医疗卫生服务体系基本形成，疾病防治能力不断增强，医疗保障覆盖人口逐步扩大，卫生科技水平日益提高，居民健康水平明显改善。中国建立了覆盖超过 95% 人口的基本医疗保障制度，农村和城市的基层医疗卫生服务体系都得到加强，初步建立了国家基本药物制度，基本公共卫生服务均等化水平显著提高。这些措施和进展，促进了中国国民健康水平的稳步提高。2010 年人均期望寿命达到 74.8 岁，其中男性 72.4 岁，女性 77.4 岁。孕产妇死亡率从 2002 年的 51.3 / 10 万下降到 2012 年的 24.5 / 10 万。婴儿死亡率及 5 岁以下儿童死亡率持续下降，婴儿死亡率从 2002 年的 29.2‰下降到 2012 年的 10.3‰，提前实现了“千年发展目标”中的第四个降低儿童死亡率的目标。5 岁以下儿童死亡率从 2002 年的 34.9‰下降到 2012 年的 13.2‰。

总之，“人权入宪”十年来，医药卫生事业得到较快发展，服务体系更加健全，服务能力不断提升，医疗保障制度不断探索发展，药品生产供应保障能力不断增强，人民群众享受到越来越多现代医疗技术进步的成果，国民健康持续改善。中国政府也将一如既往地重视卫生事业，进一步促进人人享有健康的目标实现。

Significant Improvement of Human Rights Protection in Health Services

Ma Xiaowei, Vice Minister, National Health and Family Planning Commission

China has made great achievements in protecting human rights since "[t]he State respects and protects human rights" was articulated in the *Constitution of the People's Republic of China* in 2004. Right to health is a core right for all citizens and the basis for their participation in social activities and enjoyment of all other rights. It is especially the case for China, a large developing country with a population of over 1.3 billion, where healthcare is of vital importance to hundreds of millions of people and a priority in people's livelihood. The Chinese government pays great attention to improving its people's health and public health services. As the Constitution stipulates, "[t]he State develops medical and health services... to protect people's health." Over the years, China has worked hard to develop healthcare with Chinese characteristics in accordance with the policy of "making rural areas the focus of our work, putting disease prevention first, supporting both traditional Chinese medicine and Western medicine, relying on science, technology and education, and motivating the whole society to join the efforts of improving people's health." A system of health laws have been enhanced and people's health has remarkably improved.

I. The system of public health laws is basically in place.

Since "[t]he State respects and protects human rights" was articulated in the Constitution, China has ushered in a new era of medical and health legislations, with huge progresses achieved in the development of human rights protection and health-related legal system. So far, 11 laws, 39 administrative regulations and nearly 140 department rules have been enacted in this area, covering food and drug safety, medical service and regulation, maternal and child health and community health service, disease prevention and control and bio-safety, infectious disease prevention and control, mental health, and prevention and handling of medical disputes. These laws embody the spirit of the Constitution that China fully respects and protects human rights, protects people's lives and health with concrete actions, protects patients' privacy and respects their dignity. Details are as follows:

1. Laws

The *Food Safety Law of the People's Republic of China* (hereinafter referred to as "*Food Safety Law*") was adopted at the 7th Session of the Standing Committee of the 11th National People's Congress on February 28, 2009. The law responds to the requirements of the times and establishes a scientific management system based on production management and risk monitoring and assessment in the area of food safety to address food safety issues. The system design demonstrates a comprehensive and systematic view, taking into consideration the use of food ingredients and additives, liabilities of food producers and service providers, supervision and management by the government, food safety accident prevention and emergency response. These considerations represent an effort to effectively control the food sources, thus ensuring people's safety and health. On June 17, 2013, the revision of *Food Safety Law* was started as part of the legislative work of the State Council in 2013, which indicated that food safety and hygiene are given great importance in legislation for the benefit of the people.

Tort Law of the People's Republic of China (hereinafter referred to as "*Tort Law*") was adopted at the 12th Session of the Standing Committee of the 11th National

People's Congress on December 26, 2009. *Tort Law* establishes for the first time a chapter on liability for medical malpractice so as to regulate the behavior of both doctors and patients and streamline the medical malpractice compensation system, focusing on maintaining a harmonious doctor-patient relationship, respecting patients' rights and protecting vulnerable groups. The relevant provisions cover cases of tort, determination and liability of medical institutions or medical staff, as well as the writing and provision of medical records, briefing on the standard of diagnosis and treatment, informing patients of the risks involved beforehand, protecting patients' privacy and confidentiality of their information, thus providing effective legal support in the protection of patients' legitimate rights and interests.

Mental Health Law of the People's Republic of China (hereinafter referred to as "*Mental Health Law*") was adopted at the 29th Session of the Standing Committee of the 11th National People's Congress on October 26, 2012. The people places high expectations on the *Mental Health Law*, which not only fills the gap in mental health legislation but also draws a promising blueprint for protecting the human rights of those suffering mental disorders. According to *Mental Health Law,* "[t]he personality, dignity, and personal and property safety of the patients with mental disorders are inviolable. The lawful rights and interests of the patients with mental disorders in terms of education, employment, medical treatment, obtainment of material assistance from the state and society and other lawful rights and interests shall be protected by law. The relevant entities and individuals shall keep confidential the name, portrait, address, employer, and medical records of the patients with mental disorders and other information from which the identities of the patients with mental disorders may be inferred." *Mental Health Law* contains a chapter on legal liability of the government and relevant departments, employers, schools, medical staff and prisons as well as that of the community, family, media and psychological counsellors in promoting psychological health and preventing mental disorders. *Mental Health Law* clarifies for the first time that "people with mental disorders may be hospitalized for treatment only on voluntary basis" and restriction of the personal freedom of such is forbidden by law. This law regulates the medical treatment of patients with mental disorders, protects their rights and interests and contributes to their recovery.

It took 27 years for the law to finally be adopted. From its proposal to promulgation, opinions and suggestions from different populations in society were taken into consideration. With a focus on the protection of vulnerable groups, a people-oriented approach and an endeavor to give people equal rights and equal opportunities, the law fully demonstrates the concept of rule of law in respecting and protecting human rights.

2. Administrative regulations

Currently, administrative regulations in the field of healthcare cover bio-safety, circulation and vaccination of vaccines, control of narcotic and psychoactive drugs, prevention and treatment of HIV / AIDS, prevention and control of schistosomiasis, prevention and treatment of infectious diseases, food safety, family planning, labor protection for female employees, etc. For example, the already promulgated *Regulation on the Bio-Safety Management of Pathogenic Microbe Labs, Regulation on the Administration of Circulation and Vaccination of Vaccines, Regulation on the Control of Narcotic Drugs and Psychotropic Drugs, Regulation on the Prevention and Treatment of HIV / AIDS, Regulations on Prevention and Control of Schistosomiasis, Special Rules of the State Council on Strengthening the Supervision and Management of the Safety of Food and Other Products, Nurses Regulation, Regulation on the Supervision and Administration of the Quality and Safety of Dairy Products, Regulation on the Family Planning Work for the Migrant Population, Regulation on the Implementation of Food Safety Law of the People's Republic of China,* and *Special Provisions for the Work Protection of Female Employees* all place strong emphasis on the protection of people's right to life and health and a people-oriented approach.

3. Department rules

Since 2004, various departments' rules have been set with the purpose of effectively implementing health-related laws and regulations to protect people's life and health. The rules cover radiology, healthcare quality and safety, screening of diseases of new-born babies, healthcare at nurseries and kindergartens, drugs and devices for family planning, prevention and treatment of infectious diseases, prevention and treatment of sexually transmitted diseases, diagnosis and treatment of occupational diseases, prevention and control of tuberculosis, food safety, safety in catering services, food additives, administration of food safety in railway operations, drug safety, and clinical use of medical devices, thus setting up specific protection institutions in different fields and from different perspectives.

II. Medical reform is advanced for the benefit of the people.

Under the legal system of medical and health care, China has long been devoted to forging ahead the reform of the medical and health care system, bearing in mind that protection of people's health rights and interests is the top priority. In 2009, China set the goal of establishing a basic medical and health care system covering both urban and rural residents by the year 2020. Health reform and development help ensure that each and every resident, regardless of their gender, ethnic group, or whether they live in the city or countryside, enjoy basic healthcare services that are safe, effective, convenient and affordable.

1. Establishment of urban and rural healthcare system

China has established a basic healthcare system covering the urban and rural areas, which includes the public health service system, medical service system, medical security system and drug supply system. By the end of 2012, there were 912,000 grass-roots medical and health care institutions, including 8,176 community health service centers, 25,000 community health service stations, 37,000 town and township hospitals and 653,000 village clinics, with a total of 1.234 million beds. The government has also carried out a project to send 10,000 doctors to support healthcare in the rural areas. From 2009 to 2011, over 1,100 tertiary hospitals in cities gave assistance to 955 county hospitals; and secondary hospitals in cities in central and western China gave assistance to over 3,600 town and township hospitals every year. By the end of 2012 the essential medicines system had gained a full coverage, with all grass-roots government-run medical and health facilities using and supplying essential medicines without adding a surcharge for the resale of the drugs. This system is now being extended to village clinics and non-government health service providers at the grass-roots level.

2. Remarkable improvement in ensuring equal access to basic public health services

The per capita financial input in basic public health services was raised from 15 yuan in 2009 to 25 yuan in 2012. Forty-one items in ten categories of basic public health services are provided free for all residents. In 2011, vaccination rate under the national immunization program reached over 90 percent in general and the hospitalized delivery rate stood at 98.7 percent. Patients infected with major infectious diseases such as HIV, tuberculosis, schistosomiasis, echinococcosis, leprosy and malaria can get free medication. China was the first country to eliminate filariasis among the 83 endemic countries and regions.

3. Active effort in the provision of medical assistance

The *Opinions on Pilot Programs of Medical Aid for Major and Serious Diseases* were formulated and the relevant programs have been carried out in 273 pilot areas across the country. In 2012, 22.1 billion yuan was spent in medical assistance to 91.34 million people nationwide. To help vagrants and beggars, the State promulgated *Opinions on Strengthening and Improving Assistance and Protection for Vagrant Minors* and conducted a special campaign to "send vagrant children back home". By 2012 there were altogether 1,788 aid agencies (aid and relief centers, and aid and protection centers for vagrant minors) all over the country. From 2010 to 2011, these agencies offered aid to 4,128,709 vagrants and beggars. The relevant departments have concertedly responded to major public health emergencies such as SARS, H1N9, the Wenchuan earthquake and Lushan earthquake, providing medical rescue and other services, fully demonstrating the people-oriented approach and the comprehensive effort to protect people's well-being.

III. Improvement of people's health.

Thanks to unremitting efforts of many years, a healthcare system covering both urban and rural residents has basically taken shape, with the capabilities of disease prevention and control constantly improving, the coverage of medical insurance gradually expanding. In this process, the people's health has been remarkably improved along with advancement of medical science and technology. China has established a basic medical insurance system that covers over 95% of its population, enhanced both urban and rural grass-roots health services, put in place a national essential medicine system and markedly improved equal access to basic public health services. All of these measures and progresses contribute to the steady betterment of the Chinese people's health. In 2010, average life expectancy for Chinese was 74.8 years – 72.4 years for males and 77.4 years for females; maternal mortality went down from 51.3 per 100,000 in 2002 to 24.5 per 100,000 in 2012; infant mortality and mortality of children under the age of five have kept dropping, with the former going down from 29.2‰ in 2002 to 10.3‰ in 2012, ahead of the schedule of this target under UN Millennium Development Goals, and the latter down from 34.9‰ in 2002 to 13.2‰ in 2012.

To conclude, the decade after the concept of human rights was articulated in the Constitution has witnessed rapid progress in medical and health care, with more full-fledged services, greater service-providing capabilities, better and improved medical insurance system and stronger medicine production and supply capabilities. People now enjoy more benefits from progress in modern medical science and technology and their health has been significantly improved. The Chinese Government will, as always, attach great importance to health service and work towards the goal of health for all.

(original translation by Li Xiaoyu)

推动扶贫攻坚　促进人权发展

国务院扶贫开发领导小组副组长、扶贫办主任　刘永富

中国《宪法》明确规定："国家尊重和保障人权"。生存权和发展权是首要的人权，是享有人权的基础。《世界人权宣言》第25条阐明："人人有权享受为维持他本人和家属的健康和福利所需的生活水准，包括食物、衣着、住房、医疗和必要的社会服务。"贫困尤其是绝对贫困，直接影响着人的生存权，也侵蚀着人的发展权，是对人类权利的最大剥夺。因此，中国政府将保障人民的基本生存权、发展权放在人权事业的首位，通过市场化改革调动社会创造力，不断加大扶贫力度创造脱贫环境，努力构建扶贫开发与社会保障相结合的扶贫战略和政策体系。特别重视开发式扶贫，促进贫困人口提高自我生存和发展的能力，使之成为扶贫项目的决策者、参与者和管理者。通过多年的艰苦努力，在全球率先实现"联合国千年发展目标"中贫困人口减半目标，为全球减贫事业作出了重大贡献，成功走出一条中国特色的扶贫开发道路，为中国的人权保障事业写下了浓墨重彩的华丽篇章。

一、过去十年中国扶贫开发取得显著进展

2004年，中国政府将"国家尊重和保障人权"写入《宪法》。在扶贫开发方面，实施完成了《中国农村扶贫开发纲要（2001～2010年）》。目前正在实施《中国农村扶贫开发纲要（2011～2020年）》。这两个国家中长期

减贫计划，不仅使扶贫政策覆盖了更多的低收入群体，而且开始了扶贫开发的主要任务由解决温饱转向脱贫致富，促进了扶贫战略和政策体系的不断完善，形成扶贫开发与社会保障两轮驱动，专项扶贫、行业扶贫和社会扶贫三位一体的扶贫工作新格局，中国农村扶贫开发取得显著进展。

（一）农村居民的生存和温饱问题基本解决

2004年以来，为了提高贫困人口的保障水平，国家两次提高农村扶贫标准。

一是从2004年的924元逐步提高到2010年的1274元。以此标准衡量的农村贫困人口数量，从2000年年底的9422万人减少到2010年年底的2688万人；贫困发生率从2000年的10.2%下降到2010年的2.8%，基本上解决了农村居民的生存和温饱问题。

二是2011年国家大幅提高扶贫标准，以2010年不变价2300元作为新的扶贫标准。在新标准下，农村贫困人口从2011年的1.22亿人减少到2013年年底的8249万人，贫困发生率相应地从12.7%下降到8.5%，促进了农村贫困人口的脱贫致富。

（二）贫困地区经济快速发展

贫困地区产业结构进一步优化，特色优势产业快速发展，县域经济综合实力不断增强。592个国家扶贫开发工作重点县农民人均纯收入从2004年的1582元增加到2013年年底的5389元，绝对数增长了2.4倍，增幅高于全国农民收入增长平均水平，人均地区生产总值、人均地方财政收入年均增幅水平也都高于全国平均水平，发展差距不断扩大的趋势得到遏制和扭转。

（三）贫困地区生产生活条件明显改善

国家不断加大贫困地区基础设施建设投入，全面改善这些地方的生产生活条件。2004年，国家扶贫开发工作重点县自然村通电、通电话的比重分别为95.1%、64.4%；居民人均年生活消费支出1392元；人均住房面积21平方米，住房为钢筋混凝土和砖木结构的农户比重为52.5%，有厕所的农户比重为85%。到2013年年底，国家扶贫开发工作重点县自然村通电、通电话的比重分别为99.3%、93.1%；居民人均年生活消费支出4622元；农户人均住房面积27.8平方米，住房为钢筋混凝土和砖木结构的农户比重达92.7%，农户有厕所的比重达92.3%。贫困地区农村面貌发生明显变化。

（四）贫困地区社会事业不断进步

农村义务教育得到加强，扫除青壮年文盲工作取得积极进展。到2013年年底，国家扶贫开发工作重点县7～16岁学龄儿童入学率达到97.4%，接近全国平均水平。青壮年劳动力平均受教育年限达到8年，文盲率下降到7%以下。基层医疗卫生服务体系建设不断加强，新型农村合作医疗实现了全覆盖。到2013年年底，国家扶贫开发工作重点县参加新型农村合作医疗的农户比重接近99%，乡乡建有卫生院，有合格卫生室的行政村比重为92.9%，有合格乡村医生的行政村比重为89.2%。从2007年开始全面建立并不断完善农村最低生活保障制度。到2013年年底，全国农村有5388万人口享有最低生活保障。2009年在全国开始实施新型农村社会养老保险试点，计划2015年年底基本实现与城镇居民社会养老保险制度合并，2020年前全面建立公平、统一、规范的城乡居民养老保险制度。

（五）贫困地区生态恶化趋势得到初步遏制

过去十年，中国实施了退耕还林还草、天然林保护、退牧还草、三北防护林体系建设、易地扶贫搬迁等生态工程项目，水土流失面积有所下降，森林覆盖率有所增长，一定程度上阻止了生态恶化趋势，改善了生态环境。

石旮旯里的生机——贵州晴隆石漠化治理。

河南省栾川县狮子头扶贫搬迁新村。

二、扶贫开发主要做法和政策措施

（一）制定扶贫规划，完善扶贫战略

2011 年，中国政府在顺利完成《中国农村扶贫开发纲要（2001 ～ 2010 年）》各项目标任务的基础上，颁布实施了《中国农村扶贫开发纲要（2011 ～ 2020 年）》（以下简称"新十年纲要"），扶贫开发从以解决温饱为主要任务的阶段转入巩固温饱成果、加快脱贫致富、改善生态环境、提高发展能力、缩小发展差距的新阶段。《新十年纲要》明确了"两不愁、三保障"的奋斗目标，从基本农田和农田水利、特色优势产业、饮水安全、生产生活用电、交通、农村危房改造、教育、医疗卫生、公共文化、社会保障、林业、生态和信息化等方面提出工作任务，并明确到 2015 年和 2020 年的具体指标。《新十年纲要》坚持开发式扶贫的方针，实行扶贫开发与农村低保有机结合的扶贫政策体系。《新十年纲要》明确将连片特困地区作为扶贫攻坚主战场，加大投入和支持力度，加强对跨省片区规划的指导和协调。各省（自治区、直辖市）对所属连片特困地区负总责，在国家指导下，以县为基础制定和实

施扶贫攻坚工程规划。国务院各部门、地方各级政府加大统筹协调力度，集中实施一批交通、水利、教育、卫生、文化、就业、社会保障等民生工程，大力改善生产生活条件，培育壮大一批特色优势产业，加快区域性重要基础设施建设步伐，加强生态建设和环境保护，着力解决制约发展的瓶颈问题，促进基本公共服务均等化，进一步改变连片特困地区面貌。

（二）提高扶贫标准、加大资金投入

2011 年，国家大幅度提高了扶贫标准，以 2010 年不变价的 2300 元作为新的扶贫标准，比原标准提高了 92%。伴随着扶贫标准的提高，国家中央专项扶贫资金从 2004 年的 122 亿增加至 2013 年的 406 亿元。2004 ～ 2013 年，中央财政累计安排扶贫贷款贴息资金 55 亿元，发放扶贫贷款 3283 亿元，并不断推进扶贫贷款管理体制改革，采取贫困村互助资金试点等政策措施，有效缓解了贫困群众贷款难的问题。

（三）推进重点工作，强化部门协作

过去十年，扶贫部门与农业、水利、电力、环保、交通、住建、科技、民政、人力资源社会保障、教育、医疗等行业部门和公共服务提供部门一起，推出了针对贫困地区和贫困人群的系列政策措施。扶贫部门实施贫困村整村推进、劳动力转移培训（“雨露计划”）、产业化扶贫、互助资金和贴息贷款、易地扶贫搬迁、以工代赈、特殊地区扶贫试点等政策和项目。行业部门也不断加强扶贫开发，农业部门进行农业技术推广，交通部门改善贫困地区交通条件，水利部门加强贫困地区水利建设，电力部门解决无电人口用电问题、实施电网改造，住建部门实施农村危房改造项目，科技部门实施科技扶贫，教育部门完善和加强义务教育，医疗卫生部门实施和普及推广农村新型合作医疗，民政部门实施农村最低生活保障制度，人力资源和社会保障部门加强进城务工人员的培训与权益保障，环保部门加强贫困地区生态建设，等等。行业扶贫为保证扶贫开发取得显著进展奠定了坚实基础。

江西省贫困家庭女孩接受茶艺培训。

湘西柑橘累计开发 80 万亩产量 50 万吨——产业化扶贫。

四川省贫困村互助资金借款现场。

（四）引导社会扶贫，关注特困群体

国家继续实施和不断完善中央定点扶贫工作机制，逐步实现了国家扶贫开发工作重点县定点帮扶的全覆盖。加强引导东西部扶贫协作，让东部地区的资金、技术、人才、产业等助推中西部贫困地区扶贫开发事业。通过开展“光彩事业”等活动，积极引导和鼓励民营企业、社会组织和个人参与扶贫开发。过去十年，国家把贫困人口集中的中西部革命老区、少数民族地区、边疆地区和特困地区作为扶贫开发的重点区域，把对少数民族、妇女、残疾人等特殊人群的扶贫开发纳入扶贫规划，统一组织，同步实施，同等条件下优先安排，加大扶持力度。

三、继续推动扶贫攻坚，促进人权全面发展

中国是世界上最大的发展中国家，贫困人口规模大、贫困问题程度深，扶贫开发是一项长期的历史任务。为实现“扶贫对象不愁吃、不愁穿，保障

其义务教育、基本医疗和住房；贫困地区农民人均纯收入增长幅度高于全国平均水平，基本公共服务主要领域指标接近全国平均水平，扭转发展差距扩大趋势”的目标，中国政府将继续向贫困宣战，努力打好新阶段的扶贫攻坚战。今后一个时期，扶贫开发工作将认真做好三方面工作：

（一）统筹区域发展

在“区域发展带动扶贫开发、扶贫开发促进区域发展”理念的引导下，2012～2013年，编制出全国14个集中连片贫困区域发展与扶贫攻坚规划，统筹考虑片区内城镇化进度、重大基础设施布局、特色产业发展的实际情况，优化区域资源配置，发挥区域发展潜力，改善发展条件和环境。

（二）实行精准扶贫

通过对贫困户和贫困村精准识别、精准帮扶、精准管理和精准考核，引导各类扶贫资源优化配置，实现扶贫到村到户。首先，推进贫困县、贫困村、贫困人口建档立卡工作，掌握贫困底数，分析致贫原因，研究脱贫途径，制定帮扶措施。其次，创新扶贫工作机制，在贫困县考核、干部驻村帮扶、扶贫资金管理、金融服务、社会参与等方面实现机制创新。其三，加大推进村级道路畅通、饮水安全、电力保障、危房改造、特色产业增收、乡村旅游开发、教育扶贫、卫生和计划生育、文化建设、贫困村信息化等方面的行业扶贫工作。最后，着力培育“雨露计划”、“扶贫小额信贷”、“易地扶贫搬迁”三个扶贫品牌。

（三）完善社会保障

不断完善农村社会保障制度，彻底改变中国农村过去单纯以土地为生存保障、以家庭养老的局面。完善和优化农村最低生活保障制度、农村新型合作医疗保险制度、农村新型养老保险制度，避免因病、因老致贫和返贫现象。加强对残疾人、妇女、儿童、少数民族的社会保护，增强社会弱势群体的技能和生存发展能力。实施及时有效的社会救助制度，使因灾、因风险等因素冲击的人群及时得到社会救助，化解致贫返贫风险。

Striving for Poverty Alleviation and Promoting Human Rights Protection

Liu Yongfu, Deputy Head, State Council Leading Group Office of Poverty Alleviation and Development; Director of the State Council Poverty Relief Office

It is explicitly stipulated in the *Constitution of the People's Republic of China* that "[t]he State respects and protects human rights". The rights to subsistence and development are the primary human rights and the foundation for the enjoyment of human rights. Article 25 of the *Universal Declaration of Human Rights* states that "[e]veryone has the right to a standard of living adequate for the health and well-being of himself and of his family, including food, clothing, housing and medical care and necessary social services". Poverty, particularly absolute poverty, directly affects the right to subsistence and corrodes the right to development. It is therefore the most severe deprivation of human rights. In light of this, the Chinese Government prioritizes the rights to subsistence and development in the effort to protect human rights. It has mobilized social creativity through market-oriented reform, creates a favorable environment for poverty alleviation by continuously increasing support, and works to develop poverty reduction strategy and policies that combine of poverty alleviation, development and social security. We pay special attention to development-oriented poverty alleviation and try to improve the capability of self-subsistence and self-development of the impoverished people, turning them into decision-makers, participators and managers of poverty alleviation programs. Through years of hard work, China took the lead in the world to attaining the goal of reducing the number of impoverished people by half under the United Nations Millennium Development Goals, making a great contribution to the cause of global poverty reduction. It has blazed a trail of poverty alleviation and development with Chinese characteristics, adding an illustrious and colorful chapter to the cause of human rights protection in China.

I. Remarkable progress has been made in China's poverty alleviation and development over the past decade.

In 2004, that "[t]he State respects and protects human rights" became a provision of the Constitution. The Chinese Government completed the implementation of *Outline for Development-Oriented Poverty Reduction in China's Rural Area (2001-2010)*, and is implementing the *2011-2020 Outline*. According to these two mid- and long-term poverty reduction plans, poverty relief policies now cover more low income groups and the main task of poverty reduction has shifted from meeting the need for food and clothing to getting rid of poverty and becoming rich. This contributes to the improvement of the poverty reduction strategy and policy system. A new pattern combining special programs, action by industries and social efforts driven by both development-oriented poverty alleviation and social security has been formed. Remarkable progress has thus been made in poverty alleviation and development in the rural areas.

1. Problems of subsistence, food and clothing of rural residents have been basically solved

Since 2004, the State has twice increased poverty relief standard for rural areas in order to improve the security level for the impoverished population.

The first was a gradual increase from 924 yuan in 2004 to 1,274 yuan in 2010. Based on this changed standard, the poverty-stricken rural population fell from 94.22 million at the end of 2000 to 26.88 million at the end of 2010; and incidence of poverty declined from 10.2% in 2000 to 2.8% in 2010. The problems of subsistence, food and clothing for China's rural residents have been basically solved.

The second increase took place in 2011 and 2,300 yuan at 2010 constant price was set as the new standard. Poverty-stricken rural population decreased from 122 million in 2011 to 82.49 million at the end of 2010; and incidence of poverty correspondingly declined from 12.7% in 2000 to 8.5% in 2010. Impoverished people in rural areas are helped to get rid of poverty and become rich.

2. Rapid economic development in poverty-stricken areas

The industrial structure in these areas has been further optimized, industries with special advantages have developed rapidly and the comprehensive economic strengths of counties have grown. From 2004 to the end of 2013, 592 key counties in the national development-oriented poverty alleviation program had seen farmers' per capita net income grow from 1,582 yuan to 5,389 yuan, a 2.4-fold increase in absolute numbers and one higher than the national average. Growths in per capita gross regional product and per capita local fiscal revenue were also higher than the national average. The trend of widening development gap has been stopped and reversed.

3. Significantly improved production and living conditions

The government continues to increase investment in infrastructure construction in poverty-stricken areas to help improve the production and living conditions in these areas. In 2004, the percentages of electricity and telephone access for natural villages in the key counties in national development-oriented poverty alleviation program were 95.1% and 64.4%; annual per capita living expenses were 1,392 yuan and average per capita housing area was 21 square meters; 52.5% rural households had the percentage of reinforced concrete and masonry-timber housing structure; and 85% had a toilet. At the end of 2013, the corresponding figures were 99.3%, 93.1%, 4,622 yuan, 27.8 square meters, 92.7% and 92.3%. Significant changes have taken place in rural poverty-stricken regions.

4. Continuous progress in social undertakings

Compulsory education in rural areas has been strengthened and positive progress has been made in wiping out illiteracy among those in prime of life. By the end of 2013, the enrollment rate of school-age children (aged 7-16) in key counties in the national development-oriented poverty alleviation program had reached 97.4%, close to the national average. The average length of education for young adults and the middle aged had exceeded 8 years and the illiteracy rate of this group had dropped to below 7%. Grass-roots health services have been constantly improved and the new rural cooperative medical service now has a universal coverage. Close to 99% rural households in those key counties had been covered by the service. All towns and townships have hospitals, 92.9% administrative villages have qualified clinics, and 89.2% administrative villages have village doctors. Since 2007, comprehensive efforts had been made to establish and improve rural minimum living allowance system. And at the end of 2013, 53.88 million rural residents were receiving minimum living allowance. Since 2009, the government has been implementing pilot projects for the new social endowment insurance for rural residents. The plan is to merge it with the social endowment insurance system for urban residents by the end of 2015. This will allow for the establishment of a fair, harmonized and standardized endowment insurance system for urban and rural residents by 2020.

5. Ecological degradation basically under control

Over the past decade, the government has implemented a series of ecological projects, such as Grain for Green, Natural Forest Protection, Returning Grazing Land to Grassland, The Three Northern Shelterbelts Construction, Relocation and Poverty Alleviation of Residents in Extremely Harsh Living Conditions, etc. Thanks to these projects, soil erosion has decreased and forest coverage rate has been raised, thus containing to a certain extent the tendency of ecological degradation and improving the ecological environment.

Vitality in the crack of stone: combating stony desertification in Qinglong, Guizhou.

Residents of Shizitou Village in Luanchuan, Henan Province were relocated to a new residential area for poverty reduction purpose.

Ⅱ. Major methods and policy measures in poverty alleviation and development.

1. Making plans and improving strategy for poverty alleviation

In 2011, based on the successful accomplishment of the goals set in *Outline for Development-Oriented Poverty Alleviation of China's Rural Areas (2001-2010),* the Chinese Government promulgated *Outline for Development-Oriented Poverty Alleviation of China's Rural Areas (2011-2020)* (hereinafter the *"New Decade Outline"*). According to the *New Decade Outline,* the main focus of poverty alleviation and development has shifted from providing adequate food and clothing to the new stage of consolidating the previous achievement, accelerating poverty alleviation and economic progress, improving the ecological environment, enhancing development capacity and bridging the development gap. The *New Decade Outline* sets forth the goals of "the Two No-Worries and the Three Securities" – no eating or clothing worries and compulsory education, basic medical services and housing secured. Tasks and specific indicators for 2015 and 2020 are identified in basic cropland and related irrigation and water conservancy, industries with local characteristics and advantages, safe drinking water, electricity for production and living, transportation, renovation of dilapidated housing in rural areas, education, healthcare, public culture, social security, forestry, ecology and informatization, etc. The *New Decade Outline* adheres to the guideline of development-oriented poverty alleviation and adopts a policy system that combines poverty alleviation and development with minimum living allowances in rural areas. It also specifies contiguous poverty-stricken areas as the main battlefield for combating destitution and calls for increased investment and support as well as reinforced guidance and coordination in regard to trans-provincial areas. Provinces, autonomous regions and municipalities carry overall responsibility for the trans-provincial contiguous poverty-stricken areas and, under the guidance of central government, make plans and implement projects for poverty alleviation on a county-wide basis. Departments of the State Council and local governments at all levels enhance planning and coordination to implement a series of projects that are closely related to people's livelihood, covering transportation, irrigation and water conservancy, education, health, culture, employment and social security. The purpose is to significantly improve production and living conditions, cultivate and foster a big number of industries with local characteristics and advantages, accelerate the construction of important regional infrastructure, strengthen ecological construction and environment protection, spare no effort to solve the bottlenecks that restrict development and promote equal access to basic public service, thus further changing the look of contiguous destitute areas.

2. Raising the standard of poverty alleviation and increasing capital investment

In 2011, the government substantially raised the standard of poverty alleviation by 92%, setting the new standard to 2,300 yuan at 2010 constant price. As a result, the special fund for poverty alleviation from the central government increased from 12.2 billion yuan in 2004 to 40.6 billion yuan in 2013. During this period, the central government provided 5.5 billion yuan in interest subsidy on loans for poverty alleviation, and 328.3 billion yuan in loans for poverty reduction. The government also deepened reform of the management system of loan for poverty alleviation and adopted or piloted policy measures such as mutual financial assistance among poor villages, thus effectively alleviating the difficulty that impoverished people have in obtaining loans.

3. Working on priority tasks and enhancing coordination among departments

Over the past ten years, the poverty alleviation departments, together with line departments and public service providing departments including agriculture, irrigation and water conservancy, electricity, environmental protection, transportation, housing construction, science and technology, civil affairs, human resources and social security, education and health, has introduced a series of policy measures targeting poverty-stricken areas and impoverished people. Additionally, a variety of policies and projects have been implemented, such as poverty relief for the whole poverty-stricken villages, labor transfer training (also known as "Rain and Dew Plan"), poverty alleviation through industrialization, mutual fund and subsidized loans, relocation and poverty alleviation of residents in extremely harsh living conditions, poverty relief through employment, and pilot programs for poverty alleviation in special regions. The line departments have also reinforced their efforts, with the agricultural department extending agricultural technologies, transportation department improving access to poverty-stricken areas, water conservancy department strengthening construction of water conservancy facilities, power department upgrading power grid and bringing electricity supply to those previously without access to electricity, housing construction department initiating dilapidated housing renovation program in rural areas, science and technology department implementing poverty reduction with technology; education department improving and enhancing compulsory education, public health department implementing and popularizing the new rural cooperative medical service, civil affairs department establishing the system of minimum living allowances, human resources and social security department enhancing training and rights protection of migrant workers, and environmental protection department strengthening ecological construction in poverty-stricken areas. Actions taken in these different sectors have laid a solid foundation for ensuring future remarkable progress in poverty alleviation and development.

Young women from impoverished families in Jiangxi Province are taking training courses on tea ceremony.

Poverty alleviation through industrialization: 800 thousand mu (1 mu approximates 666.67 m^2) of mandarin oranges have been grown in west of Hunan Province, adding up to a total output of 500 thousand tons.

Mutual fund loan among poverty-stricken villages in Sichuan Province.

4. Guiding the society on actions for poverty alleviation and paying close attention to the extremely poor

The government continues to implement and improve the work mechanism for target poverty alleviation and now all key counties in the national development-oriented poverty alleviation program receive target relief and assistance. It has increased effort to guide cooperation between eastern and western provinces so as to steer the flow of capital, technology, human resources and industries from the eastern region to the poverty-stricken areas in central and western China. Through activities such as "Glory Program", the government actively guides and encourages private enterprises, NGOs and individuals to contribute to poverty alleviation and development. In the past decade, the government has made extra effort in poverty reduction in old revolutionary base areas in central and western China, ethnic minority areas, border areas and areas of extreme poverty where there are more people in need. Actions targeting ethnic minorities, women, and people with disabilities have also been incorporated in overall planning and implementation and given prioritized attention and greater support.

Ⅲ. Continue advancing poverty alleviation and promote comprehensive protection of human rights.

China is the world's largest developing country, with a large poor population and deeply-rooted poverty problems. Poverty alleviation and development remain a long-term historical task. In order that "recipients of poverty relief have no worries about food or clothing and have secure access to compulsory education, basic medical service and housing; per capita net income growth of rural residents in poverty-stricken areas is higher than the national average; indicators of main areas of basic public service are close to national average; the trend of widening development gap is reversed", the government will continue combating poverty and prepare for an uphill battle in this new stage. For some time to come, poverty alleviation and development work will be concentrated on the following three aspects:

1. Make overall plans for regional development

As "regional development facilitates poverty alleviation and development; development-oriented poverty alleviation promotes regional development", the government made regional development and poverty reduction plans for 14 contiguous poverty-stricken areas from 2012 to 2013. These plans take into account the urbanization process, important infrastructures and existing industries with local characteristics and advantages and optimize regional resource allocation with a view to tapping the full development potential and improving conditions and environment for development in the relevant areas.

2. Focus on the precision of poverty alleviation

Through precise identification, support, management and evaluation of poor families and villages, the government guides optimized allocation of all kinds of resources to the villages and households. First, the establishment of a system of filing and record keeping about poor counties, villages and households should be promoted so as to get the basic data, analyze the causes for poverty, identify solutions and develop supportive measures. Second, the work mechanisms for poverty reduction should be more innovative so as to encourage creative solutions for county-level performance evaluation, resident government officials in poor villages to provide support, poverty alleviation fund management, financial services and public participation. Third, greater efforts will be made to facilitate actions by different sectors such as inter-village road construction, safe drinking water, power supply security, renovation of dilapidated housing, income increase via industries with local characteristics and advantages, development of rural tourism, educational support, health and family planning, cultural and entertainment and access to information technology. Fourth, efforts will be redoubled in promoting the three outstanding branded projects: "Rain and Dew Plan", "Microcredit for Poverty Alleviation", and "Relocation and Poverty Alleviation of Residents in Extremely Harsh Living Conditions".

3. Improve social security

The rural social security system will be improved continuously to fundamentally change the old way of relying on farmland for subsistence and relying on family for old age. The minimum living security, new rural cooperative medical insurance, and new endowment insurance for rural residents will be improved and optimized so that people will not fall into poverty because of illness or aging. Social protection for people with disabilities, women, children and ethnic minorities will be reinforced and efforts will be made to increase the survivability and development skills of these vulnerable groups. A timely and effective social assistance system will be implemented so that people affected by a disaster or risk may receive assistance in a timely manner and thus avoid poverty.

(original translation by Xu Hongchen and Zhang Yuqian)

依法履行工会职责
切实保障劳动者人权

中华全国总工会副主席、书记处书记　江广平

今年是“国家尊重和保障人权”载入中国《宪法》十周年。十年来，中国共产党和中国政府坚持以促进社会公平正义、增进人民福祉为出发点和落脚点，全面深化改革，推动经济社会文化各项事业的发展，中国人民生活水平、民主建设水平、文化发展水平、社会保障水平、环境保护水平，都迈上了一个大台阶，中国人权事业取得不断发展。

维护劳动者合法权益，是发展人权事业的重要内容。中国工会作为中国职工自愿结合的工人阶级群众组织，是党联系职工群众的桥梁和纽带，是职工合法权益的代表者和维护者，是推动劳动者人权发展的重要力量。多年来，中国工会高度重视保障劳动者人权，积极履行各项职能，为促进实现劳动者的政治、经济、文化和社会等权利发挥了积极作用。

一、主动加强源头参与，从法律层面保障劳动者人权

自2003年以来，中国工会通过多种方式和渠道主动参与立法，努力推动形成中国特色社会主义劳动法律体系。中国工会发挥工会组织优势，深入职工群众，广泛征询并收集意见，积极代表职工向立法机关反映，通过全国

人大代表、政协工会界委员积极提出立法建议和议案、提案。2012年在《劳动合同法修正案（草案）》55.7万条意见中，绝大多数是职工和工会的意见建议。工会的意见建议在《劳动合同法（修正案）》中得到了全面反映。十年来，中国工会推动和参与了包括《公司法》、《劳动合同法》、《社会保险法》、《就业促进法》、《劳动争议调解仲裁法》、《破产法》、《物权法》、《安全生产法》、《职业病防治法》、《女职工劳动保护特别规定》等120多部涉及职工权益的重要法律法规的制定和修改。对一些突出的需从立法上解决的问题而暂时不具备全国性立法条件的，积极推动地方先行立法。目前，全国已有30个省（区、市）总工会建立了与省（区、市）人民政府联席会议制度，28个省（区、市）出台了37个企业民主管理的地方性法规，27个省（区、市）制定了集体协商地方性法规或政府规章。

工会法律援助律师志愿者为农民工解答法律问题。

经过一系列的摸索与实践，具有中国特色的工会参与立法的模式和制度机制已基本形成，以《劳动法》为骨干，《劳动合同法》、《劳动争议调解仲裁法》、《社会保险法》、《安全生产法》等法律法规组成的劳动法律体系已基本确立并不断完善，为工会开展各项工作、切实维护职工权益、实现劳动者人权提供了有力的法律保障。

二、切实发挥工会作用，维护劳动者合法权益

（一）广泛开展“两个普遍”，维护劳动者的组织权和集体谈判权

面对职工队伍迅速发展壮大、流动性显著增强、企业用工方式复杂多变的状况，2004 年以来，中国工会提出并履行“组织起来、切实维权”的工作方针和“以职工为本，主动依法科学维权”的维权观。2010 年起广泛开展“两个普遍”工作，即依法推动企业普遍建立工会组织、依法推动企业普遍开展工资集体协商。

中国工会以非公有制企业和外商投资企业为重点领域，以农民工为重点对象，大力推进新经济组织、新社会组织组建工会，努力攻克沃尔玛等跨国公司在华企业组建工会难点，整顿重建国有改制企业工会组织，工会组织组建和会员发展取得了重大突破。2013 年年底，中华全国总工会基层工会组织达到 276.6 万个，覆盖单位数达到 653 万个，工会会员总数达到 2.9 亿，其中农民工会员 1.1 亿。

同时，中国工会把维护职工集体谈判权作为重中之重来抓，依法推动企业广泛开展工资集体协商，大力推进行业性、区域性集体协商。2013 年年底，全国 31 个省（区、市）已建会企业工资集体协商建制率均达 80% 以上，全国已签订集体合同 242 万份，覆盖企业 632.9 万家，覆盖职工 2.87 亿人。其中签订行业性集体合同 24.2 万份，覆盖企业 143 万家，签订区域性集体合同 33.4 万份，覆盖企业 372 万家。沃尔玛、肯德基、家乐福等世界 500 强在华企业均成功开展集体协商，在国际国内产生了较大影响。

（二）努力构建和谐劳动关系，维护劳动者的民主管理权和劳动争议权

多年来，中国工会不断推动健全协调劳动关系三方机制，发挥劳动合同、集体合同和职代会制度作用，推进企业民主管理，健全劳动关系矛盾预警、调解机制，劳动关系总体保持稳定。

截至 2013 年 9 月，全国已建立工会的企事业单位单独建立厂务公开制

度的有464.3万家，单独建立职工代表大会制度的有470.8万家，区域（行业）职工代表大会覆盖企业177.2万家。2012年年底，各级工会在企事业单位建立劳动争议调解委员会85.8万个，共有劳动争议调解员288.4万人，建立区域性行业性调解组织2.5万个，调解组织人数21.8万人。各级工会发挥工会信访部门、"12351"职工热线电话和信息中心的作用，及时汇总、分析、掌握职工的利益诉求，并与人民法院、劳动行政部门等加强协调配合，积极探索工会牵头、各方联动的劳动争议预防调处方式方法。

（三）着力健全体制机制，维护劳动者就业权、公平收入权和职业培训权

就业权是基本人权中的重要内容，稳定和扩大就业是保障劳动者就业权的重要措施。十年来，中国工会以下岗失业人员、农民工、困难职工家庭高校毕业生等就业困难群体为重点，发挥工会组织自身优势，大力开展就业服务、技能培训和创业指导。特别是2009年以来，为应对国际金融危机冲击，组织开展了千万农民工援助行动、全国女职工岗位创新技能大赛、技能培训促就业行动、全国"工会就业援助月"、家政服务工程、困难职工家庭高校毕业生"阳光就业行动"等活动。仅2014年全国"工会就业援助月"活动就组织专场招聘会7413场次，提供免费就业服务578万人次。

工会提供职业介绍服务。

中国工会积极参与收入分配制度改革，参与制定《关于深化收入分配制度改革若干意见》，推动解决职工收入分配中的突出问题，切实维护职工公平收入权。各级工会积极促进最低工资标准调整，配合政府有关部门做好农民工工资支付保障工作。2009～2013年，全国31个省（区、市）最低工资标准年均提高幅度达12.6%；全国城镇非私营企业在岗职工年平均工资由2008年的29229元增长至2012年的46769元，年均增长12.5%，私营单位职工工资五年来也有较大幅度的提高。

各级工会进一步发挥工会“大学校”作用，积极引导广大职工提高科学文化和技术技能水平，不断增强竞争能力和就业创业能力。2012年年底，共建设全国职工教育培训示范点2400家，命名全国职工技能实训基地130家。建设了5000家全国工会“职工书屋”示范点，带动各级工会自建50000余家“职工书屋”。目前，已使1226万职工提升学历层次，使2043万职工提升技术等级，对1306万城镇下岗失业人员和农民工进行了转岗就业培训、自主创业培训和职业技能培训。

（四）积极参与社会保障政策制定与监督，维护劳动者社会保障权和职业安全权

中国工会积极促进社会保障逐步覆盖全体职工，加强劳动保护工作，维护职工健康权益和生命安全，健全困难职工帮扶工作网络，丰富帮扶内容，加强法律援助。

中国工会以扩大社会保险覆盖面、提高保障水平、统筹层次和职工待遇水平为重点，积极参与有关法规政策的制定，推动实现将600多万名关闭破产国有企业未参保退休人员全部纳入城镇职工基本医疗保险，将312万名国有企业“老工伤”人员和工亡职工家属纳入工伤保险统筹管理，并将未参保集体企业和“五七工”、“家属工”等群体纳入养老保险，有力维护了职工的社会保障权利。到2013年年底，全国参加城镇职工基本养老保险、基本医疗保险、失业保险、工伤保险、生育保险人数分别达到32218万、27443万人、16417万、19917万、16392万；主动参与职业病防治工作，推广“工会参与职业病防治工作模式”，推动建立职业病防治工作联席会议机制，推动政府加强职业病防治工作和用人单位防治主体责任落实。5年来，全国基层以上工会提出事故隐患和职业危害整改意见共计176万余件；积极创新帮扶工作机制，形成"救助—维权—服务"三位一体的工作格局，打造了"送温暖工程"、"困难职工帮扶中心"、"困难女职工关爱行动"、"金秋助学"、"阳光就业"、"家政服务工程"、"农民工平安返乡"等一系列帮扶品牌，2003～2013年各级工会帮扶中心共筹集帮扶资金218.8亿元，帮扶困难职工和农民工6798.3万人次。2005年开展"金秋助学"活动以来，中国工会共筹集助学款73.6亿元，帮助574.7万人次困难职工和农民工子女走进校园。

工会提供免费体检。

（五）注重保障底线公平，维护特殊群体权利

中国工会高度关注妇女、农民工等特殊群体的权益维护，积极参与《妇女权益保障法》、《生育保险办法（草案）》、《女职工劳动保护特别规定》、《劳务派遣暂行规定》等涉及女职工和农民工权益的法律法规规章的制定与完善，最大限度地将女职工、农民工组织到工会组织中来，配合开展特殊群体保护检查和维权专项行动，使他们的特殊权益得到较好维护。

截至 2013 年 9 月，全国基层工会女职工组织数已达 261.4 万个，已建工会基层单位工会女职工组织覆盖率 97.65%，全国女职工专项集体合同签订数 121.5 万份，覆盖企业 294.6 万家，覆盖女职工 7787.1 万人；深入开展农民工帮扶工作，仅 2013 年为 345.8 万人次困难农民工提供帮扶，在 2014 年春节期间帮助 555.8 万人次农民工平安返乡。会同有关部门开展农民工工资支付专项检查，为 155 万名农民工追回被拖欠工资 108.5 亿元。

女职工健康体检。

三、积极加强国际合作，推动劳动者人权对外交流

中国工会积极参与国际交流，加强劳动者人权对话。多年来，中国工会与国际劳工组织、国外工会组织就工会权利、工资集体协商、企业劳动争议处理、职业安全卫生、性别平等、反对强迫劳动等主题开展形式多样的研讨与培训活动，相互学习保障劳动者人权的实践经验，并积极参与国际人权对话交流活动，宣传中国工会维护职工权益的工作和成果，增强外国工会对中

国工会的认识和理解。

中国工会积极参与国际劳工事务，参与国际劳工标准的制定，围绕就业、社会保障、工资集体协商、性别平等、反对强迫劳动、职业安全卫生等议题广泛开展技术合作，努力推动国家批准《国际劳工公约》并监督公约的实施。2006 年，《消除就业与职业歧视公约》(第 111 号公约)、《职业安全和卫生及工作环境公约》(第 155 号公约) 先后得到国家的批准。

中国工会积极参与国际劳工组织、二十国集团、亚太经合组织、金砖国家等国际多边治理机制，代表广大发展中国家劳动者，阐述维护工人的基本权利的主张。中国工会与国际性工会组织以及各国工会组织的对话交流与合作不断深入发展，中国工会维护职工合法权益的主张与实践受到大多数国外工会组织的赞赏，中国特色社会主义工会发展道路得到国际工运界的理解和认同。

当前，中国正致力于实现中华民族伟大复兴的中国梦，通过全面深化改革，让发展成果更多更公平地惠及全体人民，中国人权事业正在向更高的目标迈进。中国工会也将进一步履行职责，更好地维护劳动者合法权益，为促进职工群众舒心工作、体面劳动、全面发展，为推动中国人权事业的发展作出新贡献。

Fulfilling Trade Union Responsibilities According to Law to Protect Laborers' Human Rights

Jiang Guangping, Vice Chairman and Secretary of the Secretariat, All-China Federation of Trade Unions

This year is the tenth anniversary since the clause that "[t]he State respects and protects human rights" was articulated in the *Constitution of the People's Republic of China*. In the past ten years, the Communist Party of China (CPC) and the Chinese Government has borne in mind the promotion of social equity and justice as well as people's well-being and comprehensively deepened reform to promote economic, social and cultural development. Substantial improvement has been made in people's living standards, level of democracy, cultural development, social security and environmental protection, leading to constant betterment of human rights protection.

Protecting laborers' lawful rights and interests is an important element in the development of human rights. China's trade union federations are mass organizations of the working class formed voluntarily by the Chinese workers. They work as a link between the CPC and ordinary workers and act as the representative and guardian of workers' lawful rights and interests, and a driving force for the protection of laborers' human rights. The federations have for years attached great importance to the protection of laborers' human rights, actively implemented all functions and played a positive role in helping laborers to enjoy their political, economic, cultural and social rights.

I. Strengthening participation from the beginning to protect laborers' human rights at the legal level.

Since 2003, the federations have been actively pushing forward through various means and channels a system of socialist labor laws with distinct Chinese characteristics. They actively represent opinions that they solicit and collect extensively from among workers to the legislative organ and put forward legislative suggestions, proposals and draft resolutions through deputies to the National People's Congress and members of the Chinese People's Political Consultative Conference committees. In 2012, among 557,000 pieces of comments collected for *Amendment to the Labor Contract Law (Draft),* most are from workers and trade unions. As a result, the unions' opinions are fully reflected in the revised *Labor Contract Law.* In the past ten years, the federations have promoted and participated in the making and revision of more than 120 important laws related to the rights of workers, such as *Company Law, Labor Contract Law, Social Insurance Law, Law on Promotion of Employment, Law on labor-Disputes Mediation and Arbitration, Bankruptcy Law, Property Law, Safe Production Law, Occupational Illness Prevention and Treatment Law,* and *Special Regulations for the Work Protection of Female Employees.* With regard to the outstanding problems that need to be addressed through legislation and for which the conditions of national legislation are not ripe yet, the federations help create and revise local laws. Now, the federations of trade unions in 30 provinces (autonomous regions and municipalities) have established joint conference mechanisms with the provincial government. Twenty-eight provinces (autonomous regions and municipalities) have developed 37 local laws pertaining to democratic management of enterprises, and 27 provinces (autonomous regions and municipalities) have created local laws or government regulations on collective bargaining.

The union's volunteer legal aid lawyers answer legal questions of migrant workers.

After a series of exploration and practice, the mode and institutional mechanism of the federations participation in the legislation has been set up. This mechanism has distinct Chinese characteristics. A system of labor laws, including the *Labor Law, Labor Contract Law, Law on Labor-Disputes Mediation and Arbitration, Social Insurance Law, Safe Production Law* etc, has been basically put in place and constantly improved, providing solid legal basis for the trade unions to conduct various activities to protect workers' interests and realize laborers' human rights.

II. Giving full play to the role of trade unions to protect laborers' lawful rights and interests.

1. Extensive campaign to achieve "two universalities" in protection of laborers' right to organization and collective negotiation

As the number and the mobility of workers rapidly increase and forms of hiring become more complex and volatile, the federations proposed in 2004 that workers must get organized to safeguard their legal rights and that efforts to safeguard these rights must be workers-oriented and conducted in a proactive, lawful and scientific way. The federations have since acted upon these principles. Since 2010, extensive campaign has been widely carried out to achieve "two universalities", i.e., trade unions should be established in all enterprises and enterprises should all engage in collective wage bargaining.

The federations target non-public and foreign-invested enterprises as well as migrant workers as their main focuses of work and encourage the establishment of trade unions in the new economic and social organizations. The federations have overcome the difficulties and set up trade unions in the Chinese businesses of MNCs like Wal-Mart, and rectified and rebuilt trade unions in restructured state-owned enterprises, resulting in major breakthroughs in the organization and membership of trade unions. By the end of 2013, the number of the grass-roots trade unions affiliated to the All-China Federation of Trade Unions (ACFTU) had reached 2.766 million, in 6.53 million enterprises and institutions. The total number of union members amounted to 290 million, among which there were 110 million migrant workers.

The federations regard the protection of collective negotiation rights as one of their most important tasks, and push forward collective wage bargaining in enterprises and make great effort to facilitate industry-wide and region-wide collective bargaining. By the end of 2013, more than 80% enterprises with trade unions in 31 provinces (autonomous regions and municipalities) had set up collective wage bargaining system. 2.42 million collective contracts had been signed, covering 6.329 million enterprises and 287 million workers. Among these contracts, there were 242,000 industry-wide collective contracts, covering 1.43 million enterprises, and 334,000 region-wide collective contracts, involving 3.72 million enterprises. All Fortune 500 companies such as Wal-Mart, KFC and Carrefour have successfully conducted collective bargaining in their enterprises in China, which has fairly big influence both in China and the international society.

2. Work towards harmonious labor relations to protect laborers' rights in democratic management and labor disputes

In recent years, the federations have made continuous effort to improve the tripartite mechanism to coordinate labor relations, put into good use the systems of labor contract, collective contract and workers' congress, promote democratic management of enterprises and improve labor relations early warning and mediation mechanisms, thus keeping labor relations stable on the whole.

By September 2013, among the enterprises and institutions which had trade unions, 4.643 million had in place a corporate affair transparency mechanism and 4.708 million had a workers congress system. In addition, 1.772 million enterprises had joined the regional (industry-wide) workers congress. By the end of 2012, the trade unions at all levels had set up 858,000 labor dispute mediation committees in all types of enterprises, with 2.884 million mediators. There were 25,000 regional and industrial mediation organizations with 218,000 staff members. The unions' complaint departments, 12351 hotline and information centers collect, analyze and take stock of workers demands in a timely manner. Trade unions at all levels work with the people's courts and labor administrative departments to explore ways to prevent and mediate labor disputes with joint efforts led by the trade unions.

3. Focused effort to improve the system and mechanism to protect laborers' rights to employment, fair income and vocational training

The right to employment is an important part of basic human rights. To stabilize and expand employment is an important measure to protect laborers' right to employment. In the past 10 years, the federations have focused on laid-off workers, migrant workers, and university graduate students from families with economic difficulties. They have provided employment service, vocational training and entrepreneurial guidance for them. Since 2009 in particular, in light of the international financial crisis, the federations have organized a variety of activities including campaign to help millions of migrant workers, creative skills competitions for female workers, job-hunting-oriented vocational training campaign, "employment assistance month", domestic service project, and the "Sunshine Employment Campaign" for university graduates from workers' families with economic difficulties. During the employment assistance month in 2014 alone, the federations organized 7,413 special job fairs and provided free employment service for 5.78 million people.

Trade unions provide employment service.

The federations actively participate in the reform of the income distribution system and the formulation of *Several Opinions on Deepening Reform of the Income Distribution System* to help solve outstanding issues of income distribution and protect workers' right to equal income. Trade union federations at all levels actively promote the adjustment of the minimum wage standards and support relevant government departments in securing salary payment for migrant workers. From 2009 to 2013, the average annual increase of minimum wage standards in the 31 provinces (autonomous regions and municipalities) of China was 12.6%. The average annual salary of employees in service in urban non-private enterprises increased from 29,229 yuan in 2008 to 46,769 yuan in 2012, an average annual increase of 12.5%. The salary of employees in private enterprises has also registered substantial increase in the past five years.

Trade union federations at all levels act as a "big school" by actively guiding workers to improve their knowledge and skills so as to enhance competitiveness, employability and entrepreneurial skills. By the end of 2012, the federations had set up 2,400 pilot training centers and designated 130 skills training bases. ACFTU also built 5,000 workers' demonstration libraries, followed by local trade union federations with more than 50,000 libraries built for their members. Up to date, the federations at various levels have helped 12.26 million workers to improve their academic qualifications and 20.43 million workers to enhance skills. They have also provided training to 13.06 million urban laid-offs and unemployed and migrant workers to help them change jobs, start their own business or improve vocational skills.

4. Active participation in formulation and supervision of social security policies to protect laborers' rights to social security and occupational safety

The federations actively promote gradual extension of the social security system to cover all workers and strengthen labor protection so as to protect workers' health and life safety. The network to help workers with difficulties has been improved, with more services and strengthened legal aid.

The federations focus on expanding coverage and improving the security level, pooling and benefits of social insurance, and actively participate in the formulation of related laws and regulations. They have helped in the effort to include more than 6 million uncovered retired employees of closed or bankrupt state-owned enterprises in the basic medical insurance for urban employees, 3.12 million SOE employees with "old" work-related injury and dependents of those who died in work-related accidents in work-related injury insurance, and collective enterprises that have not joined the insurance, the "May 7th workers" and spouse workers – urban residents who were engaged in the state-owned enterprises in 19 industries as of the 1960s or 1970s but not covered by the basic endowment insurance – in the endowment insurance, thus protecting their right to social security. By the end of 2013, the numbers of people covered by basic endowment insurance, basic medical insurance, unemployment insurance, work-related injury insurance and maternity insurance for urban workers had reached 322.18 million, 274.43 million, 164.17 million, 199.17 million and 163.92 million respectively. The federations take an active part in the prevention and treatment of occupational disease and advocates for the inclusion of trade unions in the relevant work. They have promoted joint meetings on this issue and urged the government to strengthen the prevention and treatment of occupational diseases and to hold employers accountable. In the past five years, and trade unions above the grass-roots level have put forward 1.76 million pieces of comments about accident potentials and occupational hazards. The federations have innovated in assistance mechanisms and created a triad work pattern of assistance, rights protection and service. They have developed a series of branded assistance projects including heart-warming project, assistance centers for workers in need, campaign of caring for female workers in need, autumn education assistance program, Sunshine Employment project, domestic service project, and migrants workers' safe journey back home. From 2003 to 2013, assistance centers affiliated with trade union federations at all levels raised 21.88 billion yuan and helped 67.983 million workers and migrant workers in need. Since 2005, when the autumn education assistance program was launched, the federations have mobilized 7.36 billion yuan to help 5.747 million children of workers in financial hardships and of migrant workers to go to school.

Unions offer free medical examination.

5. Emphasis on bottom line equity to safeguard the rights of special groups

The federations pay high attention to the protection of special groups including female workers and migrant workers. They have actively participated in the making and revision of the relevant laws and regulations, including the *Law on the Protection of the Rights and Interests of Women, Measures on Maternity Insurance (Draft), Special Provisions on Labor Protection for Female Employees,* and *Provisional Regulations on Labor Dispatch.* Efforts are made to attract female workers and migrant workers to join the trade unions and better protect their special rights and interests via targeted inspection and protection campaigns.

By September 2013, the number of female workers' organizations in grass-roots trade unions had reached 2.614 million and 97.65% grass-roots trade unions had set up such organizations. Special collective contracts for female workers had amounted to 1.215 million, involving 2.946 million enterprises and 77.871 million female workers. Assistance programs for migrant workers are actively carried out. In 2013, 3.458 million migrant workers were offered help from the unions. During the Spring Festival of 2014, 5.558 million migrant workers were helped to safely return to their hometown. The federations have worked with relevant government departments on special salary payment inspections and helped, to retrieve 10.85 billion yuan in salary arrears for 1.55 million migrant workers.

Medical examinations for female workers.

Ⅲ. Actively strengthening international cooperation and advancing exchanges among laborers on human rights.

China's trade union federations actively participate in international exchanges and strengthen laborers' dialogue on human rights. They have engaged in various forms of discussion and training with the International Labor Organization and trade unions of other countries on the rights of trade unions, collective wage bargaining, settlement of labor disputes, occupational safety and health, gender equality, and opposing forced labor. With these, they have learnt from each other practices and experiences in the protection of laborers' human rights. The federations also take an active part in international human rights dialogues and exchanges to share with foreign counterparts the work and achievements in protecting employees' rights and interests and to deepen their understanding of Chinese trade unions.

The federations actively involve themselves in international labor affairs, participate in the setting of the international labor standards, develop extensive technical cooperation on employment, social security, collective wage bargaining, gender equality, ending forced labor and occupational safety and health, and push forward the ratification of *International Labor Conventions* in China and oversee its implementation. In 2006, China ratified the *Discrimination (Employment and Occupation) Convention (ILO No.111)* and *Convention Concerning Occupational Safety and Health and the Working Environment (ILO No.155)* .

The federations are also active in the international multilateral governance mechanisms like International Labor Organization, Group of Twenty, APEC, and BRICS, in which they state on behalf of laborers of developing countries the propositions on the protection of workers' basic rights. The dialogues, exchanges and cooperation with international and national unions have deepened. Their propositions and practices in the protection of workers' legal rights are widely appreciated by foreign trade unions. The path of trade unions development with Chinese characteristics is widely understood and identified in the international workers' movement community.

Now, China is committed to realizing the Chinese Dream of great national rejuvenation. Through deepened reform, development will benefit all people in a more equitable way and human rights will be better protected. China's trade union federations will further perform their functions, better protect the lawful rights and interest of laborers and make new contribution to people's decent work and comprehensive development and betterment of human rights protection in China.

(original translation by Yang Ji)

贯彻男女平等基本国策，尊重和保护妇女权益

全国妇联副主席、书记处书记　孟晓驷

中国是世界上女性人口最多的国家，在 13.35 亿人口中女性有 6.48 亿，占人口总数的 48.56%。中国高度重视性别平等和妇女发展事业。男女平等既是中国《宪法》的基本原则，也作为促进社会发展的一项基本国策予以遵循。2004 年，“国家尊重和保障人权”写入中国《宪法》，中国在人权事业取得巨大成就的同时，妇女事业也得到进一步推动和发展。

“人权入宪”十年来，中国认真落实“尊重和保障人权”的宪法原则，进一步建立和完善了妇女权益保护的一整套法律法规和政策体系，运用法律、行政、宣传、教育等多种手段予以贯彻执行。中国政府在顺利完成了前两个《中国妇女发展纲要》之后，开始实施第三个纲要，即《中国妇女发展纲要（2011 ～ 2020 年）》。妇女发展目标被纳入《国民经济和社会发展第十二个五年规划纲要》并着力推进，实现二者同步发展。2012 年党的十八大首次将“坚持男女平等基本国策，保障妇女儿童合法权益”写进工作报告，这是中国执政党引领性别平等走向主流价值的政治承诺。在中国党和政府大力推动和全社会共同努力下，妇女发展取得长足进步，妇女地位不断提高，性别平等状况不断改善。

一、进一步完善法律法规体系，为实现妇女权益提供法律保障

十年来，中国制定或修订了《妇女权益保障法》、《劳动合同法》、《婚姻法》、《就业促进法》、《女职工劳动保护特别规定》等10余部保障妇女权益的法律法规。截至2013年年底，31个省（区、市）修订了《妇女权益保障法实施办法》，29个省（区、市）人大出台了预防和制止家庭暴力的地方法规。《反家庭暴力法》已被列入国家立法计划。

《妇女权益保障法（修订案）》对总则、妇女权益领域和法律责任进行了全面补充和完善，强化了政府及相关部门、机构的责任，突出了妇女权益保护重点，对社会上普遍关心的妇女参政、就业中的性别歧视、家庭暴力、性骚扰、农村妇女土地承包及相关财产权益等问题做出新规定。《就业促进法》专门设立"公平就业"一章，要求"消除就业歧视"，"保障妇女享有与男子平等的劳动权利……不得以性别为由拒绝录用妇女或者提高对妇女的录用标准……不得在劳动合同中规定限制女职工结婚、生育的内容"。《劳动合同法》规定，女职工在孕期、产期、哺乳期期间，用人单位不得解除与她们的劳动合同。《社会保险法》规定："职工应当参加生育保险，由用人单位按照国家规定缴纳生育保险费。"在保障妇女政治权方面，国家出台了《关于修改〈中华人民共和国全国人民代表大会和地方各级人民代表大会选举法〉的决定》，规定："全国人民代表大会和地方各级人民代表大会的代表应当具有广泛的代表性……应当有适当数量的妇女代表，并逐步提高妇女代表的比例。"2010年修订的《村民委员会组织法》规定："村民委员会成员中，应当有妇女成员"，"妇女村民代表应当占村民代表会议组成人员的三分之一以上"。这些规定从法律上切实保证了对妇女的政治赋权，使妇女对国家政治生活的参与、决策和管理程度不断提高。

女村民在村委会换届选举中投下自己庄严的一票。

二、持续实施妇女发展纲要，有力推动妇女事业新发展

自 1995 年颁布实施第一个《中国妇女发展纲要（1995 ～ 2000 年）》以来，中国以十年为一个周期，先后出台了《中国妇女发展纲要（2001 ～ 2010 年）》和《中国妇女发展纲要（2011 ～ 2020 年）》。2010 年，中国政府对《中国妇女发展纲要（2001 ～ 2010 年）》的成果进行了评估和审查。在充分肯定纲要执行已取得的成果基础上，根据中国社会经济发展的现实情况，中国政府制定了未来十年的发展计划和目标。

《中国妇女发展纲要（2011 ～ 2020 年）》确定妇女的健康、教育、经济、参政、社会保障、环境、法律为发展优先领域，提出了 57 项主要目标和 88 项策略措施。纲要进一步明确了国务院及地方政府各有关部门机构的职责，要求各级政府在实施《中国妇女发展纲要》中坚持"五纳入"：纳入国家和地方法规政策、纳入经济社会发展总体规划和专项规划、纳入各级政府财政

预算、纳入为民办实事的发展项目、纳入政府工作议事日程和责任考核内容，确保妇女发展与经济社会发展同步规划、同步落实。纲要实施以来，妇女发展取得了历史性的巨大进步。

相关国家机制的进一步完善为妇女发展提供有力的组织保障。国家专门设立国务院妇女儿童工作委员会（简称“妇儿工委”），委员会成员单位由成立初的19个部门发展为目前的35个，全国所有省、地、县政府均成立了“妇儿工委”。妇儿工委发挥综合协调、督促检查和参谋助手作用，推动有关部门将妇女工作列入重要议事日程，各司其职、通力合作。全国人大及其常委会将保障妇女权益、促进性别平等作为一项重要任务，设立“工会、青年团和妇女工作办公室”，定期听取各委员会和有关部门促进性别平等的情况报告。2009年至今，数次开展《妇女权益保障法》等相关法律的执法检查和调研。全国政协社会和法制委员会设置了“妇女儿童工作小组”，对妇女发展中的重点难点问题适时提出建议，积极办理促进性别平等和妇女发展的提案。

三、多措并举，推动性别平等和妇女赋权

为妇女创业就业搭建平台。为促进妇女就业，政府和社会组织合作在200多个城市开展“春风行动”，为失业妇女、女农民工、女大学生送就业岗位和就业服务。为解决妇女创业资金问题，自2009年起实施小额担保贷款财政贴息政策，2009年至2014年一季度末向创业妇女提供贷款1800多亿元，中央及地方落实财政贴息资金120多亿元，为360多万人次妇女提供了创业启动资金，辐射带动近千万妇女创业就业。

妇女发展项目为改善妇女生活环境、促进妇女发展作出了贡献。

为保障妇女的健康增加新投入。中央和地方政府累计投资20多亿元开展“降低孕产妇死亡率和消除新生儿破伤风”项目。仅2008～2010年中央财政就投入70亿元用于全国农村孕产妇住院分娩补助，大大降低了孕产妇和新生儿死亡率。从2009年开始开展农村妇女乳腺癌、宫颈癌免费检查，并为贫困患癌妇女建立专项救治基金，截至2013年年底已累计为3700多万名农村妇女提供了免费检查。发往中国中西部地区的“母亲健康快车”，以流动医疗车为载体，努力为贫困地区妇女儿童送健康理念、送健康知识和健康服务。

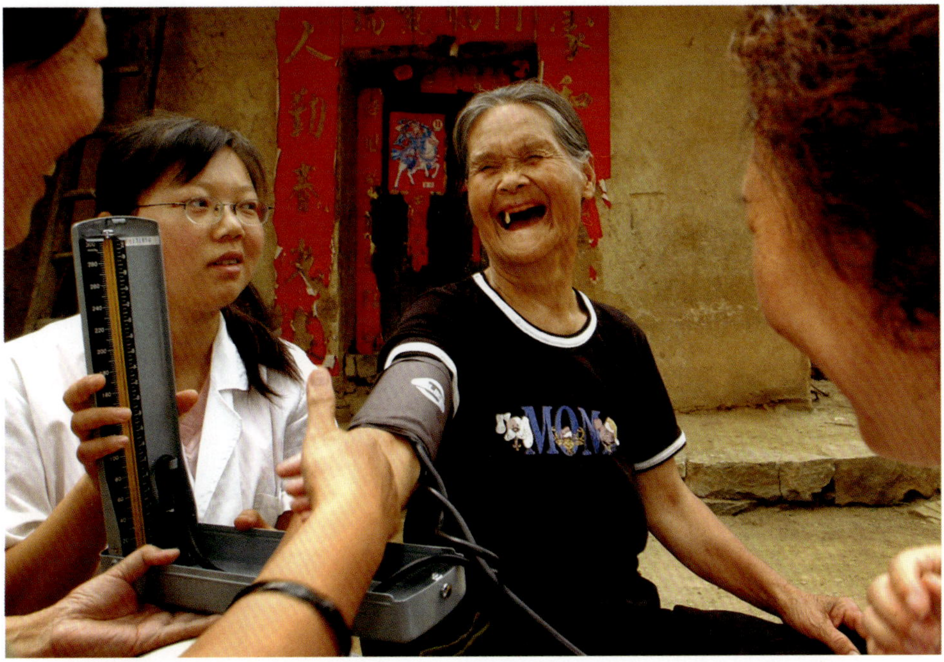

“母亲健康快车”为贫困地区妇女提供医疗服务。

努力消除教育中的性别差距。2011 年，中国在全国范围内普及九年义务教育，人口覆盖率达到 100%。2012 年，小学学龄男、女童净入学率分别为 99.84% 和 99.86%，初中阶段毛入学率为 100%，基本消除了性别差异。高学历人群中女性比例大幅提高，2012 年在校研究生（硕士、博士）中女生占总数的 48.95%，在校普通本专科中女生占总数的 51.36%。男女平均受教育年限差距从 2000 年 1.3 年缩小到 2010 年的 0.76 年。

加强普法宣传和法律援助。充分发挥妇女组织的网络优势，多部门联合，通过开展“法律六进”活动（进机关、进乡村、进社区、进学校、进企业、进单位），加强维护妇女权益和男女平等基本国策法制宣传；连续 14 年开展“三八”妇女维权周活动，将法制宣传与维权服务送到基层、送到家庭、送到广大妇女身边。从 2010 年起实施“中国妇女法律援助行动”，为妇女儿童侵权案件提供法律援助，保障了弱势群体利益。不断加强维权服务机构建设，妇女维权站（点）、妇女法律援助中心在全国各地广泛建立。各级法院普遍设立“妇女维权合议庭”、“反家暴合议庭”。建立家庭暴力投诉站、报警点 1.2

万多个，在近 60 个城市的救助站建立家庭暴力庇护中心。在全国 2800 多个县区开通了妇女维权热线，接受并处理妇女维权投诉。

法院成立女子合议庭。

四、开展国际交流与合作，促进世界妇女人权事业发展

中国举办了纪念联合国第四次世界妇女大会十周年会议（“北京 +10”）、“妇女与城市发展暨纪念第四次世界妇女大会十五周年论坛”（“北京 +15”），推动各国进一步落实《北京行动纲领》、促进妇女赋权与发展。与联合国减灾秘书处合作举办妇女与减灾国际会议，首次将性别意识纳入减灾主题。此外，围绕国际热点妇女问题举办了妇女与可持续发展国际论坛、东亚性别平等部长级会议、亚太经济合作组织妇女与经济论坛等大型国际会议。

中国积极参与联合国系统妇女人权领域的活动，积极推动国内落实《消除对妇女一切形式歧视公约》、《儿童权利公约》等与妇女儿童利益息息相关的人权公约。积极参与中美、中英、中欧、中澳人权对话机制的活动，主动与不同社会制度、不同文化背景和发展水平的国家进行深入的人权交流。

第六届中美妇女领导者交流与对话会（2014年）。

中国与联合国相关机构以及德国、澳大利亚、日本等国家广泛开展妇女人权项目合作。十年来，共争取国际合作项目100余个，资金约1.7亿元，惠及亿万妇女儿童。

针对不同国家的特殊需求，中国以小额物资援助形式先后在老挝、泰国、毛里求斯、莱索托、吉布提、津巴布韦和苏丹建立了中外妇女友好交流（培训）中心，向非洲国家派遣专家，为当地妇女开展生产技能培训，受到热烈欢迎。

中国不断巩固与亚非拉发展中国家妇女姐妹的传统友谊，并开展对发展中国家妇女领导人的培训。十年来，全国妇联面向亚非拉国家和东盟、上合组织等地区组织举办妇女研训班，内容涉及减贫、反对暴力、改善妇女教育与健康水平等。来自世界55个国家的百余名代表参加了培训。参加者对活动给予高度评价，认为这是“推动妇女共同发展的创新之举”。

在实现中华民族伟大复兴中国梦的进程中，不断改革创新的中国必将为男女两性创造更加公平和谐的生存发展环境，妇女的优势和潜能必将得到更加充分的发挥。

Implementing Basic National Policy of Gender Equality, Respecting and Protecting Women's Rights and Interests

Meng Xiaosi, Vice President and Secretary
of the Secretariat, All-China Women's Federation

China has the largest female population in the world. In its total population of 1.335 billion, there are 648 million women, accounting for 48.56%. China attaches great importance to gender equality and women's development, with the former being a basic principle of the *Constitution of the People's Republic of China* and a basic state policy to promote social development. In 2004, that "[t]he State respects and protects human rights" was articulated in the Constitution, marking a milestone in human rights protection and also advancing the women's cause.

The decade after "human rights" articulation in the Constitution has witnessed China's efforts to adopt and improve laws, regulations and policies for women's rights protection in earnest implementation of the relevant constitutional principle. This has involved leveraging various tools, including legislation, administration, publicity and education. The successful completion of the first two *Outlines for the Development of Chinese Women* has been followed by the third *Outline for 2011-2020*. Goals for women's development are incorporated into the Outline of the 12th Five-Year Plan for National Economic and Social Development and has been promoted in parallel with the latter. In 2012, the 18th CPC National Congress included in the work report a vow to "implement basic national policy of gender equality and protect the legitimate rights and interests of women and children" for the first time. This demonstrates the political promise of the CPC to integrate gender equality in mainstream values. With the support of the CPC and the government, and with the concerted efforts of the whole society, women's development has seen great progress with enhanced women's status and improved equality between the two genders.

I. Further improvement of legal system to legally secure rights and interests of women.

Over the last decade, more than 10 laws and regulations on the subject of women's rights protection including *Law on the Protection of the Rights and Interests of Women, Labor Contract Law, Marriage Law, Law on Promotion of Employment and Special Provisions for the Work Protection of the Female Employees* have been enacted or revised. By the end of 2013, 31 provinces (autonomous regions and municipalities) had revised the *Measures for the Implementation of Law on the Protection of the Rights and Interests of Women,* and 29 provincial-level people's congresses had promulgated local regulations on preventing and ending domestic violence. *Anti-Domestic Violence Law* has been put in the national legislation plan.

The Amendment to *Law on the Protection of the Rights and Interests of Women* supplements and improves the law in terms of the general provisions, areas of women's rights and interests as well as legal liability, stresses the responsibilities of the government and relative departments and institutions, highlighted the focus of protection, and contains new provisions on issues of interest to the whole society such as women's participation in politics, gender discrimination in employment, domestic violence, sexual harassment, rural women's land contracting and related property rights. *Law on Promotion of Employment* has a chapter devoted to fair employment, which requires all levels of government to "eliminate discrimination in employment" and "guarantee that women enjoy equal right to work as men". The employing units are forbidden to "refuse to employ women or raise recruitment standards for females by using gender as an excuse" or "have such provisions as restrict female workers from getting married or bearing a child included in the labor contract." *Labor Contract Law* forbids employers to terminate labor contract if the female employee is pregnant, perinatal or breast-feeding. *Social Insurance Law* provides that employees shall be covered by maternity insurance with premiums paid by employers in accordance with the relevant regulations. To guarantee women's political rights, the *Decision on Amending the Electoral Law of the National People's Congress and Local People's Congresses of the People's Republic of China* was issued, providing that "[d]eputies to the National People's Congress and the local people's congresses shall be broadly representative… there shall be an appropriate number of women deputies, and the proportion thereof shall be raised gradually". *Organic Law of the Villager's Committees of China* revised in 2010 stipulates that "the villagers' committee shall include an appropriate number of women", and that "female representatives should account for more than one third of all representatives to the villagers' committee". The above mentioned regulations legally guarantee women's political empowerment, raising their presence in decision making and management of state political affairs.

The female villager cast her solemn vote in the election of the villagers committee.

Ⅱ. Implementation of the Outline to boost new development in women's cause.

The first *Outline for the Development of Chinese Women (1995-2000)* is followed every 10 years by the issuance of another. They have included an *Outline for 2001-2010* and another for 2011-2020. In 2010, the government evaluated and reviewed the results of implementing the 2001-2010 Outline. On the basis of the results already achieved in the implementation of the Outlines and in light of the current level of socio-economic development society and economy, the government formulated the development plans and goals for the next 10 years.

Outline for the Development of Chinese Women (2011-2020) prioritizes women's health, education, economic status, political participation, social security, environment and legal system and identified 57 major objectives and 88 strategies and measures. It further clarifies the responsibilities of the State Council and local governments and agencies in the implementation of the Outline. Governments at all levels are required to incorporate its implementation in national and local regulations and policies, general and special plans for socio-economic development, fiscal budgets at all levels, development projects with tangible benefits to the people, and government agenda and performance assessment, making sure that women's development and socio-economic development are planned and implemented in a synchronized way. Women's development has seen historic progress since the implementation of the Outline.

The improvement of related national mechanisms provides effective organizational guarantee for women's development. The National Working Committee for Children and Women has been instituted under the State Council and its membership has grown from 19 to 35. This body has been set up at the provincial, prefectural and county government levels and functions as the coordinator, supervisor, inspector and assistant in the effort of pushing relevant government departments to list women's development on the top of their agenda, with each playing its due role and all engaging in full cooperation. The National People's Congress and its standing committee consider the preservation of women's rights and interests and promotion of gender equality an important task. It has set up for the work an office of the labor unions, youth leagues and women to listen to the reports on gender equality promotion presented by the committees and related departments regularly. Since 2009, inspections and investigations have been conducted on the enforcement of laws like *Law on the Protection of Rights and Interests of Women.* The Committee for Social and Legal Affairs of the National Committee of Chinese People's Political Consultative Conference established the "work group on women and children's affairs", which offers timely advice for the resolution of key and difficult problems in women's development and actively processes proposals for gender equality and women's development.

Ⅲ. Promotion of gender equality and women's empowerment by taking various measures.

Efforts are made to build platforms for women's employment and entrepreneurship. In order to promote women's employment, the government and social organizations together launched the "Spring Breeze Action" in over 200 cities, providing job opportunities and employment services for unemployed women, female migrant workers and college graduates. To address problems related to capital for women who intend to start their own businesses, secured micro loans are provided with interest discount since 2009. From 2009 to the end of the first quarter in 2014, loans worth over 180 billion yuan were provided for female entrepreneurs and central and local financial discount capital worth over 12 billion yuan was allotted, which was used as start-up capital for over 3.6 million women and provided examples for nearly 10 million women who followed suit in seeking employment and business opportunities.

Women's development projects help improve women's living environment and promote their development.

Additional investment has been made to protect women's health. The central and local governments have invested over 2 billion yuan in a project intended to lower maternal mortality rate and eliminate tetanus among newborns. From 2008 to 2010, the Central Government allocated 7 billion yuan in maternity subsidy for delivery in hospital by rural mothers across the country, which brought down considerably maternal and neonatal mortality rates. Since 2009, free breast cancer and cervical cancer screening has been offered to rural women and a special treatment fund has been established to help impoverished female cancer patients. By the end of 2013, a total of 370 million rural women had received the free screening. The "Healthy Mother Express" program of mobile medical vehicles for central and western areas have taken health concepts, knowledge and services to women and children in poor regions.

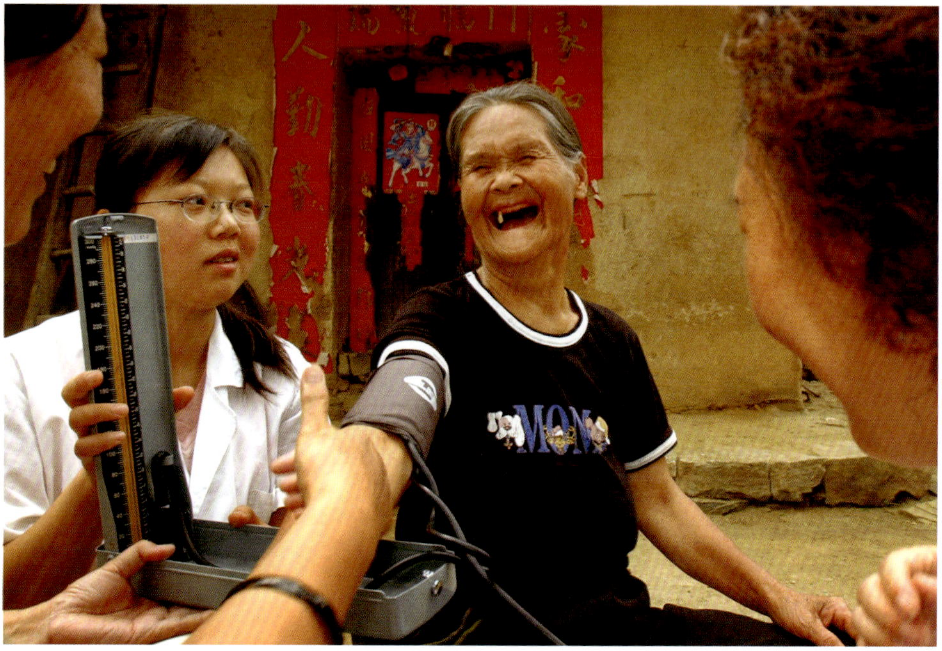

The "Healthy Mother Express" brings medical services to women living in poor areas.

Actions have been taken to eliminate gender disparities in education. In 2011, China realized universal nine-year compulsory education across the country with a population coverage of 100%. In 2012, the net enrollment rates of school-age boys and girls were 99.84% and 99.86% respectively, and the gross enrollment rate for junior middle school was 100%, indicating that gender differences were basically eliminated in this regard. Female proportion in people with higher education has increased by a large margin, as in 2012 the proportion of female postgraduate students on master's and doctorate programs was 48.95%, and female students accounted for 51.36% of all university students. The gender gap in average years of education has narrowed from 1.3 year in 2000 to 0.76 in 2010.

Campaigns to publicize legal knowledge and offer legal aid have been strengthened. Women's organizations give full play to their network advantages in carrying out inter-sectoral activities such as the "six entries of law" that spread legal knowledge in government agencies, rural areas, communities, schools, enterprises and work units to promote the publicity of the basic state policy of protecting women's rights and interests and gender equality. The March 8th Women's Rights Week activity has been celebrated 14 years in a row, bringing legal education and rights protection services to the grass-roots level for individual households and women. The Chinese Women's Legal Aid Action starting in 2010 involves provision of legal assistance in cases concerning infringement of women or children's rights, thus protecting the interests of vulnerable groups. Institution building has been enhanced with the establishment of women's rights protection stations and women's legal aid centers throughout the country. Courts at all levels have set up collegiate benches for the safeguarding of women's rights and against domestic violence. Over 12,000 domestic violence complaint stations and alarm centers have been established and domestic violence shelters have been set up in the rescue and assistance centers in nearly 60 cities. Hotlines are in operation in over 2,800 counties and districts to receive and address women's complaints.

Women collegiate bench in court.

Ⅳ. International exchange and cooperation to promote the protection of women's human rights all over the world.

China hosted the conference to commemorate the 10th anniversary of the Fourth World Conference on Women (Beijing+10) and the Forum on Women and Urban Development and in Commemoration of the 15th Anniversary of the 4th World Conference on Women (Beijing+15) promote the further implementation of *Beijing Platform for Action* by all countries and the empowerment and development of women. Together with UNISDR secretariat, China held the International Conference on Gender and Disaster Risk Reduction and brought the gender concept into the realm of disaster reduction for the first time. In addition, on hotspot issues concerning women, China has also held other major international conferences such as the International Forum on Women and Sustainable Development, East Asia Gender Equality Ministerial Meeting and APEC Women and the Economy Forum.

China takes an active part in activities related to women's human rights within the UN system and actively works for the implementation of international human rights conventions closely linked to women and children's rights such as *Convention on the Elimination of All Forms of Discrimination Against Women* and *Convention on the Rights of the Child.* China actively participates in human rights dialogues with the US, UK, EU and Australia and engages in in-depth exchanges on human rights with countries of different social systems, cultural backgrounds or development levels.

The 6th China-US Women's Leadership Exchange and Dialogue, 2014.

China has cooperated extensively with related UN agencies, Germany, Australia, Japan and other countries in the field of women's human rights. Over the last decade, more than 100 international cooperation projects have been jointly carried out with a total investment of nearly 170 million yuan, benefiting hundreds of millions of women and children.

To suit the various needs of different countries, China has provided micro material assistance to establish centers for women's friendship and exchanges (training) in Laos, Thailand, Mauritius, Lesotho, Djibouti, Zimbabwe and Sudan. It has also sent experts to African countries to teach local women production skills which are very well accepted.

China continues to consolidate the time-honored friendship with sisters from developing countries in Asia, Africa and Latin America and has launched training programs for women leaders in developing countries. Over the past 10 years, All-China Women's Federation has organized women's training workshops for Asian, African and Latin American countries as well as regional organizations such as

ASEAN and SCO, the contents of which cover a wide range of subjects including poverty reduction, anti-violence, improvement of women's education and health. Over a hundred representatives from 55 countries in the world have been trained under these programs, which received positive feedback from the trainees as an innovative initiative to promote women's common development.

In the journey towards the Chinese Dream of great national rejuvenation, China will, in the process of continuous reforms and innovations, create a fairer and more harmonious environment for the subsistence and development of both genders, thus enabling the full play of women's advantages and potentials.

(original translation by Li Xiaoyu)

保障残疾人人权是中国残疾人事业发展的根本使命

中国残疾人联合会主席　张海迪

中国目前残疾人人口总数为8500多万。残疾人是中国特色社会主义建设事业不可或缺的重要力量，是国家经济社会发展的积极参与者和贡献者。2004年，随着“国家尊重和保障人权”写入《中华人民共和国宪法》，包括广大残疾人在内的所有中国公民的人权被明确纳入国家根本大法的保护范畴。中国政府采取了诸多行之有效的措施，切实保障残疾人的基本人权和自由不受侵犯。弘扬人道主义始终是中国残疾人事业发展的主旋律，保障残疾人人权始终是中国残疾人事业发展的根本使命。

一、保障残疾人人权的法律体系不断健全

立法是保障残疾人人权的基础。改革开放以来，中国高度重视残疾人人权保障立法工作，逐步形成以《中华人民共和国宪法》为依据，以刑事、民事、行政等法律为基础，以《中华人民共和国残疾人保障法》为核心，以《残疾人教育条例》、《残疾人就业条例》、《无障碍环境建设条例》等行政法规和大量地方法规为配套的残疾人人权保障法律体系。国务院正在制定《残疾预防和残疾人康复条例》、修订《残疾人教育条例》，努力使保障

残疾人人权的法律体系更加健全，从而为残疾人人权保障奠定更为坚实的法律基础。

确保法律的贯彻实施是保障残疾人人权的关键。全国人大常委会多次开展《中华人民共和国残疾人保障法》执法调研活动，并于2012年对《中华人民共和国残疾人保障法》进行执法检查和立法后评估。地方各级人大每年开展《中华人民共和国残疾人保障法》执法检查1000余次。通过不同层级的执法检查和调研活动，有效促进了《中华人民共和国残疾人保障法》的贯彻实施，进一步强化了政府部门执行《中华人民共和国残疾人保障法》的主体责任，进一步提高了社会各界遵守《中华人民共和国残疾人保障法》的自觉意识。

2008年8月30日，国际残奥委会主席菲利普·克雷文（左）和中国残联名誉主席、北京奥组委执行主席邓朴方（右）在北京残奥村和平广场为《残疾人权利公约》纪念墙揭幕。

获得法律服务是保障残疾人人权的重要方法和途径。各级人民法院积极为残疾人提供司法救助服务，对符合条件的残疾人当事人的诉讼费用实行缓、减、免；为涉及案件的残疾人提供便利和无障碍服务，减少残疾人诉讼拖累，降低残疾人的诉讼成本。各级法律援助机构积极为残疾人提供法律援助服务，确保残疾人不因经济原因打不起官司。各级残疾人联合会积极为残疾人提供法律救助服务，努力维护残疾人的各项合法权益。截至 2013 年年底，全国司法行政机关建立专门的残疾人法律援助中心 2821 个，全国残联系统建立残疾人法律救助工作站 901 个；2013 年为残疾人提供法律援助和救助服务 8 万多人次，有效维护了残疾人的各项合法权益。

残疾人人权保障状况主动接受国际社会监督。中国是联合国《残疾人权利公约》的积极倡导国和参与国，为公约的制定和通过作出了实质性贡献，是公约的首批签署国和批准国。中国积极履行缔约国的责任和义务，全国人大常委会于 2008 年修订了《中华人民共和国残疾人保障法》，各级立法机关也对相关法律法规进行了修订，从而确保国内立法与《残疾人权利公约》的基本原则相协调。中国政府按时提交《残疾人权利公约》履约报告，积极接受联合国残疾人权利委员会的审议，确保中国的残疾人人权保障情况接受国际社会的监督。中国政府全方位加强与联合国相关机构、国际残疾人组织、其他国家在公约框架下的交流与合作，共同分享残疾人人权保障的经验，携手研究解决残疾人人权保障面临的困难与挑战。

二、保障残疾人人权的各项制度日趋完善

中国将残疾人事业发展纳入国民经济和社会发展规划。各级政府每五年制定一次残疾人事业发展规划，确定残疾人事业发展的总体目标、指导原则、任务指标和主要措施；同时制定康复、教育、就业、削减贫困、社会保障、文化体育、权益保障等领域的配套实施方案。通过这些五年规划的实施，分阶段、有步骤地推进残疾人事业发展和残疾人人权保障工作。

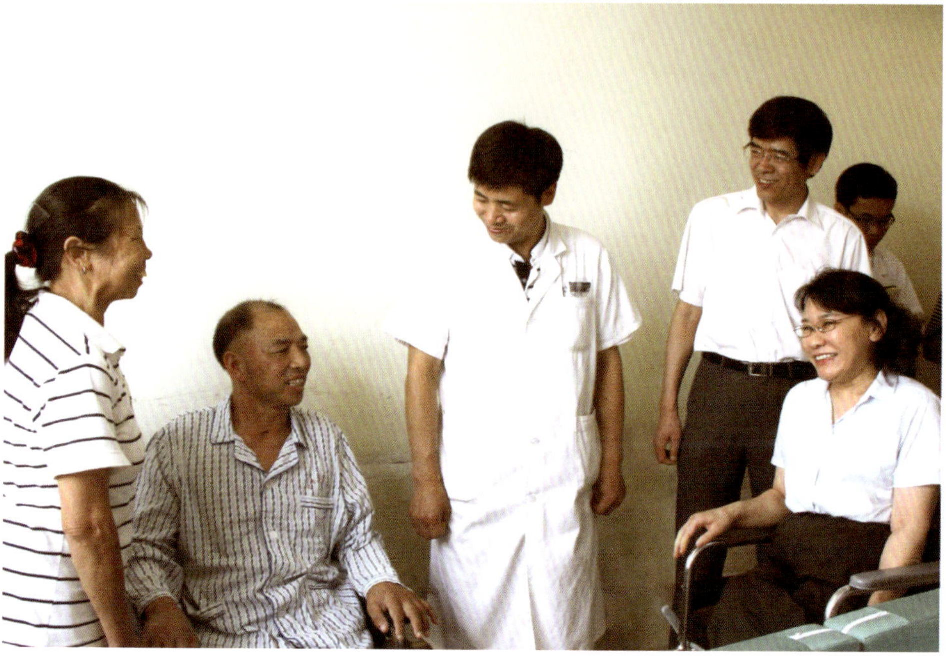

2014 年 7 月 21 日，中国残联主席张海迪、中国残联理事长鲁勇看望在中国康复研究中心进行治疗的残疾人患者。

积极制定和完善相关社会保障制度，确保残疾人的生存权。制定落实消除残疾人贫困的方案，每年帮助 120 多万农村残疾人摆脱贫困，努力缩减残疾人总体生活状况与社会平均水平之间的差距；采取针对性措施，确保符合条件的残疾人被纳入最低生活保障范围；建立困难残疾人生活补贴重度残疾人护理补贴制度，减轻残疾人的生活负担；制定专项补助政策，为重度残疾人参加城乡基本养老保险和医疗保险提供资金补贴；实施“阳光家园计划”等支持项目，每年为 90 多万名残疾人提供多种形式的托养服务。通过一系列措施的贯彻落实，残疾人的基本生活得到制度性保障，残疾人生活状况得到显著改善。

农村残疾人喜获丰收。

不断改进对残疾人的服务，充分保障残疾人的发展权。国家基本公共服务规划中对残疾人作出重点安排和部署，要求各级基本公共服务机构针对残疾人需求提供个性化服务。普遍开展残疾儿童抢救性康复，实施重点康复工程，每年使700多万名残疾人得到不同程度的康复，在2900多个县(市、区)开展社区康复服务，保障残疾人获得康复服务权利。实施特殊教育提升计划，切实保障残疾人受教育权利，目前义务教育阶段在校残疾学生近36.8万人，特殊教育普通高中班和残疾人中等职业学校在校学生1.9万人，高等教育阶段在校学生3万余人。对残疾人就业实施保护政策，为残疾人提供具有针对性的就业培训和服务，城镇残疾人每年新增就业30多万人，不断改善残疾人就业环境，消除残疾人就业歧视，确保残疾人的劳动就业权不受侵犯。残疾人深度参与和全面融入社会的能力得到大幅度提升，越来越多的残疾人实现人生和事业的梦想。

视力残疾儿童正在上课。

大力促进残疾人政治权利的享有和实现。国家积极保障残疾人的选举权和被选举权，为残疾人参加选举提供无障碍服务和便利。据不完全统计，目前有1700多名残疾人、残疾人亲友和残疾人工作者当选为县级以上人大代表，代表全国各类残疾人参加国家事务管理；3200多名残疾人、残疾人亲友和残疾人工作者被推荐为县级以上政协委员，行使参政议政权利。全国乡镇（街道）建立残疾人联合会4万个，社区（村）建立残疾人协会58万个，建立各类残疾人专门协会1.5万个。国家充分尊重残疾人对残疾人事务的知情权、参与权、表达权、监督权，在制定涉及残疾人的法律法规和政策时，各级立法机关和政府部门主动征求和积极听取残疾人、残疾人组织的意见和建议。

三、残疾人平等融入社会的良好环境逐步形成

中国正视环境障碍给残疾人带来的巨大不利影响，充分认识到消除环境障碍不仅是残疾人融入社会的前提，也是保障残疾人人权的关键。中国积极

制定相关法律法规和标准，加大监督和实施力度，致力于消除阻碍残疾人融入社会的物理环境障碍、交流障碍和社会环境障碍，努力营造残疾人平等融入社会的良好环境。

全面推行城乡无障碍环境建设，积极推进行业无障碍服务。分阶段重点推进大中城市、小城镇、农村的无障碍建设，对城乡建筑物、道路、公共交通、信息交流、公共服务的无障碍提出了明确具体要求，确保城乡无障碍环境建设平衡发展，不同领域的无障碍环境建设同步进行。人民法院系统集中对 1300 个审判法庭和人民法庭进行无障碍改造和相关设施配备，方便残疾人参加诉讼。铁路系统对 5000 节旅客列车车厢进行改造，设置残疾人专座和无障碍卫生间，并建立了为残疾人预留车票制度。航空系统在机场旅客航站区和航空公司配备无障碍设施和轮椅。公安系统开通聋人手机短信报警服务。银行业系统普遍提供金融无障碍服务。广播电台和电视台积极开办残疾人专题栏目和手语节目，影视节目普遍加配字幕。596 个地市级以上图书馆开设了盲人阅览室，部分药品开始标注盲文。各级政府提供资金支持，为 55 万贫困残疾人家庭实施危房改造，为 30 万户贫困残疾人的家居环境实施无障碍改造。

积极消除基于残疾的歧视，为残疾人全面融入社会创造条件。加强对社会公众的引导和教育，在主流媒体广泛宣传残疾人人权保障的基本理念，大力弘扬人道主义思想，积极传播反映残疾人生活和精神世界的优秀文学艺术作品，将保障残疾人人权的法律法规纳入国家普法宣传规划，积极同歧视残疾人的错误观念和陈规陋习作斗争，严厉打击侵犯残疾人人权的各种违法犯罪行为，推进建立尊重、关心、帮助、支持残疾人的良好社会氛围。鼓励和支持残疾人参与文化体育活动，影响和带动社会各界形成对残疾人的积极评价和客观认识。中国政府先后承办了 2007 年上海世界特奥会、2008 年北京残奥会、2010 年广州亚残运会，并在世博会 159 年历史上首次在上海设立残疾人主题馆，不仅为国际残疾人运动作出了贡献，更对全社会产生了持续而深远的影响。

中国残疾人艺术团“千手观音”演出剧照。

残疾人是中华民族大家庭的重要成员，是中华民族伟大复兴的重要依靠力量。中国残疾人事业发展将始终秉承弘扬人道主义的理念，始终坚持保障残疾人人权的根本使命，努力实现残疾人与全国人民同步小康，让残疾人生活得更有尊严、更加殷实、更加幸福，与全国人民一道早日实现美好生活的中国梦！

Protecting the Human Rights of Persons with Disabilities Is the Ultimate Mission of the Cause of Persons with Disabilities in China

Zhang Haidi, Chairperson, China Disabled Persons' Federation

There are over 85 million people with disabilities in China. They play an essential part in the building of socialism with Chinese characteristics and are active participants in and contributors to the socio-economic development of the country. In 2004, that "[t]he State respects and protects human rights" was articulated in the *Constitution of the People's Republic of China*, thus the human rights of all Chinese citizens, including people with disabilities, are clearly enshrined in China's fundamental law. The Chinese Government has employed a variety of effective measures to protect the basic human rights and freedom of people with disabilities from violation. Promoting humanitarianism has always been the central theme and protecting human rights has been ultimate mission of the cause of people with disabilities in China.

I. Continued improvement to the legal system for the human rights protection of people with disabilities.

Legislation is the cornerstone of protecting the human rights of people with disabilities. Since the reform and opening-up policy was adopted, increasing value has been placed on the development of a legal system to protect the human rights of people with disabilities. This system is founded on criminal, civil and administrative laws in accordance with the Constitution. The core legislation is the *Law of the People's Republic of China on the Protection of Disabled Persons,* supported by administrative regulations and local bylaws, such as *Regulation on the Education of the Disabled, Regulation on the Employment of the Disabled* and *Regulation on the Construction of Barrier-Free Environments.* The State Council is currently formulating the *Regulation on Prevention of Disability and Rehabilitation of Disabled Persons* and revising *Regulation on the Education of the Disabled* in order to improve the legal system and strengthen the legal foundation for the protection of their human rights.

The key to protecting the human rights of persons with disabilities lies with the implementation of relevant laws. The Standing Committee of the National People's Congress has carried out multiple investigations into the enforcement of *Law on the Protection of Disabled Persons* and performed inspection and post-legislation evaluation in 2012. Local People's Congresses perform over 1,000 inspections each year over its implementation. Inspections and investigations at different levels effectively promote implementation of the law, further strengthen government departments' responsibilities in the implementation process and raise social awareness across all sectors to abide by the law.

Access to legal services is an important means and path to protecting the human rights of persons with disabilities. The People's Courts at all levels actively provide legal aid service to people with disabilities. Court costs may be deferred, reduced and even exempted for eligible persons with disabilities. Conveniences and accessible services are provided for disabled people involved in lawsuits so as to reduce the burden and cost of lawsuits for them. All legal aid organizations make active efforts to provide legal aids for people with disabilities to remove the financial hindrances for them to pursue legal action. Disabled persons associations at all levels act proactively with legal services for the disabled so as to safeguard their legitimate rights and interests. By the end of 2013, the judicial administrative organs had set up 2,821 legal aid centers and the CDPF system had 901 legal assistance stations. These institutions provided legal aid and assistance for over 80,000 people, effectively defending their various rights and interests.

On August 30, 2008, Philip Craven (left), chairman of International Paralympic Committee, and Deng Pufang (right), Honorary Chairman of China Disabled Persons' Federation and Executive President of the Beijing Organizing Committee for the Games of the XXIX Olympiad, unveiled the monumental wall of *Convention on the Rights of Persons with Disabilities* at the Peace Square, Beijing Paralympic Village.

The state of human rights protection of people with disabilities has been placed under international supervision. China has been an active advocate of and participant in the UN *Convention on the Rights of Persons with Disabilities* process with substantive contribution to its formulation and adoption, and was among the first to sign and ratify it. The Chinese Government has made active efforts to fulfill its obligations and responsibilities as a signatory. The NPC Standing Committee amended the *Law on Protection of the Disabled* in 2008 and legislative organs at all levels amended all related laws and regulations to ensure consistency with the basic principles enshrined in the Convention. The Chinese Government submits in timely manner implementation reports and accepts review by the United Nations Committee on the Rights of Persons with Disabilities, thus ensuring the placement of the protection of the disabled persons' human rights under international supervision. The Chinese

Government comprehensively strengthens exchanges and cooperation with the related UN agencies, international organizations of people with disabilities and other states parties in the framework of the Convention, sharing experiences in the protection of disabled persons' human rights and working together to deal with difficulties and challenges confronting them.

Ⅱ. Increasingly improved systems for the protection of disabled persons' human rights.

The development of persons with disabilities has been included in the planning for national economic and social development in China. Governments at all levels formulate their plans for the development of persons with disabilities every five years to define the overall objectives, guiding principles, tasks and indicators, and major actions. In addition, they develop supportive implementation programs in the fields of rehabilitation, education, employment, poverty reduction, social security, culture and sports as well as rights protection. With the implementation of these five-year plans, the cause of persons with disabilities and the protection of their human rights have been furthered in a phased and step-by-step way.

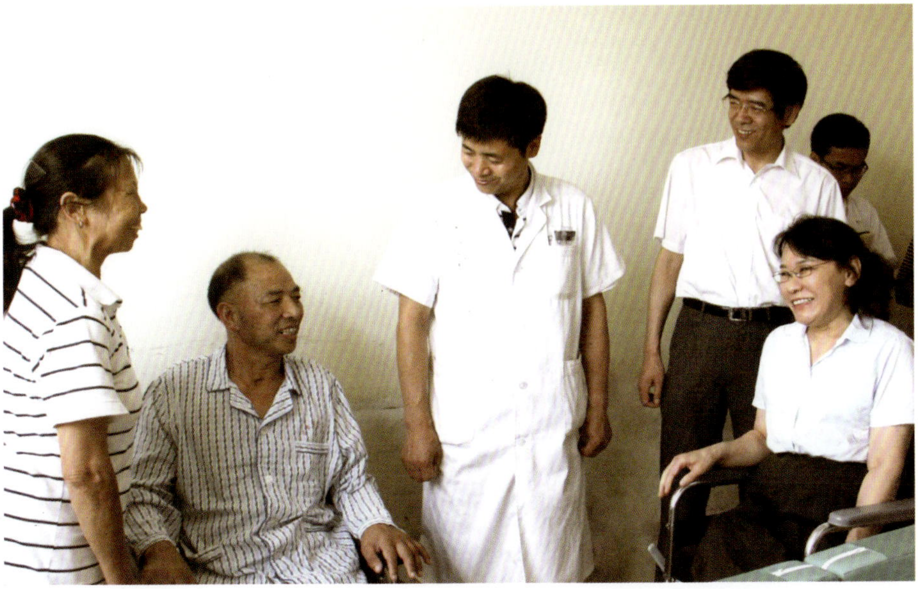

On July 21, 2014, Mme. Zhang Haidi, Chairperson of China Disabled Persons' Federation (CDPF), and Mr. Lu Yong, Director of the Executive Council of CDPF, visited disabled persons treated at the China Rehabilitation Research Center.

The relevant social security systems are actively formulated and improved to ensure the right of persons with disabilities to subsistence. Plans are made and implemented to reduce poverty among persons with disabilities and help 1.2 million disabled people in rural areas out of poverty every year. Efforts are made to narrow down the gap in living standards between the disabled and an average person in society. Targeted measures are taken to make sure that eligible disabled persons are provided with minimum living allowances. Subsidies are provided for those in financial hardships and those with severe disabilities so as to reduce for them the burden of life. Earmarked funds are provided to enable people with severe disabilities to participate in urban and rural basic endowment insurance and medical insurance. By implementing supportive programs such as "Sunshine Home Project", a wide variety of foster cares are provided for more than 900,000 people with disabilities every year. With the implementation of a series of measures, the basic living of people with disabilities is systematically secured and has improved significantly.

A harvest for persons with disabilities in the countryside.

Services for people with disabilities are continuously improved and their right to development is comprehensively protected. The national basic public services plan contains arrangements for people with disabilities as a priority and requires basic public services institutions to provide personalized services for them. Emergency rehabilitation is widely provided for children with disabilities. Key rehabilitation projects are implemented, with over 7 million people rehabilitated to various extents. Community-based rehabilitation services are provided in over 2,900 counties (cities and districts) with a view to protecting the disabled persons' right to rehabilitation service. A special education improvement plan is implemented to protect their right to education. Currently there are nearly 368,000 students with disabilities at school for compulsory education, 19,000 at special education high schools and special secondary vocational schools, and over 30,000 at institutions of higher education. Employment protection is provided for persons with disabilities, who enjoy targeted employment training and services. Each year over 300,000 people with disabilities in urban areas find jobs. With improved employment environment and elimination of discrimination against persons with disabilities, their right to work is protected from violation. With markedly enhanced capability of taking an in-depth part in and fully integrating into the society, increasingly more persons with disabilities are realizing their dreams in life and career.

Children with vision impairments in class.

Redoubled efforts are made for persons with disabilities to enjoy and exercise the political rights. The government actively protects their right to vote and stand for election and provides accessible services and facility for them to take part in election. According to incomplete statistics, over 1,700 persons with disabilities, their families, and people working with them have been elected as deputies to People's Congress at and above the county level, representing all persons with disabilities to participate in management of state affairs. Over 3,200 have been recommended as members of the CPPCC committees at and above the county level, exercising the right to participate in and deliberate state affairs. There are 40,000 federations of disabled persons' associations in towns and subdistricts all over the country, about 580,000 disabled persons' associations in communities and villages, and about 15,000 special associations. The right to information about matters related to persons with disabilities as well as rights to participation, expression and supervision are fully respected. When making laws, regulations, and policies concerning persons with disabilities, legislative organs and government departments at all levels proactively solicit and listen to the opinions and advices of people with disabilities and their organizations.

III. An emerging sound environment for persons with disabilities to integrate into the society as equals.

China faces up to the huge adverse effect of environmental barriers on the life of persons with disabilities. It regards the removal of those barriers as both a precondition for disabled people to be integrated in society and a key to protecting their human rights. China has actively made laws, regulations and standards and strengthened supervision over and implementation of them. It is committed to removing the barriers in physical environment, communication and social environment that keep persons with disabilities from being integrated into the society and creating an agreeable environment for them to be integrated into the society as equals.

Comprehensive efforts are made to promote accessibility in both urban and rural areas and accessible services in different sectors. The construction of accessible facilities are advanced stage by stage in large and middle-sized cities as well as smaller towns and the countryside. Explicit accessibility requirements are put forward with regard to buildings, roads, public transportation, information communications and public services to ensure urban and rural accessibility in a balanced manner and synchronize accessibility development in all areas. The People's Courts have renovated about 1,300 court rooms for accessibility and related facilities so as to bring convenience to persons with disabilities attending lawsuits. The railway sector has reformed 5,000 railroad cars to install special seats for persons with disabilities and accessible toilets. It has also set up the mechanism to reserve train tickets for disabled people. Airports and airliners are equipped with accessible facilities and wheel chairs. The public security organs have launched alarm service by text messages for deaf persons. Banks usually have accessible services. Radio and television stations offer special programs focusing on persons with disabilities, sign language programs and subtitled movies and TV series. Libraries of 596 prefectures and higher level administrative regions have reading rooms for blind people and instructions for some medicines are provided in braille as well. Governments at all levels provide funds to renovate dilapidated houses for 550,000 poor families with disabilities and conduct accessibility renovation for 300,000 such households.

We take active actions to eliminate disability-based discrimination so as to create conditions for persons with disabilities to integrate into the society. The public is educated and guided by extensively communicating through the mainstream media the basic concept of human rights protection for the persons with disabilities, advocating humanitarianism and promote literary and art works that reflect the life and spiritual world of persons with disabilities. The laws and regulations protecting disabled persons' human rights are important contents in the national campaign to popularize legal knowledge. We fight against the misconception and bad customs of discrimination against persons with disabilities, harshly crack down on illegal and criminal activities violating the human rights of persons with disabilities, and promote a sound social atmosphere in which disabled people are respected, taken care of, helped and supported. Persons with disabilities are encouraged and supported to take part in cultural activities and sports and people from all walks of life are steered to form positive and objective views of persons with disabilities. The Chinese Government hosted the 2007 Shanghai Special Olympics, Beijing 2008 Paralympic Games and Guangzhou 2010 Asian Para Games and set up a theme pavilion for disadvantaged people at Expo 2010 Shanghai China, the first ever in the 159 years of world expos. These events not only contributed greatly to international para games but also have a lasting and far-reaching influence on the society.

A stage photo of China Disabled People's Performing Art Troupe performing *Thousand-Armed Avalokiteśvara.*

People with disabilities are important members of the big family of the Chinese nation and constitute an important force for the great national rejuvenation. The CDPF will always bear in mind the ideal of humanitarianism and its ultimate mission of protecting the disabled persons' human rights, and work for the realization of a better-off society for all people in China so that people with disabilities will, as their compatriots, live a life of greater dignity, wealth and happiness and realize the Chinese Dream sooner together with all people of the country.

(original translation by Yang Shouxun)

西藏人权的发展与进步

中国西藏文化保护与发展协会副会长　拉巴平措

西藏的人权事业在不断发展与进步，西藏人民今天享有的人权是旧西藏无法比拟的。中央政府和西藏地方各级政府为保障和促进西藏的人权作出了巨大努力，实施了许多特殊政策和措施。西藏的民族区域自治制度在不断巩固和发展，西藏人民在政治上当家做主，在经济社会发展中享有成果，在继承发展传统文化和宗教信仰上享有自由。

一、政治进步与人民当家做主

按照《中华人民共和国宪法》和《中华人民共和国民族区域自治法》的规定，西藏自治区享有广泛的自治权利，包括立法权、对国家有关法律的变通执行权、使用民族语言文字的权利、人事管理权、财政管理权和自主发展文化教育权等。

自成立以来，西藏自治区人民代表大会及其常委会先后制定了 290 多部地方性法规，对多项全国性法律制定了适合西藏特点的实施办法。在全区干部队伍中，藏族及其他少数民族干部占 82.05%，其中县、乡两级领导班子中藏族和其他少数民族干部占 80.06%。

随着中国民主政治的发展和完善，西藏的民主制度不断健全，民主形式日益丰富，有序政治参与渠道不断扩大。2012 年，经过直接和间接选举产生的现任34244名四级人大代表中，藏族和其他少数民族代表31901名，占93%以上。目前，西藏自治区共有全国人大代表20名，其中14名为藏族和其他少数民族，共有全国政协委员29名，其中26名为藏族和其他少数民族。

西藏逐步发展形成了具有中国特色、西藏特点的农牧区基层民主制度。目前，西藏95%以上的村建立了村民代表会议制度。西藏192个城市社区全部建立了社区居民代表大会、社区居委会等社区组织，社区居民自治有充分的组织保证。

西藏农牧民行使选举权。

二、经济发展与民生改善同步

西藏实现了经济总量的历史飞跃，并持续保持较快发展，西藏人民也充分享受到了经济发展的成果。西藏地区生产总值连续19年实现两位数以上增长，年均增速12.7%。2013年，西藏自治区国内生产总值达807.67亿元，比上年增长12.5%；农牧民人均纯收入达到6578元，比上年增长15%，连续11年保持两位数以上的增长；城镇居民人均可支配收入达20023元，比上年增长11.1%。2013年，西藏农牧民人均居住面积为30.51平方米，城镇居民人均居住面积为42.81平方米，各项民生事业显著改善。特别是，连续8年累计投资273.57亿元的农牧民安居工程全面完成，全区46.03万户、230万名农牧民住上了安全适用的房屋，农牧民生产生活条件得到历史性改善。

西藏最传统的卡垫编织业得到发展。

西藏自治区在水、电、路、讯、气、广播电视、邮政等农村综合配套设施上的建设加快推进，乡镇通邮率、乡镇通公路率和行政村通公路率分别达到 94.6%、99.7% 和 97.4%。目前，西藏次高级以上路面里程达到 8896 公里，公路通车里程达到6.52万公里，基本实现县县通公路、乡乡通公路。2014年，青藏铁路拉萨至日喀则段建成通车。截至目前，西藏已建成通航机场 5 个，9 家航空公司在藏运营，开通国内航线 48 条。2013 年，接待游客 1290 万人次，旅游总收入 165 亿元。农畜产品加工业、藏医药业、民族手工业稳步发展。

藏民自家种的西瓜喜获丰收。

三、藏文化保护事业欣欣向荣

多年来，中央政府和西藏自治区政府倾力保护和弘扬西藏优秀传统文化。

藏语文学习使用受到法律保护。《中华人民共和国宪法》、《中华人民共和国民族区域自治法》和《中华人民共和国国家通用语言文字法》均明确规定，保障少数民族使用和发展本民族语言文字的自由。西藏自治区还颁布实施《西藏自治区学习、使用和发展藏语文的规定》，将学习、使用和发展藏语言文字工作纳入法制化轨道。

西藏的孩子们正在学藏文。

西藏教育系统推行以藏语文授课为主的双语教学体系。目前，所有农牧区和部分城镇小学实行藏汉语文同步教学，主要课程用藏语授课。中学阶段也同时用藏语文和汉语授课，并在内地西藏班开设藏语文课。截至目前，西藏实施双语教学的小学在校学生 28 万多人，占小学在校生总数的 97%；中学在校学生 17 万多人，占中学在校生总数的 91%。

藏语文在生活中得到广泛应用。西藏各级人民代表大会通过的决议、法规，西藏各级人民政府的正式文件和公告都使用藏、汉两种文字。公共场所的各种标识、标牌等都使用藏、汉两种文字。西藏共有 14 种藏文杂志、10 种藏文报纸，西藏人民广播电台开办有 42 个藏语栏目，西藏电视台藏语卫视 24 小时播出。2013 年，西藏自治区出版藏文书籍 780 种，印数达 431 万册。藏语文使用迈入了信息化。通过互联网和手机浏览、阅读、收听、收看国内外新闻和各类资讯，成为众多藏文用户日常生活的一部分。

文物古迹得到有效保护。目前，西藏有各类文物点 4277 处，其中国家级 55 处，馆藏文物 232 万件(套)。2000 年以来，中央先后投入资金 20.4 亿元，实施了一系列重点文物保护维修工程。其中，布达拉宫、罗布林卡、萨迦寺三大重点文物保护维修工程投资 3.8 亿余元。

打阿嘎（“打阿嘎”即用西藏最传统的打造屋顶或地面的方式维修寺院）。

非物质文化遗产得到有效保护、传承和发展。目前，西藏有非物质文化遗产项目近800个，其中国家级项目76个，传统戏剧演出机构80多个，传承人1177名。藏戏和《格萨尔》史诗被列入联合国教科文组织人类非物质文化遗产代表作名录。158部珍贵古籍入选国家珍贵古籍名录。西藏自治区把藏医药事业发展作为医疗卫生工作的重点。目前，西藏有藏医医疗机构19所，在50多所县医院设有藏医科，藏医服务网络基本覆盖全区。藏药生产由手工作坊向现代工业化生产迈进，藏药加工实现了标准化、规范化、规模化，一些藏药产品销往全国各地和部分国家，藏药产值达数亿元。

四、宗教信仰自由获得充分保障

中央和西藏自治区各级政府一贯尊重并依法保护西藏信教群众的宗教信仰自由权利。

在雪域高原，处处可见从事宗教活动的信教群众，到处悬挂着经幡，堆积着刻有佛教经文的玛尼堆。信教群众家中几乎都设有小经堂或佛龛，每逢婚丧嫁娶还请高僧念经祈祷。在西藏每个传统的宗教节日里，信教群众都可以按照自己的心愿转经、朝佛、烧香、磕头、布施、还愿。每年到拉萨朝佛敬香的信教群众达百万人次以上。一年一度的雪顿节、羊年转纳木错圣湖、马年转冈仁波切神山等宗教活动，都正常进行并受到社会各方面的尊重。

僧人获得藏传佛教最高学位拉让巴格西。

目前，西藏有各类宗教活动场所 1787 座，住寺僧尼 4.6 万余人，活佛 358 名。寺庙学经、辩经、晋升学位、受戒、灌顶、修行等传统宗教活动正常进行，每逢重大宗教节日都循例举行各种活动。活佛转世作为藏传佛教特有的传承方式得到国家的尊重，目前已有 60 多位新转世活佛按历史定制和宗教仪轨得到批准认定。

许多藏传佛教经典和文化获得抢救性保护和科学管理。国家投资 3500 万元、历时 16 年完成了藏文《大藏经》的整理和出版，满足了僧尼和信教群众的学修需要。寺院的壁画、雕刻、塑像、唐卡、经卷、法器、佛龛等宗教文化载体，得到保护和修缮。各寺庙的传统印经院得到继承和发展，现有木如寺印经院、布达拉宫印经院等大型传统印经院近 60 家，年印经卷 6.3 万种，民间经书销售摊点 20 家。

根据藏传佛教的实际，西藏自治区政府制定了《西藏自治区实施〈宗教事务条例〉办法》、《西藏自治区藏传佛教僧人学经晋升格西拉让巴学位管理暂行办法》等八个地方性法规。从 2005 年起，西藏自治区恢复了藏传佛教学经僧人考核晋升制度，截至目前，已有 18 位僧人获得了格西拉让巴学位。中央政府还于2004年创立了藏传佛教高级学衔制度，截至目前，共有110位僧人荣获拓然巴高级学衔，84位僧人荣获智然巴中级学衔。西藏各级政府还将寺庙在编僧尼全部纳入社会保障体系，僧尼年满60周岁的按月领取养老金，标准为每月120元，尼姑年满60周岁、僧人年满65周岁的终身享受基本医疗保险。目前，一批爱国爱教、宗教造诣较高、德行服众的宗教界人士进入西藏自治区各级人大、政协并担任领导职务。

五、教育、医疗等各项事业充分发展

西藏自治区的科学教育事业迅猛发展。目前，西藏有专业技术人员56264人，其中，少数民族43552人，占总数的77.41%。他们在农牧业生产、工业生产、藏药产业、新能源、旅游业、文化创意、民族手工业等领域的科技创新和成果转化方面发挥了积极作用。

西藏首届藏医博士学位获得者。

现在，西藏已建立起一个涵盖学前教育、基础教育、职业教育、高等教育、成人教育、特殊教育等的完整现代教育体系。2013 年，教育投入达 108 亿元，比上年增长 15%。实施对接受义务教育阶段教育的农牧民子女包吃、包住、包学习费用的"三包"政策，先后 12 次提高补助标准，惠及 51.04 万人。目前，"三包"标准提高到年生均 2700 元，奖学金、助学金政策全面落实。2012 年，在全国率先实现 15 年 (学前教育 3 年、小学 6 年、初中 3 年、高中 3 年) 免费教育。目前，西藏青壮年文盲率下降到 0.8%，15 周岁以上人口人均受教育年限达到 8.4 年。

西藏已建立以拉萨为中心，遍布全区城乡的藏医、西医、中医相结合的公共医疗卫生服务体系，实现了"一村一卫生室"的目标。以免费医疗为基础的农牧区医疗制度覆盖全区农牧民。2013 年，农牧民免费医疗经费补助标准提高到人均 340 元。近年，西藏自治区政府还安排专项资金 2300 万元，建立了农牧民群众大病补充医疗保险。县乡医疗机构全部配备救护车、流动服务车。西藏一直实行宽松的生育政策，对占总人口 80% 以上的农牧民不限制生育数量。2010年，西藏人口增长到300.2万人，其中藏族人口271.6万人，占总人口的 90% 以上。西藏人均寿命提高到 68 岁，孕产妇死亡率和婴儿死亡率均大幅下降。

第一位藏族女列车长。

近年来，西藏的社会保障体系日趋完善，老有所养、病有所医、困有所助成为现实。截至目前，以基本养老保险、基本医疗保险和失业、工伤、生育保险为核心的覆盖城乡居民的社会保障体系在西藏全面建立，全区各项社会保险参保总人数达到248.9万人次。2013年，为改善民生共投入53亿元。企业基本养老金提高到月人均3018元，新农保基础养老金提高到月人均105元。城镇职工和居民基本医疗年度最高支付限额分别提高到30万元、20万元。城乡居民最低生活保障标准分别提高到月人均440元和年人均1750元。

第一次坐上火车的藏北牧民兴奋地望着窗外的风景。

结束语

西藏人权的发展进步离不开中央政府的支持和全国人民的帮助。截至2012年，中央财政对西藏安排各项补助达4543.4亿元，占西藏地方财政成立以来累计支出的96%。中国国家制度的优越性和中华民族互帮互助的优良传统，为西藏的发展进步提供了强大动力，推动了西藏人权的发展与进步。

Progress in Protection of Human Rights in Tibet

Lhagpa Phuntshogs, Vice Chairman, China Association for Preservation and Development of Tibetan Culture

The human rights cause in Tibet is constantly developing and improving. The level of human rights protection Tibetan people enjoy today is beyond imagination in old Tibet. The Central Government and local governments in Tibet have made great efforts to protect and advance human rights by implementing many special policies and measures. The regional ethnic autonomy in Tibet is continuously consolidating and developing. The Tibetan people manage their own political affairs, harvest fruits of socio-economic development and enjoy freedom in carrying forward and developing traditional culture and religious belief.

I. Political progress and people being masters of the country.

According to the *Constitution of the People's Republic of China* and *Law on Regional Ethnic Autonomy*, the Tibet Autonomous Region enjoys extensive rights of autonomy, including legislation, flexible implementation of relevant national laws, use of the Tibetan language, personnel management, fiscal management, and independent development of culture and education.

Since its institution, the regional people's congress and its standing committee have made over 290 local laws and regulations and formulated measures for the implementation of national laws in Tibet suited to local conditions. Among government officials in the region, Tibetans and other ethnic minorities account for 82.05%, and 80.06% at county and township levels.

With the development and improvement of socialist democracy around the country, the democratic system in Tibet has also been improved, with increasingly diversified forms of democracy and expanding channels for orderly political participation. In 2012, among the 34,244 deputies elected directly and indirectly to the four levels of people's congresses, 31,901 were of Tibetan or other ethnic origin, accounting for more than 93%. Among the 20 regional deputies to the NPC, 14 are ethnic Tibetan or other minorities. Tibet also has 29 members of the CPPCC National Committee, among whom 14 are Tibetans or other ethnic minorities.

Tibetan people exercise their right to vote.

Tibet has gradually put in place a system of grass-roots democracy with both Chinese characteristics and Tibetan specialty and covering both farming and pastoral areas. Currently, over 95% villages in Tibet have established the system of villagers' representative conferences. 192 urban communities have set up community residents' congresses and community residents' committees, providing a solid organizational guarantee for the self-governance of local residents.

II. Synchronized economic development and livelihood improvement.

Historical leapfrog development has been realized in terms of economic aggregate. The Tibetan economy is growing steadily and quickly and the Tibetan people have fully enjoyed the fruit of economic development. The regional GDP has had double-digit growth for 19 consecutive years, with an annual growth rate of 12.7% on average. In 2013, Tibet Autonomous Region's GDP reached 80.767 billion yuan, a 12.5% increase over the previous year. Per capita net income of farmers and herdsmen had maintained double-digit growth for 11 consecutive years, reaching 6,578 yuan in 2013, 15% increased over the previous year. The per capita disposable income of urban dwellers was 20,023 yuan, 11% more than that of the previous year. In 2013, the per capita floor space of farmers and herdsmen was 30.51 square meters and that of urban dwellers 42.81. All elements of people's livelihood have improved remarkably. In particular, the housing projects for farmers and herdsmen with an investment of 27.357 billion yuan over 8 consecutive years had been completed and 2.3 million farmers and herdsmen in 460,300 households moved into safe and affordable houses, marking a historical improvement of their living and working conditions.

Tibetan traditional weaving industry has also developed.

Tibet Autonomous Region has sped up construction of comprehensive rural infrastructures including drinking water, power, road and railway, telecommunication, natural gas, radio and television broadcasting, and postal services. Now, townships having access to postal service and road network account for 94.6% and 99.7% of the total respectively, and 97.4% administrative villages can be reached by road. At present, Tibet has 8,896 km of high-grade roads and the total length of roads open to traffic is 65,200 km. Every county and township now has access to road transportation. In 2014, the Lhasa to Shigatse section of the Qinghai-Tibet railway was completed and open to traffic. Tibet now has 5 airports and 9 airlines operate 48 domestic routes to and from the autonomous region. In 2013, Tibet received 12.9 million tourists and the total tourism income reached 16.5 billion yuan. Agricultural and livestock products processing, Tibetan medicine and handicraft industries are developing steadily.

A Tibetan farmer was all smiles at watermelon harvest.

Ⅲ. Thriving cause of Tibetan culture protection.

For these years, the Central Government and Tibet Autonomous Region government have spared no effort to protect and promote Tibetan traditional culture.

Learning and using of the Tibetan language is protected by law. The *Constitution of the People's Republic of China, Law on Regional Ethnic Autonomy* and *National Common Language Law* all clearly stipulate that ethnic minorities' freedom to use and develop their own languages is protected. Tibet Autonomous Region issued *Provisions of Tibet Autonomous Region on Learning, Using and Developing Tibetan Language,* legalizing learning, using and developing of the Tibetan language.

Tibetan children are learning Tibetan language.

Bilingual education, with Tibetan as the primary language, is widespread in Tibet. At present, primary schools in all farming and pastoral areas and some urban areas use both Tibetan and Chinese in synchronized teaching, with the major courses mostly using Chinese. Middle schools also use both languages, and Tibet classes in middle schools in inland areas also have a Tibetan language course. At present, there are more than 280,000 primary school students and 170,000 middle school students receiving bilingual education, accounting for 97% and 91% of the total respectively.

The Tibetan language is widely used in daily life. Resolutions and regulations adopted at people's congresses at all levels in Tibet and formal documents and public announcements published by people's governments at different levels are all in both Tibetan and Chinese languages. Both languages are also used in identifiers and signs in public areas. There are 14 Tibetan-language magazines and 10 Tibetan-language newspapers in Tibet. Tibet People's Radio has 42 programs in Tibetan. The Tibet TV Station has a Tibetan-language satellite channel broadcasting 24 hours a day. In 2013 some 780 titles of books in the Tibetan language were published in the autonomous region, with a total of 4.31 million copies. The use of Tibetan is becoming more and more IT-based. Through the Internet, mobile phones and other means, Tibetans read, listen to and watch domestic and international news and get all types of information, which has become part of their daily life.

Cultural relics and historical sites have been effectively preserved in the Tibet Autonomous Region. Currently, Tibet has 4,277 cultural relics sites (including 55 national-level ones), and 2.32 million items of cultural relics are in their collection. Since 2000 the Central Government has invested 2.04 billion yuan in key projects for the preservation and maintenance of cultural relics in Tibet, among which more than 380 million yuan has been used in the three major cultural relics sites: the Potala Palace, Norbulingka and Sakya Monastery.

Tibetan people are maintaining monastery in the traditional way.

The region's intangible cultural heritage has been effectively preserved, carried forward and developed. Currently, Tibet has nearly 800 intangible cultural heritage items (including 76 at the national level), over 80 performance troupes of traditional dramas and 1,177 inheritors of intangible cultural heritage. Tibetan opera and *the Gesar epic* have been included in UNESCO's Masterpieces of the Intangible Heritage of Humanity. 158 Tibetan classics have been put on the State List of Valuable Ancient Books. The People's Government of the Tibet Autonomous Region has made the development of traditional Tibetan medicine a key part of its health strategy. There are now 19 Tibetan medical establishments over 50 county hospitals have a department of Tibetan medicine, and Tibetan medicine service network covers the whole region. Instead of small manual workshops, traditional Tibetan drugs are now produced in modern factories in scale, with standard products and according to standardized procedures. The products are sold all over China and in some foreign countries, with a total output of several hundred million yuan.

IV. Fully protected freedom of religious belief.

The Central Government and the government of Tibet Autonomous Region has always respected and protected citizens' freedom of religious belief according to law.

On the snow-covered plateau, it is not difficult to see prayer flags, Mani stones inscribed with Buddhist scriptures, and believers taking part in religious activities. Ordinary believers usually have a scripture hall or a Buddha shrine at home and invite lamas or nuns from monasteries to hold religious wedding and funeral ceremonies. During every Tibetan traditional festival, religious believers circumambulate, worship Buddha, burn incense, kowtow, donate, and redeem vows according to their will. Every year, more than a million religious people pay pilgrimage to Lhasa to worship Buddha and burn incense. All religious activities such as annual Shoton Festival, circumambulating the sacred Lake Namtso in the Year of Goat and Mount Kailasa in the Year of Horse are carried out normally and respected by all sectors of society.

Monks received the highest academic degree of Tibetan Buddhism.

Currently, Tibet has 1,787 venues for different religious activities, over 46,000 resident monks and nuns, and 358 Living Buddhas. Traditional religious activities such as scripture learning and debate, degree promotion, initiation into monkhood or nunhood, abhisheka (empowerment ceremony) and self-cultivation are held on a regular basis, while ceremonial activities are also held at important religious festivals. Living Buddha reincarnation is a special succession system of Tibetan Buddhism and is respected by the State. So far, over 60 reincarnated Living Buddhas have been confirmed through traditional religious rituals and historical conventions.

Many Tibetan Buddhism classics and culture are under rescuing conservation and managed scientifically. China invested 35 million yuan and spent 16 years to finish the collation and publication of *Tripitaka* in Tibetan language, satisfying the learning needs of monks, nuns and believers. Tibet has protected and repaired such carriers of religious culture as murals, carvings, statues, Thangka, sutras, religious ritual implements and shrines. There are now nearly 60 traditional sutra printing houses, including one in the Moru Monastery and one in the Potala Palace. They print 63,000 sutra titles every year. There are also 20 private shops selling these sutras.

In light of the reality of Tibetan Buddhism, Tibet Autonomous Region has enacted 8 local laws and regulations including *Tibet Autonomous Region's Implementation Measures of Regulations on Religious Affairs* and *Provisional Method of Tibet Autonomous Region for the Management of Tibetan Buddhist Monks' Promotion to the Highest Degree in Scripture Learning.* Since 2005, Tibet Autonomous Region restored the evaluation and promotion system for monks learning scriptures of Tibetan Buddhism. Until now, 18 monks have received the highest degree. In 2004, the Central Government set up a system of senior academic titles for Tibetan Buddhism and up to now 110 monks have received the rdo-rams-pa title and 84 monks received an intermediate title. The Tibetan government also included monks and nuns in monasteries into the social security system. Monks and nuns at the age of 60 and above receive a pension of 120 yuan every month. Nuns aged over 60 and monks aged over 65 enjoy basic medical insurance for the remainder of their life. Many respectable people of the religious conscience who love the country and religion and have high religious attainment, have join the people's congresses and political consultative conference committees at all levels in the Tibet Autonomous Region and take on leadership roles.

V. Comprehensive development of education, healthcare and other undertakings.

Tibet Autonomous Region's science and education have achieved rapid development. Currently, Tibet has 56,264 technical professionals, of whom 43,552 are from ethnic-minority groups, accounting for 77.41 percent. They play an active role in scientific innovation and application in agriculture, animal husbandry, industrial production, Tibetan medicine, new energy, tourism, cultural creativity, ethnic handicrafts and other fields.

The first PhDs in Tibetan medicine.

Now, Tibet has established a modern education system covering pre-school education, basic education, vocational education, higher education, adult education and special education. In 2013, education investment reached 10.8 billion yuan, an increase of 15% over the previous year. The government covers all tuition, food and boarding expenses for students from farmers and herdsmen's families in the stage of compulsory education, with the amount of subsidies increased 12 times, benefiting 510,400 people. At present, the standard is raised to 2,700 yuan for every student, and the scholarship and subsidies policies are fully implemented. In 2012 Tibet became the first province in China to offer 15-year free education (three-year preschool, six-year primary school, three-year junior middle school and three-year senior middle school). In Tibet, the illiteracy rate among young and middle-aged people has decreased to 0.8 percent, and the average length of education for people above the age of 15 has reached 8.4 years.

Now Tibet has a public medical and health service system combining Tibetan medicine, Western medicine and traditional Chinese medicine and covering all urban and rural areas of the autonomous region with Lhasa as the center. The objective of "one clinic per village." A medical system based on free medical services is now accessible to all the farmers and herdsmen in the autonomous region. In 2013, the subsidy for these medical services was raised to 340 yuan annually per person. In recent years, the autonomous region government has also allocated a special fund of 23 million yuan to set up a major disease supplementary health insurance for farmers and herdsmen. Medical institutions in counties and villages are equipped with ambulances and mobile service cars. Tibet has been implementing a flexible family planning policy, which exempts the farmers and herdsmen, who account for over 80% of Tibet's total population, from the limit set on the number of children one couple could have. In 2010, population in Tibet increased to 3.002 million, of which 2.716 million were Tibetans, accounting for more than 90% of the total. The average life expectancy in Tibet has increased to 68 years; maternal and infant mortality rates have dropped greatly.

The first Tibetan female train conductor.

In recent years Tibet's social security system has increasingly improved, so that the sick may seek medical treatment, the elderly are cared for and the financially strained may receive aid. Tibet has put in place a social security system which consisted of basic endowment insurance, basic health insurance, unemployment insurance, work-related injury insurance and maternity insurance, and covered all urban and rural residents, with an insured population of 2.489 million. In 2013, the government invested 5.3 billion yuan to improve people's livelihood. Company's basic pension rose to average 3,018 yuan per person per month and basic pension from the new rural social endowment insurance increased to average 105 yuan per month. The annual maximum payment limit for urban workers and residents' basic medical insurance rose to 300,000 yuan and 200,000 yuan respectively. The urban and rural subsistence allowances standard rose to average 440 yuan per person per month and 1,750 yuan per person per year respectively.

Tibetan herdsmen are looking outside the window in their first train ride.

Conclusion

Tibet would not have this development and progress without the support of the Central Government and the assistance of the rest of the country. By 2012, the Central Government has transferred 454.34 billion yuan to Tibet in various financial subsidies, accounting for 96% of the accumulated fiscal expenditures of the local government since it was founded. The superiority of China's state system and the fine tradition of helping one another within the Chinese nation, have given the development of Tibet much momentum, and has promoted the development and progress of human rights protection in Tibet.

(original translation by Niu Ya'nan)